# Home Buying Strategies for Resale Homes

# Alan Silverstein's Home Buying Strategies for Resale Homes

Stoddart

Published in 1989 by
Stoddart Publishing Co. Limited
34 Lesmill Road
Toronto, Canada
M3B 2T6

Hardcover edition published in 1986 by
Stoddart Publishing Co. Limited.
Third printing September 1993.

---

**CANADIAN CATALOGUING IN PUBLICATION DATA**

Silverstein, Alan, 1951–
    Alan Silverstein's home buying strategies for resale homes

Companion volume to the author's: Hidden profits in your mortgage.

ISBN 0-7737-2155-3 (bound) ISBN 0-7737-5325-7 (pbk.)

1. House buying — Canada. I. Title.
II. Title: Home buying strategies for resale homes.

HD1379.S54 1989      643'.120971      C86-093154-4

---

"Zero Lot Line" illustration by Jane Edmonson
Cover: Brant Cowie/ArtPlus Limited
Cover Photo: Peter Paterson

Printed and bound in Canada

# Table of Contents

# *Preface*

Buying a house should be an exciting and fulfilling experience. From the first house-hunting expedition until closing and beyond, prospective purchasers should experience feelings of happiness, enthusiasm and anticipation about themselves, their new dwelling and their futures. While this heady euphoria cannot continue indefinitely, no buyer wants to suddenly have to deal with the unanticipated, the unexpected and the unforeseen just before closing. Concern easily can turn to crisis, and demoralize a buyer. How can the peaks and valleys — the mixed emotions — be smoothed out, so the initial buoyancy can be maintained throughout?

Buying a house has remained basically the same procedure over the generations. Too often it has been a "learn by doing" proposition, the buyer wishing he knew at the beginning what he knows at the end. Traditionally, buying a house began with the signing of the Offer to Purchase. Only in the interval between acceptance and closing were fundamental questions asked — many of them concerning finances — and crucial information sought. Few buyers ever challenged this approach; it was simply the way things were done.

Until the 1980s! Today, the new consumer awareness is reflected in buying a home. More and more purchasers realize that all the key decisions must be made *before, and not after,* the offer is signed. *The interval between acceptance and closing is the time to implement those decisions, not to initiate them.*

With signing the offer climaxing the transaction, these buyers give themselves more time to investigate, make inquiries and seek out answers before being legally committed to a property. Armed with more information obtained much earlier than usual, these buyers are less likely to face the unanticipated, the unexpected and the unforeseen. They put pen to paper better prepared than their predecessors, having carefully thought out and analyzed their needs, wants and financial ability to handle the transaction. Little is left to chance.

Reflecting this new approach to buying an owner-occupied home is what I call HOBS — Home-Buying Strategies. In its simplest form, HOBS emphasizes the need to plan and arrange *every* aspect of a transaction prior to signing an offer. Buyers must have a thorough understanding of what they are committing to, before making that commitment. The information buyers need to know, the pitfalls to avoid, the questions to ask and the answers to seek are examined in detail in this book, so buyers can create and implement their own unique home-buying strategy. Once the offer is signed, everything should simply fall into place, the important tasks having been completed.

*Alan Silverstein's Home-Buying Strategies* has been written with two goals in mind. The first is to unravel some of the mysteries associated with buying a house, making buyers more comfortable with the topic. As our educational system does not offer courses such as "Home-Buying 101," too many people learn about buying a house on hearsay, through someone else's painful experiences or in the "School of Hard Knocks." *Alan Silverstein's Home-Buying Strategies* provides Canadian buyers with a straight bill of goods on what to do, what to avoid, and who to consult and when. Buyers will be guided through every step of the transaction, from the time a decision is made to start looking for a home until well after closing. Second, this book will encourage buyers to think, ask questions, rethink and constantly refine their ideas when buying a house for their own personal use. Many decisions have to be made beyond selecting the actual house. Properly applied, these strategies will help buyers make those decisions appropriately, enabling them to acquire the right home at the right price — the house that best satisfies their needs and wants.

With the bulk of the work in buying a house taking place at the pre-contract stage, a considerable portion of the book is devoted to the preliminary questions buyers must consider before even looking for a house. Detailed discussions follow on the selection of real estate professionals, mortgage financing and the contents of the offer — all before the question of signing the offer is raised! The commentary on the post-signing period is considerably slimmer, the transaction at that stage being etched in stone and unalterable.

Just as the purchase of a used car differs dramatically from the purchase of a new car, so too with buying a home. Purchasers of newly constructed (or yet-to-be constructed) homes must deal with numerous issues that purchasers of resale homes never face, such as purchasing from plans; new home warranties; unique mortgage concerns; onerous one-sided contractual terms; and missed closing dates. Rarely is the purchaser of a newly built home represented by a separate real estate agent, forcing the purchaser to "go it alone," unless an experienced real estate lawyer has been consulted in advance. Mixing resale and newly built homes would not do justice to either. For that reason, the focus of this book is the purchase of a resale home — one that has been previously owned and occupied. Buyers of homes from builders, however, will still find many of the insights extremely relevant and useful.

When designing a home-buying strategy, the purchaser must know the right questions to ask. Checklists and charts appear throughout the book to help buyers (record pertinent information) when they make their inquiries.

*Alan Silverstein's Home-Buying Strategies* is the companion volume to *Hidden Profits in Your Mortgage*, published by Stoddart Publishing. Together, the books are an invaluable reference tool, whether the acquisition, financing or refinancing of a resale home is involved. Their message is the same — to deal with the complex issues of the 1980s, both buyers and borrowers must devise a sound, personal strategy before making any commitments whatsoever.

The home-buying strategies appearing in this book have been developed and refined from both my experiences as a real estate lawyer as well as the experiences — good and bad — of clients over the years. Experience is such a valuable teacher, and gaining experience is such a difficult process. Readers of this book are benefiting from other people's experiences. Can we benefit from yours? Have you faced a particular problem or do you have a home-buying strategy others should know about? Address your correspondence to me, c/o Stoddart Publishing, 34 Lesmill Road, Toronto, Ontario M3B 2T6. When writing, please include copies of any relevant documents that might assist in understanding the situation.

# *Acknowledgments*

On any major project, be it a movie, stage presentation or book, the contributions of the people who play vital roles behind the scenes should be acknowledged. My sincere appreciation to those who typed the manuscript — Donna Boisselle, Elaine Haft, Maureen Jarrett, Eileen Kohls, Connie Romanyshyn and Danny J. Rosenzweig. For technical and other assistance, thank you to two good friends, Jack Haft and Ellen Roseman. As always, recognition is in order for the fine staff at Stoddart Publishing. Most importantly, I would like to thank and dedicate this book to my wonderful family — my wife, Hannah, and my sons, Elliott and Darryl. Their strength, support and encouragement made this work possible.

# 1

## *What Is HOBS?*

---

Buying a resale house is not something that is done overnight. It takes time — a lot of time. And thought. Many questions have to be asked and the answers carefully analyzed before any commitment whatsoever can be made. Sports teams devise a game plan before taking the ice or the field, to guide them through the game. Doesn't it make sense for home buyers to do the same?

Think about buying a car for a moment. With so many different models, options and features available, would anyone ever think of buying a car without doing considerable homework first? Would anyone ever make a commitment without knowing the overall cost of buying that car, including the true cost of financing it? By the time most car buyers are ready to purchase, they have spent hours doing preliminary research, investigating the market, the dealerships, the product and car loans. They have clearly spelled out their needs, their wants and what they can afford to pay. Only then will they start negotiating. Should it be any different when that same person buys a house, for a price anywhere five to ten times more than the cost of a car?

Considering the high level of consumer awareness today, why should home buyers even consider making a commitment to proceed without having marshalled all pertinent information? Key decisions can only be made after going on a fact-finding expedition, asking pointed questions and obtaining satisfactory answers. Acknowledging this need for information, two questions then must be asked:

1. What are these critical preliminary decisions to be reached?
2. When should they be made?

HOBS stands for Home-Buying Strategies. A modern, practical approach to buying a home in Canada in the 1980s, it requires that *all* the important decisions be made *before* signing and submitting an Offer to Purchase. Instead of the offer being one of a buyer's first acts, with HOBS it is one of his last. These other decisions, some too often left in the past until after the contract was signed, relate to the selection of the real estate professionals (agent, inspector and lawyer) and a detailed examination of a buyer's financial ability to pay, plus informal pre-approval for mortgage financing. Buyers who have a HOBS also will demand full, complete and timely disclosure of *all* costs they will face when buying a home, including the so-called hidden costs. Only this way can they plan and budget early for these expenses. In short, a home-buying strategy will take the guesswork out of acquiring an owner-occupied property.

Each buyer will ask a multitude of questions and demand thorough answers in designing his or her own HOBS. It will be constantly refined and revised over time, based on the many different decisions reached and strategies developed along the way. Understandably, then, each buyer's HOBS will be different.

HOBS is the master plan buyers prepare to guide them as they complete the purchase of their home. When the offer is signed, relevant information affecting the *entire* transaction has been obtained and all fundamental decisions have been made. The remainder of the time to closing becomes anti-climatic. With HOBS, a purchaser will only make a commitment once he knows what he is committing to. Developing and applying a home-buying strategy represents the common sense approach to buying a house in Canada in the 1980s.

Why is HOBS so important? Contrast it with the situation, far too common, where buyers sign first and make decisions and inquiries later. For example, if the selection of a lawyer is left until after the offer is signed, how then can a lawyer best represent a purchaser's interest, when the contract is a *fait accompli*, unalterable. Does that make sense? The same holds true for a mortgage. Too often buyers do not even think about getting a mortgage (although they know they will need one) until after the contract is signed. With a very short period in which to arrange financing, buyers lack the time needed to adequately shop for a loan. More often than they should, buyers in this situation take whatever mortgage package is presented, simply because it is available. Is that wise? Considering the costs involved in closing a real estate transaction — the fees, disbursements, transfer taxes, adjustments, mortgage deductions and other expenses — how can a buyer sign a contract without having even asked what these charges will total? How can a buyer properly budget his funds for closing without this information? How can a buyer know how large a mortgage to apply for, until he knows the size of these expenses? Time becomes the greatest enemy of a buyer who does not prepare a home-buying strategy. Important decisions must be made under pressure. Choose a lawyer. Choose a home inspector. Choose a lender. Budget finances. You may possibly even find yourself short of funds for closing, if your budget is drawn too fine!

As no commitments are made until all decisive questions have been answered, HOBS encourages buyers to take stock of themselves and to seriously analyze their situation before signing any contract. Is this such a bad idea? No buyer wants the high hopes and expectations generated on signing an offer to be destroyed soon afterwards, if he cannot qualify for a mortgage loan. No one wants the bubble of enthusiasm to burst several days before closing upon learning that he lacks sufficient funds to complete the transaction.

Developing a home-buying strategy obviously will require a considerable investment of time to thoroughly investigate every step. Yet it is an easy and inexpensive method of ensuring that the commitment made is ultimately the right one. With a home-buying strategy, the initial level of optimism and excitement purchasers have can be maintained throughout the transaction, until the keys are delivered on the day of closing.

# 2

## *Rent or Buy?*

Rent or buy? — an age-old question. The answer primarily depends on one's financial health — the ability to purchase and then "carry" a property — personal lifestyle, and other intangible factors.

Obviously, home ownership is not for everyone. Your lifestyle may not require the facilities nor permit some of the benefits home ownership offers. Like Steve and Mona, some people prefer to rent because of the freedom from responsibility it provides. From shovelling snow in the winter and cutting the grass in the summer, to being home when the electrician or plumber has to answer your call, owning a home requires a regular expenditure of time and money on its management, upkeep and maintenance. Mobile people can relocate much more quickly and easily if they rent their premises. Tenants also can avoid both the long-term mortgage obligations and the commitment of funds that most buyers face.

Renting has a unique advantage in those provinces where rent controls are in effect. While mortgage rates, taxes, utilities and repairs may increase dramatically from year to year, rent increases will be kept to fixed maximums in most cases. Leasing is often cheaper than owning from a monthly cash-flow point of view. Security of tenure, which permits tenants to remain in possession on a long-term basis, is another important reason encouraging people to continue as tenants.

Aside from the mortgage commitment, an owner-occupied

home is certainly not a "liquid" investment because it cannot be converted readily into cash, as is the case with Canada Savings Bonds and term deposits. Yet despite all these reasons, buying real estate has always been viewed as an excellent hedge against inflation. Capital appreciation has always motivated people to invest in property. As prices rise in the economy, so too, the argument goes, should house prices. With the increase in value for a principal residence being totally exempt from capital gains tax, the owner-occupied home has been one of the most popular forms of investment in Canada. By contrast, tenants pay their rent and other charges every month without ever having anything to show for it.

Anyone who lives in a property he or she owns benefits from the imputed income it generates. Just like the handyman who fixes up his own house, or the family which bakes its own bread, a home owner finds himself in a better economic position because of the rent he does not have to pay when he occupies his own home. If a similar property rented for $750 a month, the home owner saves himself $9,000 a year by owning, rather than renting, subject to the cost of financing the mortgage. This explains why Canadians whose homes are mortgage free often find it cheaper to remain where they are, rather than moving to rental accommodation.

The allure of home ownership, though, goes much deeper than monetary concerns. Many of its benefits do not have a monetary value. Security, stability, privacy and a feeling of permanence are just some of the reasons why people strive to own their own home. The backyard in which the kids can play, the roominess in which to live, the pride of owning a home coupled with the fun of decorating it as an expression of personal taste, inspire many Canadians toward the goal of home ownership. As rapidly and dramatically as the world is changing around us, it is clear that not all the old virtues are dead yet!

Deciding whether to rent or buy requires a clear and rational decision. Developing a home-buying strategy will help you to see what is involved in a home purchase and whether home ownership is right for you.

# 3

# *The Advantages of the Resale Home*

A world of difference separates the purchase of a resale home from one that is being bought from a builder. A resale home actually exists. Purchasers see what they get, and get what they see. They can touch it, inspect it and measure it. No need to speculate, visualize and imagine what the house will look like, when it is finally completed. On the other hand, builders are not selling homes; they market plans, "architectural impressions," and a choice of color selections.

Buyers of newly constructed (or yet-to-be-constructed) homes often are more concerned with the builder than the homes the builder constructs. Questions commonly asked are: What is its reputation? How has it handled previous buyers? What happens if it becomes insolvent before or after closing? In the resale situation, none of these concerns ever surfaces. While the purchaser may wish to know who the builder was, the focus of attention is the home, plain and simple.

As part of their sales brochure, builders include a detailed list of 30, 50 or even 100 features or "appointments" that accompany the house. These lists appeal to many purchasers of new homes because potential buyers can easily compare what different builders offer. Purchasers of resale homes who like this approach need only prepare their own checklist of features and appointments based on the information in chapter 17. Each time a resale home is viewed, those items accompanying the property are marked off on the checklist. Any promotional information or lists of features highlighting the resale property can be attached as well. With just a little effort, a list that is more thorough, more detailed and more indicative of a purchaser's needs and wants can be easily prepared.

Without question, newly built homes provide their owners with modern equipment that should last for many years to come. Unfortunately, the purchase of a new home today parallels ordering dinner in a fine restaurant *à la carte*. Many items buyers want, from air conditioning to extra electrical plugs, are only available for an additional charge. When a used car is bought, factory-installed extras may warrant a slightly higher sale price. Rarely, though, does the increase cover the initial cost of those extras. So too with resale homes. Buyers consider the house "as is" — as a package. Rarely are they prepared to pay considerably more for a house, simply because a premium lot, upgraded carpeting and better quality windows were acquired initially. Sellers of resale homes know this, and they often lament how they will not get out of a house the money they put into it!

Resale homes are sold in communities and neighborhoods that have a certain level of charm and maturity. By contrast, many purchasers feel that new homes built in new subdivisions have a cold, stark look that takes many years to soften. Until grass is laid and roads are paved, mud is a major inconvenience that new-home purchasers face, especially after a rainstorm. Newly built homes in developing communities also may lack the support services, transportation facilities, schools and shopping available in more established areas. This topic is discussed in more detail in chapter 9, "Know the Community and Neighborhood."

Offers to purchase newly built homes are a buyer's nightmare. Both lengthy and complex, they impose onerous restrictions and responsibilities on buyers, far beyond what they anticipate. New home contracts also contain a catalogue of hidden charges that buyers expect the builder to bear. Not so with resale offers. While they do exhibit a distinct pro-seller slant, they are not nearly as one-sided as the offers builders pay their lawyers to prepare. Most real estate associations and boards develop standard form resale offers, which agents and lawyers in the area become familiar with. Being much shorter contracts, they are much easier to understand for that reason alone. Unlike new-home contracts, few "termination" or "unusual" clauses appear in resale offers. Any that do are quite noticeable, being specifically added to the printed form of offer.

Probably the biggest problem and the most common complaint about buying a new home involves missed or delayed closing dates. Builders are notorious for not completing their homes on time, placing the blame on everyone at all involved in its construction. Too often this means that purchasers must scurry about, making alternative arrangements with very little notice. Not so with a resale house. As it already exists, there is no reason why it should not be ready for occupancy when anticipated. Closing dates in resale transactions are meaningful, and provide buyers with a level of stability and security that buyers of new homes can only wish for. Many a person has shunned a new home for this reason alone.

Most buyers of newly built homes anticipate having to cope with a certain level of aggravation after closing. Work remains unfinished, defects begin to materialize, and problems ultimately begin to surface. Rarely is the rectification work completed when buyers want and expect it done. Resolving these outstanding issues can mean spending considerable time on the phone calling the builder's service department. Time off work may also be necessary, meeting with the service rep on site to address the problem face to face. These headaches are one of the non-monetary expenses buyers have to pay when buying a house from a builder.

This is not to say that buyers of older resale homes do not inherit any problems. Yet that is the very point. Those buying resale homes *expect* to face these problems in the future. Purchasers of new homes feel their homes should be trouble-free for a considerable time after closing. The purchase price paid may reflect these different degrees of anticipation.

The risk of finding hidden defects in a resale property can be reduced considerably if a home inspector is retained to conduct a thorough investigation of the property *before* the offer becomes firm. Detailed knowledge about its share of repair not only allows a possible readjustment of the purchase price, but also helps buyers properly budget for the ongoing costs of maintenance and repair.

Buying a resale home actually can save money for a buyer. Just because a property is new does not mean it is in move-in condition immediately after closing. Windows need to be covered (sheets on the windows are not very appealing!). A fence may have to be erected, a driveway may have to be laid, and plants, bushes and shrubbery may be desired. By contrast, the older home Wayne and Lavern bought included many improvements and features as part of the purchase price. These items, which would not have accompanied a newly built house, included drapes and drapery tracks; blinds, sheers and other window coverings; upgraded electric light fixtures; an outdoor patio; landscaping and four appliances (fridge, stove, washer and dryer). While not everyone is as fortunate as Wayne and Lavern, many of these improvements accompany most resale homes. Buyers operating on a tight budget always find a resale home in a move-in condition very appealing.

Older homes also have a certain charm associated with them that buyers like. Fine woodwork, ornate brickwork, leaded glass doors and windows and solid concrete walls are just some of the features of resale homes.

Obviously the debate between resale and newly built homes will never end. A market exists for both; it is simply a matter of personal choice. Despite the immediate appeal of a new home, many buyers opt for a resale home for one simple reason. A known quantity will be transferred to them on a fixed, pre-arranged date. To many people, this reason outweighs all others.

# 4

## *When Is the Best Time to Buy?*

The "seasons" of the real estate market closely parallel the cycles in nature. After a winter lull, the market blooms and blossoms in the spring and summer. The market slows with the coming of fall, although there is usually an exciting Indian Summer. HOBS — the development and application of a unique home-buying strategy — encourages buyers first to consider when they wish to close the purchase and take possession of their home. Then they must work backwards, leaving ample time to find the property, negotiate the offer and close the transaction.

The quietest time for the real estate market is the beginning of December to the middle of February. With the onset of winter and the inconveniences that it brings, fewer buyers are prepared to go "house-hunting" or to view open houses. Moving in winter presents a set of different problems. Trekking through ice and snow with heavy furniture or boxes inevitably leads to blotches of dirt, grime and slush on carpets and floors. Extra care must be taken with weather-sensitive plants and other foliage, to avoid damaging or even killing them. A severe snow storm might even cause the move to be delayed. Christmas, of course, and mid-winter holidays also account for the softness of the buying market at this time of year.

Like holiday package trips, many good deals are available for those prepared to buy "off-season." Although the supply of resale homes declines over the winter because of the weakened demand, many homes continue to be available for a variety of reasons. Anxious sellers tend to be more flexible on both price and term at this time of year, fearing the loss of an interested prospective purchaser. After all, heating a home in Canada throughout the winter is not inexpensive!

Some buyers who sign winter contracts choose a "long closing," the actual closing date being well in the future. Fred and Shirley, with two children in school, are a perfect example. Changing their children's schools in mid-year could cause considerable disruption and a possible loss of a school year. By signing an offer in March with closing set for June, Fred and Shirley benefited from a winter contract, while minimizing the effects of a winter closing. Winter sellers often will accept an offer with a long closing, for the piece of mind it provides. Those who have already purchased another house now know that the uncertainty of selling their existing property is over. Sellers who have not yet bought another home now can look for it without feeling the pressures of time. A long closing also allows them to negotiate its purchase from strength, knowing the sale of their present home will not be a problem. Anyone not buying another house now can begin looking for suitable rental accommodation with a precise occupancy date in mind.

First-time home buyers should remember that real estate agents are not very busy during the winter. The sluggish winter market affords an excellent opportunity for buyers to meet agents, learn about the market, and seek answers to the many questions they have. Over the winter, agents will have more time to spend solidifying relationships for an immediate or not-too-distant purchase. Even if they are not ready to buy at this stage, buyers will have a valuable head start when they finally decide the time is right.

Inspecting a home in the winter affords an opportunity not available in summer to check the effectiveness of the home insulation. A roof free of snow is a sure sign of poor insulation in the attic. A sizeable area free of ice and snow around the perimeter of the house at ground-level also is a sign of heat loss from the walls due to inadequate insulation.

In late February, as good weather reappears if only occasionally at the outset, many people's thoughts turn to buying a home. With a long, cold winter behind them, people's interest in the real estate market grows like the buds on a tree. The number of prospective buyers attending open houses or just out looking on nice weekends in late winter and early spring is astounding. Homes show well in early spring. Tulips are in bloom with lawns and trees beginning to green. A fresh coat of paint on the exterior, coupled with some outside clean-up work can make a tired house look young again, and more marketable.

The delay between the acceptance of the offer to purchase and the actual closing of the transaction also explains why interest in the resale real estate market picks up in February and March. Several weeks of exploring and negotiating may be necessary before a suitable house is located. More time will pass before the offer is accepted and any conditions are satisfied. Generally speaking, this interval between acceptance and closing lasts a minimum of 30 days. Those out house-hunting in early March may finally strike a deal sometime in April. A 60-day closing makes it a June transaction. April showers may bring May flowers, but spring contracts spawn summer closings.

Having children attending school, more than any other factor, determines when a buyer wishes the transaction to close. Danny and Marilyn are like most young couples with school-age children. They decided to move in the summer, between the school years. While the week before Labour Day is a very busy time for real estate closings, the last week in June usually surpasses it. Danny and Marilyn opted for a June 29th closing. This way their children had more time to meet and make friends over the summer, instead of facing a new group of children on the first day of school. This early summer closing also provided more opportunity for them to freshen up the property during the warm weather.

Midsummer is a quiet time in the real estate market. Buyers, sellers and agents alike are on holidays. People like to enjoy beautiful weekends resting and relaxing, rather than searching for new quarters. As in the winter months, agents selling resale homes will have more time to devote to first-time buyers. Sellers tend to be more flexible at this time, in response to the lessened demand.

After Labour Day, life returns to normal. The kids are back at school and "everyone" is back to work. But surprising as it may seem, the fall real estate market traditionally is strong. Fall buyers of resale homes may wish to relocate before winter unleashes its fury, or before their children are too far along in school. Other purchasers are anxious to move before Christmas, the house itself being the Christmas present for the family. Handymen who are intent on renovating, remodelling or upgrading a property, often wish to do so before the fall weather sets in.

When is the best time of year to buy a house? Individual circumstances are the key, and advance planning is essential. Spring and fall generally are sellers' markets, in response to the lessened supply of resale homes listed for sale. The reverse holds true during the summer and winter. Remember, too, that real estate transactions do not just happen overnight. Purchasers preparing their home-buying strategy will ask, "When would we like to close the purchase and move?" Working back from that date, allowing sufficient time to locate a property, negotiate the terms of the offer and close the transaction, will help buyers determine the best time to start looking for a home. Even the most straightforward resale transaction takes several months from start to finish. Deciding first when to move is the key to knowing the most opportune time to enter the market.

# 5

## *Which Comes First — The Purchase or the Sale?*

This chapter is designed for the existing home owner who will be selling his home and purchasing another. "Back-to-back" or "double-ender" transactions like these are very common. First-time home buyers, though, will find the commentary interesting as a further application of the home-buying strategy all buyers need to effectively purchase a home.

Home owners who are planning to move frequently ask: "Do I buy first or do I sell?" Good arguments exist for each approach, and there is no "right" answer. Cautious buyers applying HOBS lean towards selling first, although a "best-of-both-worlds" option also exists.

Some purchasers fear having two contracts in existence at the same time, selling their current home and acquiring a new home. They ask: What happens to the purchase if the sale does not close? Where do they live if the sale closes but the purchase does not? Despite these legitimate concerns, practically speaking, what is the alternative? Although it is small consolation, it should be remembered that the vast majority of residential resale real estate transactions do close when scheduled. Most problems can be resolved well before closing, usually leaving ample time to make alternative arrangements if they cannot.

Realistically, when the decision is made to move, buyers first begin thinking about where to relocate, the type of house to buy, and the features to be sought. Selling the existing house is always assumed as a foregone conclusion. Practically speaking, once a home owner has found the resale property he wishes to acquire, all his attention is focused towards getting *that* house. A buyer who has done his homework and followed HOBS will know exactly where he is going, when he is moving, what the purchase price and other closing costs will be, and the price needed on the sale of the existing house to make the move economically viable *before* the Offer to Purchase is accepted.

Michael and Susan are cautious buyers who insisted on purchasing their new home first. On the advice of their lawyer, they made the offer conditional on selling their existing home. This way, if they could not sell it within a specified time (30 days), Michael and Susan were not obligated to complete the purchase of the new home. Conditional offers go a long way in resolving the "chicken-and-egg dilemma" of whether to buy or sell first.

When a conditional offer is signed, buyers benefit from arranging the longest period of time until closing. This gives people like Michael and Susan ample opportunity to list and sell their current home. Set a closing date at least 60 days away, and make the conditional period 30 days. Conditional offers are discussed in more detail in chapter 25.

An unconditional offer, though, carries more weight with a seller, as a firm and binding contract results from its acceptance. Acknowledging this, Cliff and Clair submitted an unconditional offer to purchase even though they still had to sell their existing home. The potential danger they faced was obvious: what do they do if they cannot sell their present house before the purchase transaction is scheduled to close?

People like Cliff and Clair, who buy first, must recognize they now have an interest in two properties. Selling their existing home within a short period of time then becomes their number-one priority. With the clock ticking, they lack the luxury of time to haggle over prices and other terms in an offer. The expression "vendor has bought" is a sure sign prospective buyers can strike a harder bargain. Lower prices, additional appliances and other personal property, a new survey — sellers who have bought often must make concessions on these and other points, depending on how desperate and pressing the situation happens to be. No seller can afford to lose a willing buyer if the price is acceptable but at the lower end of the range, even if it means sacrificing a fridge or stove. The alternative is to be stuck with two homes!

Selling first and purchasing later gives buyers like Sam and Diane considerable piece of mind. Knowing their home is sold, they now can devote their time and energy to looking for another residence. Knowing how much money they will be receiving on the sale of that house helps in establishing a price range for their new home. With the existing home already sold, Sam and Diane also can avoid having to submit a conditional Offer to Purchase.

Yet selling before buying has its drawbacks, too. Buyers unable to locate a satisfactory alternative home before the sale closes could face the possibility of having no place to live. With time ever becoming a factor, buyers who have sold might have to compromise their position and negotiate the purchase less forcefully, perhaps even exceeding their financial budget. No buyer in this situation can afford to lose an acceptable property over a small amount of money, a survey, or a few used appliances that the seller will not include in the purchase price.

Timing and the state of the market are two important factors to keep in mind when deciding whether to buy or sell first. In a rising market, buying first fixes the price for the new home, allowing the existing home to be sold at the highest possible price. George and Louise were planning to "trade-up"; that is, buy a more expensive home. By selling their home first during a rising market, they realized a good price. That same rising market, though, worked to their disadvantage, as the new home cost them considerably more than anticipated. The reverse holds true during the time of a falling market. Many purchasers who bought first obtained lower-than-anticipated sale prices when the bottom fell out of the real estate market in 1981. The additional funds that had to be borrowed to finance the purchase, coupled with extremely high interest rates at that time, created financial havoc for many purchasers. Buying first in a rising market and selling first in a slumping market is good advice. Only one problem: How do you determine the state of the market at any given time, considering how volatile it is?

The most prudent home-buying strategy is to sell first, buy later. Inevitably, though, people tend to buy first, thinking the existing home always can be sold later at a good price. While fighting human nature is hard, an offer to purchase that is made conditional on the buyer selling his existing property helps ensure that the head, and not the heart, ultimately carries the day.

# 6

## Know What's Out There

Many different types of homes, styles of homes and forms of legal ownership are available to choose from today. Yes, life was much simpler years ago! Let's look at these categories separately.

### Types of Homes

a) **Single-Family Detached Dwelling:** The house is not attached to any other dwelling. More expensive than other types of housing because detached homes occupy larger lots. They offer the greatest amount of privacy.

b) **Semi-Detached or "Side-by-Side" Dwelling:** Two houses which are attached with a common wall between the houses, or a common wall between garages.

c) **Link Houses:** A variation of semi-detached, where two houses appear detached above ground, but are attached below ground.

d) **Duplex (Triplex):** Two (or three) dwelling units, stacked one above the other. The owner may live in one unit and rent out the remainder to generate investment income.

e) **Row Housing:** A number of homes similar in design, linked together with common walls. Each home owner owns the building plus the property comprising his lot. Sometimes called "freehold townhouses."

f) **Street Townhouses:** A variation on row housing. While they visually resemble row housing, all the land for the complex is owned by a condominium corporation, and not the individual owners. Only the unit and an interest in the land is acquired.

## Styles of Homes

a) Bungalow: A one-storey house.
b) Two-Storey: The entire property is two stories high.
c) Split-Level: Sometimes called a one and one-half, part of the house is one level and part of the house is two levels. A side-split has the second level on the side of the house, while a back-split has the second level at the rear.
c) Condominium Apartment: Exactly the same as a rented apartment, except that the unit is owned, together with an interest in the common areas.

## Forms of Legal Ownership

a) Freehold: Where the home owner owns the building as well as the land on which it sits.
b) Leasehold: The home owner owns the building and leases the land, usually from the government or a government agency.
c) Condominium: (Usually in an apartment building or a townhouse complex.) The purchaser owns his individual residential unit, together with a proportionate interest in the common areas. This is discussed further in chapter 19.
d) Co-Op: Instead of owning a specific unit, the home owner is a shareholder in the corporation that owns the building. On a sale, the share, not the unit, is transferred to the purchaser. The owner has exclusive use of his premises. Restrictions on the sale of the share may exist, or approval from the board of directors may be needed. Not overly popular in Canada.
e) Co-Ownership: Instead of being a shareholder in a corporation, a percentage interest in the building is owned in common with everyone else. Exclusive use of a specific unit is permitted. Often used to avoid registering the complex as a condominium, when a rental apartment is converted. Stay away from this arrangement — it is full of problems.

# 7

# *Preliminary Considerations —*
# *Your Needs and Wants*

Once the commitment to buy a house has been made, you, the purchaser, must design your own HOBS. What are you looking for in a home? What do you expect from a property? As part of your home-buying strategy, it is essential to carefully analyze your needs and wants as well as your financial ability to handle the purchase before even embarking on any house-hunting expedition. Answering the questions raised in this chapter will help determine the type of property to buy, plus what the house should contain. The next chapter will help in calculating how large a home can be afforded.

Most people, especially first-time purchasers, would like to buy the biggest and nicest property available. To avoid financial disaster though, buyers must have both feet on the ground and lower their sights. Very few people have the financial ability and security to make their first home their "dream home." Most first-time home buyers purchase a "starter" home, one that is within their means, that satisfies present needs and wants and those of the foreseeable future. Families expand in size, tastes change and incomes increase. Over time this house is traded in, to be replaced by another. This procedure may be repeated a number of times until a "permanent" residence is acquired.

Buyers following the HOBS approach will find it helpful to prepare two different lists:

a) Those features you need in a house (the "must have" list of essential items); and

b) Those features you would like to have, if available and affordable (the "wants" list — the optional items). These wants should be weighed according to personal preferences, the most important items appearing first.

Armed with these two shopping lists, the home eventually selected should satisfy all your needs and as many of your wants as possible while still remaining within your price range. Preparing these lists is best done in the privacy of your own home or apartment before you see a real estate agent.

When buying any house, remember that it eventually will have to be sold. This may be a strange thought, considering that a house has not even been selected yet. Buyers applying HOBS will not overlook the importance of this point. The house selected should contain features that will make it easier to sell in the future.

The basic features for any house are the bedrooms and bathroom, kitchen, living room, dining room and storage space. After that, individual tastes take over. Is a three-bedroom home required, or will two do? Three-bedroom homes are much more common, and are considerably easier to market. How many bathrooms? What about a usable basement? What size rooms do you want and need? Measuring your furniture, plus your present-sized rooms, would help decide this question. Is air conditioning required? Is a garage essential? Is a one-car garage sufficient? Private drive or mutual drive? How much room do the children need to play without disturbing anyone? Is the increasingly popular "family room" desired? How large should the kitchen be? Should the kitchen be at the rear of the house so that the children can be seen while they play in the rear yard? Where should the laundry room be located? How many levels of stairs are acceptable? What about a garden? In short, what type of house is best for *you*?

How large a house can be afforded? Starter homes in the 1100 to 1400 square-foot range should satisfy most of these needs by providing three fair-sized bedrooms, plus other good-sized rooms.

A purchaser's position often determines the most suitable type of house to buy. A handyman may find an older home to his liking, the only cost of upgrading the house being materials. A condominium would be inappropriate for this buyer. Childless couples, or empty-nester couples whose children have grown up and moved from the house, enjoy the lifestyle afforded by condominium townhouses and apartments. At their stage in life, paying for the maintenance of the property is easier than physically doing it themselves. Young couples with children may find that a semi-detached or link house will give them most of the benefits of a detached home, at a lesser cost.

Subjective elements should not be downplayed. People are attracted to end units of condominium townhouses or row houses because they give a feeling of living in a semi-detached home. Other purchasers totally shun condominiums, street townhouses, semi-detached and link houses, fearing the damage a fire in an adjoining property would cause.

In the space below, continue developing your unique HOBS — Home-Buying Strategy — by listing those items which are essential in a house, and those which are greatly desired.

|  | NEEDS | WANTS |
|---|---|---|
| Size of House | | |
| Bedroom | | |
| Bathrooms | | |
| Kitchen | | |
| Living Room | | |
| Dining Room | | |
| Basement | | |
| Garage | | |
| Driveway | | |
| Storage Space | | |
| Backyard | | |
| Laundry Room | | |
| Other Rooms (Family Room) | | |
| Other Features (Air Conditioning) | | |

It is never wise to put your last cent into a home. A cushion of money is needed for personal emergencies or those unexpected costs. For help in deciding whether a financial commitment can be made to purchase a particular home, read on!

# 8

# *Preliminary Considerations — Financial*

Buying a house demands that purchasers be both practical and realistic. Sacrifices and a change in lifestyle are inevitable. A holiday may have to be cancelled and weekends may be spent entertaining at home rather than on the town. More disposable income may have to be applied towards the cost of shelter than previously was the case.

A key element of HOBS is to look for a home in the proper price range. A potential buyer must ask himself and *honestly answer* the following: What can I afford to buy? This key question is so important, it deserves repeating. What can I afford to buy?

In determining the range of price he can afford, a buyer must consider *both* the amount of the downpayment as well as the ongoing costs of ownership. Purchasers must set a *realistic maximum price range* for a house and stick to it. The upper end of the range is the maximum price a buyer can afford to pay. The bottom end is perhaps 5 percent lower. "Maximum price range" is a more important consideration than just maximum price. Inevitably, the best attainable price for a property turns out to be several thousand dollars more than anticipated. By looking for property at the lower end of the range, the buyer has left himself some leeway to negotiate.

As difficult as it is to say no, setting and keeping to a fixed maximum price range will avoid numerous problems in the future. Overextending yourself financially will cause grief and anxiety, could jeopardize your continued ownership of the property, and has led to the ruin of many marriages in the past. "Living within one's means" is an old virtue, but has never been more applicable than in today's financial world.

Sam and Helen calculated their maximum price range to be $95,000 to $100,000. Although they valiantly tried to hold to a price of $95,000, the property was ultimately sold to them for $97,900, a figure well within their maximum price range. With this approach, Sam and Helen came well within budget in buying this property.

The next step is to determine the applicable maximum price range. Several rules of thumb exist, which are just that — rules of thumb. One says the maximum price to pay for a house is 2.5 times your gross income. Both 3 times as well as 3.5 gross income are also used as guidelines. Some include the income of a working spouse, while others do not if the spouse's income is not ensured on a long-term basis.

Purchasers of owner-occupied homes should put as much money down as possible on closing, considering the closing costs involved. The more money down, the lower the mortgage payments no matter what the interest rate. Since a mortgage is needed to make up the difference between purchase price and downpayment, the answer to the question "What can I afford to buy" is squarely tied in with the question of qualifying for a mortgage.

While mortgage financing is considered in more detail in chapter 20, several points should be noted at this time. Lenders examine both the property and the borrower in deciding whether to grant a mortgage. Conventional mortgages do not exceed 75 percent of the appraised value of the property. Mortgages exceeding that limit can be arranged, the purchaser having to bear extra costs.

As a purchaser, you should determine early, and well before any offer is submitted, whether you will qualify for a mortgage loan and, if so, how large. This will maximize the time to negotiate the best possible mortgage. And, most important, it allows you to negotiate the Offer to Purchase from a position of strength. You know already that once the offer is accepted and a mortgage application made, all that is needed is formal written approval.

Buyers who are keen on knowing at this stage how large a property they can afford to purchase should follow this practical three-step approach.

1. Look at your available downpayment. A small portion of the total downpayment is paid as a deposit when an offer is signed, the rest being paid on closing. Remember to leave sufficient money for the many closing costs. Then determine how large a conventional mortgage can be arranged to finance the purchase. To see how large a property can be bought, financing it with a conventional mortgage, simply multiply the available downpayment by four. Eric and Marla have $20,000 available as a downpayment. By arranging a conventional mortgage, they could afford to pay $80,000 for a home ($20,000 x 4). By comparison, if Eric and Marla decided to arrange a "high-ratio" mortgage with a 20 percent downpayment, and could meet all other criteria, they could buy a house worth $100,000.

2. Carefully examine what it will cost to "carry" the house. Two types of operating costs exist. Hydro, water, heating, insurance, maintenance and repairs fall into the first category. Much information about these costs can be acquired simply by calling the utilities and your insurance agent. The second, and most important type, is known as the debt service costs — the cost of paying the mortgage (principal and interest), realty taxes and condominium maintenance, if applicable. A phone call to the local municipality should reveal the amount of the realty taxes for a particular property.

   For a conventional mortgage, no more than 30 percent of your gross income can be applied towards the mortgage, realty taxes and condominium maintenance. The link between the size of a mortgage and the borrower's gross income means the same question can be viewed from two different viewpoints. How large a mortgage can be supported by the borrower's gross income? How large must the borrower's gross income be to support a mortgage? The first approach is examined in this chapter; the second approach is examined in the chapter dealing with mortgage financing.

Eric and Marla have gross incomes totalling $32,000. They are not thinking of buying a condominium. To determine how much of their incomes can be applied each month towards the mortgage and taxes, their gross incomes are divided by 40. Up to $800 ($32,000 ÷ 40) can be applied towards the principal, interest and taxes each month on a conventional mortgage. Assuming the tax component is $100 monthly, Eric and Marla still have $700 to pay each month towards the mortgage. How large a mortgage they can arrange depends on the interest rate they will be charged. The following chart shows the amount to be paid per month *for each $1,000* borrowed, amortized over 25 years.

| Interest Rate | $ per Thousand | Interest Rate | $ per Thousand |
|---|---|---|---|
| 10  % | 8.95 | 15% | 12.46 |
| 10.5 | 9.28 | 15.5 | 12.83 |
| 11 | 9.63 | 16 | 13.19 |
| 11.5 | 9.97 | 16.5 | 13.56 |
| 12 | 10.32 | 17 | 13.93 |
| 12.5 | 10.67 | 17.5 | 14.29 |
| 13 | 11.02 | 18 | 14.66 |
| 13.5 | 11.38 | 18.5 | 15.03 |
| 14 | 11.74 | 19 | 15.41 |
| 14.5 | 12.10 | 19.5 | 15.78 |
|  |  | 20 | 16.15 |

By dividing the amount available for the monthly mortgage payment ($700) by the amount for any given interest rate, Eric and Marla will learn how large a mortgage they can afford to carry depending on interest rates. For example, if the current mortgage interest rate was 12%, dividing $700 by 10.32 means they could carry a mortgage of approximately $67,800. Repeating this approach for 10% and 13% indicates that mortgages of $78,200 and $63,500 respectively could be carried at those interest rates. Obviously, the lower the interest rate, the larger the mortgage that can be arranged!

With a $20,000 downpayment and gross incomes of $32,000, Eric and Marla could easily arrange a conventional mortgage of $60,000, allowing them to purchase a home for $80,000. If they decided to go "high-ratio" their gross incomes would allow them to carry a mortgage of $78,200 if the interest rate was 10%, and $63,500 if the mortgage rate was 13%. Coupled with their $20,000 downpayment, Eric and Marla could purchase a property with a high-ratio mortgage for a maximum price anywhere between $83,500 and $98,200, depending on the interest rate.

3. After all this has been done, reduce the maximum price by at least 5 percent. This establishes the maximum price range referred to earlier. The maximum price previously calculated becomes the upper end of the limit, while the "adjusted" figure becomes the lower end of the range and the target price. Purchasers now have some room to maneuver and still stay within budget. To carry a conventional mortgage, Eric and Marla would argue that the highest price they could afford to pay is the adjusted figure at the lower end of the range, namely $76,000 ($80,000 less 5 percent). Knowing (but concealing) that the true maximum price they could afford to pay is $80,000, Eric and Marla can continue negotiations with peace of mind, even if the purchase price begins creeping towards the $80,000 threshold. They also know that $80,000 figure can be exceeded, depending on the interest rate, *while still qualifying for a mortgage*, if they are prepared to arrange a high-ratio mortgage. With just a few minutes of advance planning, Eric and Marla have discovered the maximum price range which is appropriate for them.

Wise buyers will stay away from acquiring a principal residence putting no cash down, or in other words, financing the purchase entirely by mortgage. Assuming the purchase price is $100,000, that sum must come from somewhere — cash, mortgage or a combination of both. The mix might be $60,000 mortgage and $40,000 cash, $90,000 mortgage and $10,000 cash or $100,000 mortgage and $0 cash down. Without investing any of his own money on closing, what could keep a purchaser attached to the property? Some people argue that the purchaser with nothing down has nothing to lose by abandoning the property. That is not so. Walking away from a home when prices fall is not all that easy in most provinces.

Assume Owen and Melodye bought that $100,000 property with nothing down, arranging instead three mortgages. The first is for $75,000, the second for $15,000, the third being held by the seller for $10,000. If the property value fell to $95,000 and Owen and Melodye could not afford its upkeep, walking away from the property would not solve their problems but instead would compound them. The seller/holder of the third mortgage still has the right to sue Owen and Melodye for the $5,000 shortfall on his mortgage when the property is sold for $95,000. (The right to sue for a shortfall of funds in this situation does not exist in Alberta.) Whatever may be the merit in buying investment property with no downpayment, it should not apply to buying an owner-occupied home.

Using the chart below as a guide, record the estimated annual operating costs for several different properties.

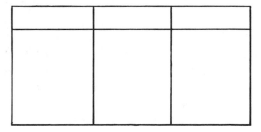

| ADDRESS OF PROPERTY | | | |
|---|---|---|---|
| Hydro | | | |
| Water | | | |
| Heating | | | |
| Insurance | | | |
| Maintenance/Repairs | | | |

Then calculate the maximum mortgage you can carry by completing the chart that follows. Eric and Marla's completed chart is given as an example.

WHAT CAN ERIC AND MARLA AFFORD TO BUY?

STEP 1   Maximum Downpayment Available/$20,000

STEP 2   *Determine the upper end of the range:*

| Gross Income | ÷ 40 = | Gross Monthly Payment |
|---|---|---|
| $32,000 | ÷ 40 = | $800 |
| Less: 1/12th of annual taxes | | $100 |
| Maximum monthly amount available for principal and interest payments | | $700 |

Divide this figure by the interest factor on page 27 to calculate the largest mortgage available at various interest rates, in thousands (i.e., $700 ÷ 9.97 = $70,210)

at x%, Maximum Mortgage is $ _____ +
Maximum Downpayment = Maximum Purchase Price (upper end of the range)

at 10%, $700/8.95 produces $78,200 + $20,000 = $98,200
at 11%, $700/9.63 produces $72,800 + $20,000 = $92,800
at 12%, $700/10.32 produces $67,800 + $20,000 = $87,800
at 13%, $700/11.02 produces $63,500 + $20,000 = $83,500

STEP 3   *To determine the lower end of the range (the target price), reduce the Maximum Purchase Price for any given interest rate by 5%*

| at x % | upper end of range is $ _____ | while lower end of range is $ _____ |
|---|---|---|
| at 10% | $98,200 | $93,290 |
| at 11% | $92,800 | $88,160 |
| at 12% | $87,800 | $83,410 |
| at 13% | $83,500 | $79,325 |

WHAT CAN I AFFORD TO BUY?

STEP 1    Maximum Downpayment Available $ _____

STEP 2    *Determine the upper end of the range:*
Gross Income      ÷ 40 =    Gross Monthly Payment
$ _____    ÷ 40 =    $ _____
Less: 1/12th of annual
taxes                            $ _____
Maximum monthly
amount available for
principal and interest
payments                    $ _____

Divide this figure by the interest factor on page 27 to calculate the largest mortgage available at various interest rates, in thousands (i.e., $700 ÷ 9.97 = $70,210)

at x%, Maximum Mortgage is $ _____ +
Maximum Downpayment = Maximum Purchase Price (upper end of the range)

| | | | | | |
|---|---|---|---|---|---|
| at 10% | $ ____ | + | $ ____ | = | $ ____ |
| at 11% | $ ____ | + | $ ____ | = | $ ____ |
| at 12% | $ ____ | + | $ ____ | = | $ ____ |
| at 13% | $ ____ | + | $ ____ | = | $ ____ |

STEP 3    *To determine the lower end of the range (the target price), reduce the Maximum Purchase Price for any given interest rate by 5%*
at x% upper end of                while lower end
            range is $ _____        of range is $ _____

| | | | |
|---|---|---|---|
| at 10% | $ ____ | | $ ____ |
| at 11% | $ ____ | | $ ____ |
| at 12% | $ ____ | | $ ____ |
| at 13% | $ ____ | | $ ____ |

# 9

# Know the Community and Neighborhood

By now, prospective purchasers applying the HOBS approach will have clearly defined needs and wants, and a sound understanding of what is affordable. Yet, it is still premature to contact a real estate agent to go house-hunting. Buyers must first decide which of the many communities and neighborhoods are of interest and "get a feel" for house prices and values in these neighborhoods.

Most real estate agents agree that there are only three important factors in buying a house — location, location and location. The resale potential and market appeal of a property is of great importance, as not everyone views the strengths and weaknesses of a location in the same fashion. A significant feature of developing a home-buying strategy is to purchase a property with the best possible location.

What does this emphasis on location really mean? Does it refer to the community in which a property is situated? The neighborhood within that community? A specific house on a particular street? The factors to consider in choosing a community and a neighborhood are explored in this chapter. Factors affecting specific properties are examined in chapter 15. Most purchasers decide first to move to a certain community. Later, a particular neighborhood is selected, containing the most desirable features of the community.

A community and neighborhood must reflect your own lifestyle and station in life. Without question, the very first thing buyers applying HOBS should do is spend some time driving or walking around the communities and through the neighborhoods that appear promising. Even before you examine them in further detail, ask yourself: What kind of "gut feeling" has it generated? Do you like what you see? What does it offer, compared to other areas? Is it well maintained? Would you like to be part of it? Can you visualize being part of it?

If possible, go back at a different time during the week (weekday and weekend). Don't forget to travel through communities and neighborhoods where you might like to live both by day and night. They tend to take on a different character in the dark, both visually and audibly. With noise travelling much further at night, a district considered acceptable by day could be totally unacceptable by night. Ask yourself if the streets appear adequately lit. Does the area appear safe and serene at night? To learn more about an area, stop and talk with some of its residents. Who better to tell you what an area is really like?

For those communities and neighborhoods that pass this preliminary hurdle, examine them more thoroughly against the following factors. Some involve a trade-off, meaning how they are ranked and weighted will differ from purchaser to purchaser. Yet each factor should be considered from both a personal as well as an objective viewpoint. One affects your buying the property, and the other will determine its resale potential. The fewer the negative factors, the greater its future marketability.

## Older vs. Newer Communities

It is fascinating how people's opinions differ in the on-going debate between older and newer communities. Besides newly built homes, numerous resale properties are available in newer communities, as people sell or "trade-up" several years after moving into an area. Well-kept established areas exhibit a certain maturity, charm and character. The impression generated is more laid-back and relaxed. By contrast, a newly developed community projects a feeling and image of freshness, vitality and youthfulness in its outward appearance. Older communities have a complete list of the support services most residents need — schools, shopping, hospitals and the like. Development of these services takes time, and they are not readily available to "residents" in newer or outlying communities. Buyers of resale homes in growing areas must be prepared to acknowledge the necessary trade-off between some of these features, and the newness associated with a developing area. A community and its neighborhoods are like the trees that line the street — both take many years to develop and mature.

## Proximity to Work and Convenience

Access to and within a community is of crucial importance to most people. Not everyone wants to be a commuter. The difference between a half-hour trip and a one-hour trip (one way) to work every day is over 10 complete days each year. Less time spent commuting to work means more time to spend with the family, or enjoying some of the other pleasures of life. Commuter communities, on the other hand, are generally more reasonably priced, being somewhat distant from the hub of activity.

Before deciding to move to a suburban community, George and Pauline did a "test run" to see how long it would take to get to work in peak rush hour. They also learned how long a trip to the city centre would take in off-hours. By checking this out ahead of time, George and Pauline did not face any surprises the first day they headed to work after moving.

## Transportation

The availability of public transportation in built-up areas far surpasses that in newer communities. This is an important consideration for families with one car. Nonexistent, irregular or limited transit service could be very inconvenient. Residents in newer areas should not rely too heavily on the projected date for new transit routes or the extension of existing lines. Even rush-hour transit service is only inaugurated when warranted. If public transportation is available, check out how frequently it is provided, especially at night and on weekends. Is an extra fare payable? Finally, considering our harsh Canadian climate, consider how far the walk is to the nearest transit or commuter stop. One kilometre is probably the farthest anyone would want to walk from the nearest commuter bus or train in the worst winter storm! Also look at the network of roads and highways in the general area. How close is the nearest highway or expressway? Many people want to be close, but not too close. Will noise be a factor? Is an interchange located nearby or planned? Do the roads have sufficient lanes to avoid traffic congestion?

## Schools

The availability of primary and high schools, both public and separate, is important to most people. Newer communities often lack the necessary "infill" of schools, making busing of children to school a necessity. The school system itself should not be ignored, as it varies considerably from municipality to municipality. Different types of programs are offered (i.e., French Immersion or services for the disabled) depending on the local Board of Education. Education is a high priority. Check out all aspects of the educational system in a community early.

## Shopping

Different classes of commercial development exist within a community. Large regional malls and plazas, generally commuter oriented, are built to service an entire community. Intermediate-sized plazas which are both commuter and pedestrian oriented have smaller trading areas. Neighborhood or convenience shopping also exists to satisfy local shopping needs.

Just a short trip through both an older and a newer community will illustrate how commercial development lags considerably behind the growth of new residential areas. Something must come first — typically it is the homes and the people. Commercial development only takes place when sufficient residents live in an area to make it economically viable. Until then, purchasers of resale properties in newer communities and neighborhoods will find themselves travelling much further to the types of shopping they are accustomed to. When travelling through these areas, learn where the different classes of commercial development are located.

Purchasers of homes in smaller communities should also determine ahead of time where they can shop. Reflecting the nature of the area, smaller shopping centres predominate. If a large regional mall exists in the area, learn its location and how long it will take to travel there.

While being close to shopping has its advantages, being *too* close has its disadvantages. Traffic congestion, noise and visual pollution, such as loose trash, may be a problem. Living adjacent or even near a commercial development, whether large or small, may not bother some people, but could deter others from buying a specific home. When analyzing these factors, remember to look at them from two different points of view — in terms of *buying* the property now, and in terms of *selling* it to someone else at a later date.

## Support Services

One of the most marked contrasts between established and growing communities is in the area of support services. Everyone needs a doctor, dentist, druggist — perhaps even a paediatrician. While buyers in older areas know exactly where these services are available, rarely are they in the vanguard of development. Usually they are part of the "in-fill" that occurs after significant residential development has taken place.

Adequate police protection, fire stations, day-care centres, ambulance service, nearby hospitals and frequent garbage pick-ups also follow in the wake of residential growth. Residents in newer developments practically everywhere complain about inadequacies of these services, when compared to the levels to which they were accustomed in more established areas. Before making any commitment, check this point out carefully!

## Religious Facilities

Being close to religious facilities such as churches, synagogues or religious schools is important to some people. Neighborhoods that are religiously oriented are found in some areas, and are centred around a religious facility.

## Recreational Facilities

Older communities far surpass newer ones in having parks, playgrounds, community centres, skating rinks, swimming pools, tennis courts, libraries, theatres and museums. Residents of newer areas constantly are demanding that high quality recreational facilities be established in the early years of community growth. The key question, of course, is how to pay for them. What swayed Gord and Connie to one community was the novel approach increasingly being followed by local municipalities. A "lot levy" fund was created, assessed to the developers of the community. The lot levy money was used to build a major recreational complex in the heart of the community. Following construction, the facilities are being maintained from the nominal fees charged to people like Gord and Connie on a user-pay basis when swimming or skating. Both this new community and its residents acquired magnificent recreational facilities without the municipality having to make a major capital expenditure.

## Other Factors

Many other factors must be considered and explored *now* before deciding on a community and neighborhood, including:

a) Telephone Service — It is surprising how small the local calling area becomes outside major metropolitan areas. Many people are shocked to learn, following a move, that former local calls are now subjected to long distance tolls.

b) Potential Deterrents — Many homes are located on or near major thoroughfares, gas stations, apartment buildings, airports, cemetaries, railway tracks and industrial parks. Although these may seem insignificant, do not simply dismiss them as frivolous concerns. Not everyone thinks the same way. What one person chooses to ignore, could totally dissuade another. Remember that the property being bought now eventually will be sold. When considering these factors, look at them *objectively* to maximize the resale potential of the property.

## Peer Pressure

Probably this is the greatest factor motivating people to consider specific communities and neighborhoods. "All our friends are moving there" is a commonly heard rallying cry. Similarly, people move to particular areas to be compatible with neighbors in ethnic, cultural, religious and socioeconomic terms; in terms of children and their ages; and also in terms of lifestyles. Sometimes the composition of the community is an overwhelming priority for a purchaser.

Be frank with yourself when considering a proposed move. Stand back and ask if it makes sense for the right reasons in terms of needs, wants and ability to pay. Has the proper home-buying strategy been devised? Let your head decide, not your heart. As pleasant as moving with friends to a community or neighborhood may appear, resist the temptation if it otherwise cannot be justified.


Don't forget how important it is to become better acquainted with the real estate market in those communities and neighborhoods. Check the ads for homes in the weekend edition of the local newspaper. Call several real estate agents whose phone numbers you noted in the ads or on "For Sale" signs in front of appealing properties. Ask them about the listing price, key features of the property, and what the purchase price includes. Try to visit several open houses too, not with a view to buying, but rather to learn more about prices and values in the area.

Finding the most suitable community and neighborhood in which to relocate will take some time. With every expedition, new thoughts will come to mind, helping refine your decision. With a properly planned HOBS, home buyers will realize when they have found the area that is most appropriate for them. Like love, it may be hard to describe in words, but when it has been found, you know it.

To help rate the factors involved in selecting a community and neighborhood, jot down some notes using the chart below as a guide.

COMMUNITY/NEIGHBORHOOD
Type of community — New or Old
Proximity to work
Transportation
Schools
Shopping
Support services
Religious facilities
Recreational facilities
Other factors

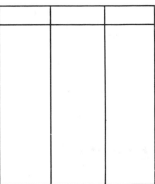

With so many decisions already having been made, buyers would think they are ready to rush right in and submit an Offer to Purchase. Not just yet! It's still premature! There's still more work to be done! The next stage in a proper HOBS involves contacting the real estate professionals with whom you must work. These are the people who will transform your ideas into reality.

# 10

## *The Three Real Estate Professionals*

The process of selecting and purchasing a home has become increasingly complex over the years. No one is expected to know all the details and technicalities involved, from the pre-offer stage until the transaction is closed and the deed is registered. A key component of the HOBS approach includes using the services of three well-qualified real estate professionals. These are specialists in whom the buyer has total and unqualified trust — a real estate agent, a home inspector and a real estate lawyer. Simply put, buyers cannot afford to ignore *any* of these experts. Otherwise, once the money changes hands on closing, a buyer will have acquired not only the property, but also the headache of any unrevealed problems.

The experience and expertise these professionals bring to a transaction cannot be overlooked. Individually, each has an important, yet distinct, role to play. Real estate agents help locate the right house at the right price for a buyer. Home inspectors carefully examine it, to determine whether it is sound or in need of repair. The lawyer processes the transaction, ensuring that title to the property is transferred properly on closing. Together, these real estate experts professionally and objectively guide buyers through a nervous yet extremely exciting time in their lives, providing ideas and support to make the transaction and the transition as smooth and worry-free as possible.

Where do you find a well-qualified real estate agent? Home

inspector? Real estate lawyer? These questions will be answered separately in later chapters. While the real estate agent is needed first, remember to select all three real estate professionals early, *before* an offer is signed. Each specialist should be "on standby," ready to participate when "the house" — suitable and affordable — has been found.

# 11

## *Choosing A Real Estate Agent*

Very few people buy a home without using a real estate agent. Choosing the right agent is almost as important as — and is a prerequisite to — selecting the right property. A knowledgeable, sincere agent in whom a buyer has complete confidence will save valuable time and effort while also reducing the headaches that accompany any home purchase.

Real estate agents are licensed, commissioned salespeople who are paid by sellers for being a "matchmaker"; that is, they bring buyers, sellers and homes together. The agent who has listed the property is commonly called the "listing agent." Any other agent who introduces a purchaser to the property is called the "selling agent" or the "sub-agent." Although the purchaser may feel the selling agent is "his agent," by law both agents are paid by and work for the person who has put his property up for sale.

Most buyers prefer to do business with a separate selling agent, so the listing agent does not represent both parties. Where two agents are involved, the commission is usually split between them. Obviously listing agents prefer dealing with purchasers who do not have a selling agent, to avoid having to split the commission.

Some buyers feel that where only one agent is involved, more subtle pressure is exerted on them to sign an offer. For this reason, buyers of resale properties are encouraged to have a separate selling agent to represent their interests.

Many real estate agents are licensed in every community.

How does a buyer decide which agent to deal with? Where do buyers new to the market, and who do not yet have an agent, meet agents? As a service industry, satisfied customers and the referral business they generate are the cornerstones of the real estate agent's success. Asking friends, relatives and neighbors for the names and phone numbers of agents they have dealt with in the past is an excellent way of being introduced to an agent. Open houses should be considered as well. An open house is held to show the features of a property to other agents and to purchasers. Equally important for buyers is the opportunity it presents to meet the listing agent for that property. By attending several open houses, prospective buyers can kill two birds with one stone; while viewing the features and learning the values of properties, buyers also can meet and talk with a number of listing agents. One of these agents could very well become the buyer's selling agent on another property.

Another way of meeting agents is to check the newspaper ads. List the names and phone numbers of agents who are active in the area where you are looking. Other purchasers simply call the agent whose number appears on a "For Sale" sign to arrange an appointment at which both the property and the agent can be assessed.

Sometimes the selection of a real estate agent can have hidden consequences. Brian recently bought a home, conditional on selling his existing home. Victoria, the agent who sold Brian the new home, also became the listing agent for Brian's present home. Victoria made two commissions this way, and Brian was unable to retain his nephew, Dennis, to sell his current home. Detailed information on these "back-to-back" transactions appears in the chapter on conditional offers.

Buyers must feel totally at ease with their agent. A good rapport is needed, coupled with a sincere feeling the agent is working for you. A good agent is a good listener, one who will hear what you need and want and who will find it for you within your price range. Expect the agent

- to know the market thoroughly, both in general as well as in the proposed neighborhood. Knowing what homes are worth is an agent's job.
- to provide you with a comparative market analysis for com-

munities and neighborhoods that interest you. Most real estate boards and associations have full details on the price at which comparable properties in the area sold.

- to pre-screen properties, so that only those which are both appealing and affordable are viewed.
- to help inspect prospective homes at mutually convenient hours, but not at a mere beck and call.
- to keep abreast of new homes constantly entering the market.
- to know about and advise on the various methods of financing the purchase, including some of the innovative financing schemes.
- to know how the asking price of a property compares with current resale values.
- to have full details about a property on which an offer will be submitted.
- to be candid in setting a realistic price when submitting that offer.
- to negotiate skillfully in setting the price and other terms in the offer.
- to move quickly, yet efficiently, to be both a mother hen and yet a catalyst, a confidant and yet a devil's advocate.

In short, a real estate agent should be an agent in the truest sense of the word, a person employed to act on behalf of another.

Once an agent has been selected, be candid and honest with him or her. Once an agent has been selected, stick with him or her. Because the agent's job involves considerable leg work, for which no money is received until the transaction is completed, agents expect loyalty from a buyer. Rarely do buyers give only one agent a written "exclusive" to act on their behalf, yet this is practically what happens. After all, a purchaser who deals with five different agents should not expect the same level of interest and closeness from any of them as he could expect by working with only one agent. Being fair with a real estate agent can only benefit the buyer. One the other hand, because no written contract exists, it is easy to "fire" an agent if he or she does not live up to expectations, or is too high-pressured. Remember, *you* have retained the agent and must be happy with his or her performance.

Spend some time talking with the agent before even looking at a house. Give the agent a copy of your shopping lists. The more familiar the agent is with your needs, wants, personal tastes and financial position, the easier it will be for the agent to locate the right house at the right price with the right financing.

The exception is if the purchaser is new to the community (a company transfer, for example). Otherwise, selecting a neighborhood and community is the purchaser's responsibility, not the real estate agent's. To be fair, a buyer must have some preliminary homework done before contacting an agent. Otherwise, the agent will be on a perpetual wild goose chase, never knowing what is acceptable.

Properly informed, an agent can review your tentative decisions, help firm them up with necessary modifications and use them to act on your behalf in the shortest possible time. A real estate agent must know the market thoroughly, but he or she can only help by knowing you— the purchaser — thoroughly as well.

If you already have selected an agent, *do not* go to an open house without "your agent." It could cost him or her a lot of money. Mac and Karen had been house-hunting with a real estate agent, Cheryl, for weeks. Cheryl did not accompany them to one open house, where Maureen, the listing agent, showed them the house. By doing this, Maureen became their agent for this property. When Mac and Karen submitted an offer on this property, Cheryl could not be shown as the selling agent, as she had not introduced them to this property. Although Cheryl had spent considerable time previously with Mac and Karen, she did not earn any commission on the sale of that house. As both listing and selling agent, Maureen made double what she would have made if Cheryl had been involved.

Once a prospective property has been located, ask your agent to find out more about the background to the sale. This information could have a great bearing on the purchase price submitted in the offer. How long has the property been on the market? Has the price been reduced already? Has the vendor bought another house? Is the vendor being transferred out of town? Is the property a "distress sale," arising from death or marriage breakdown? In all of these cases, a lower-than-expected price might be accepted, especially with a "quick closing," since the seller may not have the luxury to negotiate extensively.

Occasionally problems arise in the period between acceptance and closing. Delays could occur in the delivery of documents to your lawyer, or a seller may not cooperate in providing access to the property, despite the wording of the contract. In these situations, the real estate agent should go to bat for you. After all, it is the agent's commission which is in jeopardy if the deal doesn't close! Despite what may be said, an agent's job is only completed when the deal has closed and you are in possession of your house, and *not* simply when the offer is signed. Never hesitate to call on your agent before closing, if need be.

The importance of working with a real estate agent is best demonstrated by comparing the problems that often arise in private sales. As no agent is involved, buyers and sellers are constantly in direct contact. Emotions may run high, frustration may turn to anger and face-to-face discussions may develop into confrontations — all of which may defeat the transaction. A real estate agent, on the other hand, is an impartial, objective intermediary whose role as a "go-between" may be the difference between a "deal" and a wasted effort.

Some real estate boards are now offering computerized listings to its members. To use this system, an agent will feed information into the computer which then lists those properties that satisfy the data. The goal of this system is to eliminate much of the dreary manual work involved in finding a suitable property. To be effective, though, the agent must know what you, as a buyer, want and can afford to pay.

Finally, let the agent know at the outset how much you rely on his or her experience and expertise. Being professionals, most agents will respond to the challenge and see that you — and they — are satisfied.

# 12

# Private Listings, Exclusive Listings and MLS Listings

Houses are like toothpaste! Neither can be sold effectively without proper marketing. The greater the exposure a house receives, the greater the likelihood interested buyers will be attracted to it.

Real estate commissions are sizeable. On even the most inexpensive properties, commissions run into the thousands of dollars. Before listing a property with a real estate agent, some sellers will try and sell it privately, if only to test the waters. Often this involves little more than putting a "For Sale-Private" sign on the front lawn and an ad in the newspaper. Because no one in the real estate industry is actively "flogging" the house, the amount of exposure this private listing will get is very limited. No purchaser would be introduced to a private listing by a real estate agent since there is no commission for an agent in the event of a sale.

Once a real estate broker is engaged, the property may be listed one of two ways: "exclusively" or "MLS" (Multiple Listing Service). With an exclusive listing, the property is listed and advertised for sale only within the listing broker's office or other branches of the same company. Exclusive listings are sold most often where a large broker has a network of offices to give them wide exposure, or where the listing agent's firm concentrates its activities in a narrow area. With an exclusive listing, details of the house and its features are not distributed to all of the members of the local real estate board or association, as they would be with an MLS listing.

Multiple listings give detailed information on the lot, premises, items included in the sale price and proposed financing of the property, usually accompanied by a photo. Listings of 60 to 90 days are quite common, providing an agent ample time to generate interest in a property, market it and sell it. In an attempt to save money, some sellers list their property exclusively for a limited period of time (30 days) following which the property "goes MLS" for another 60 days if still unsold. Far and away, most properties are listed on the Multiple Listing Service.

While a seller pays the agent's commission on closing, indirectly it is the buyer who foots the bill, because sellers build the amount of commission into the sale price. Commission rates are not etched in stone. Generally accepted standard charges do exist in each area, which are virtually non-negotiable. Real estate agents are not known for cost-cutting or discounting. Exclusive listings carry a lower commission charge than MLS listings, which are available much more widely. In urban centres, the usual commission payable on an exclusive listing is 5 percent of the sale price. Six percent is the norm for properties listed on MLS. Cottage or rural properties may bring a commission as high as 10 percent of the sale price.

Buyers seeking the greatest selection of homes should consult the MLS listings first.

# 13

## *The Home Inspector*

When buying a used car, it's what's under the hood that counts. In recent years, a whole new industry, the diagnostic centre, has developed, where used car buyers can get an independent evaluation of a car's condition before buying it. Isn't there even more need for such information when purchasing a resale (used) house, when the financial commitment often is ten times as large? You would think so! Yet too often buyers only make a brief, cursory inspection of the key operating features of a house before purchasing it, stressing instead its cosmetic condition. Even when inquiries are directed to items like the roof, the electrical and plumbing systems, the furnace and insulation, the answers provided by a seller too often are accepted strictly at face value.

Most buyers feel that obvious flaws can be dealt with in subsequent negotiations, before an offer is signed. Unfortunately, it is the not-so-obvious flaws, maintenance deficiencies and structural defects that will cost home buyers enormous sums in the future, after the property has changed hands. How can a buyer know what it will cost, in addition to the purchase price, to bring a house up to standards without having it inspected first?

Resale properties do not carry any kind of warranty. Instead, the rule "caveat emptor" (let the buyer beware) still applies to the purchase of an existing home. Problem: How can a buyer beware, if he does not even know the deficiencies to look for and beware of?

Understandably, not all purchasers would feel confident when inspecting the "guts" of a resale house. To help buyers make an educated decision that a home is "fit," a new professional, the home inspector, has begun to appear in Canada. Home inspectors are not new; they have operated in the United States and the United Kingdom for years. The cost of having a home inspected is minimal, compared against the expense and agony of unforeseen repairs, hidden defects and unpleasant surprises. Proper development and application of a home-buying strategy means an impartial home inspection status report will be obtained when buying a resale property. Without this essential disclosure, it is like buying a used car blindly.

Often professional engineers, home inspectors visually examine and inspect the property internally and externally, and provide a detailed itemized written evaluation report on the present condition of the house. Estimated life expectancies should be provided for items like the roof, furnace and the driveway. Better reports include recommendations for preventative maintenance and cost estimates for major repairs and improvements. This way, home buyers can budget for these anticipated costs in the future.

Don't expect the home inspector to comment on value and price, or to decide or even recommend whether you should proceed with the transaction. As home inspectors do not know all the factors involved in the transaction, the ultimate decision must rest with you — the purchaser.

Rarely is a home inspection conducted before an offer is submitted. If the offer is not accepted, the cost of the report would be money thrown away. Instead, when a suitable property has been found and all other terms successfully negotiated, an offer is signed and accepted which is made conditional on the purchaser obtaining a satisfactory home inspection report within a set number of days after acceptance. Otherwise, the deal is off.

"Conditional on home inspection" clauses are no longer a novelty. Most sellers do not object to them appearing in an offer, as the "conditional" period usually is quite short. Sellers who are confident their property will stand up to scrutiny have nothing to fear from this type of clause. Suspicions are bound to be raised, on the other hand, if a seller strenuously objects. Most real estate agents no longer discourage buyers from including this clause in an offer. Better agents will even recommend that a home inspection clause appear in the Offer to Purchase.

Usually home inspectors are given very little time in an offer — perhaps as little as three days — to conduct an examination and prepare their written report. While they know that timing is critical, it is very easy for a buyer to maximize the amount of time available for the inspection. Instead of contacting an inspector for the first time once an offer is signed, do so *before* an offer is submitted. Find out his charges. Shop around and get at least three different price quotes. Learn more about the home inspection company. How long has it been in business? Does it have errors and omissions (liability) insurance? How extensive a written report does it prepare? What is excluded? (Probably appliances, and security systems). Once you have selected a home inspector, ask him to be "on standby" until an offer is accepted. With the necessary preliminary work concluded early, little time will be lost during that condensed "conditional" period immediately after acceptance.

When compared against the cost of the house itself, the charge for the home inspection is small. Although fees vary, many inspections run in the $200 to $300 range. If unsure which home inspector to use, check with friends, your real estate agent and your lawyer. See if they are familiar with any of the home inspection services in your area, and the quality of their reports. Like other service industries, home inspectors rely very heavily on referral business.

A home inspection should cover all the major areas of a house. Of course, the structure itself will be inspected. Features that should be examined include the electrical, plumbing, wiring, heating and air-conditioning systems; fireplace; walls (for fresh plaster and wallpaper over cracks); floors, ceilings and the state of kitchen and bathroom fixtures; waterproofing and signs of water infiltration or dampness; foundation structure; insulation and ventilation; signs of termite infestation and wood rot; condition of doors and windows and condition of the basement. External evaluations should be given on the roof and gutters; siding, eavestroughs and downspouts; soffits and fascias; garage; foundation, porches; chimney; driveway; masonry and brickwork. In short, a home inspection report gives buyers a realistic, objective appraisal of those items which too often were overlooked, ignored or taken for granted in the past.

Only with a home inspection can a purchaser be properly assured that the house does not have, and never has had, urea formaldehyde foam insulation.

A home inspection is not an appraisal of the property for mortgage purposes. That is a separate investigation, conducted to determine its fair market value. Buyers arranging a new mortgage will be paying the cost for both a home inspection report, as well as an appraisal report of the property.

Usually a verbal report is given following the inspection, the written report following within a day or so. Whenever possible, accompany the inspector when he examines the house. First hand he can point out defects and problem areas, the written report providing the detailed commentary needed. This also provides an excellent opportunity to familiarize yourself with the house (i.e., the location of the main water shut-off and the fuse box/circuit breaker), to ask questions and to raise issues when they are fresh in your mind.

Armed with a home inspection report and depending on its contents, buyers may

1. Proceed with the offer as is.
2. Walk away from the transaction, if serious defects or deficiencies are found, by giving the proper notice. Of course, this assumes the offer was made conditional on obtaining a satisfactory report.
3. Renegotiate the purchase price downwards (in a conditional offer situation), if major problems need to be rectified.

Mark and Angela found themselves in this situation recently. Although the house was only two years old, the home inspection report disclosed serious electrical problems that would cost $1,500 to correct. After lengthy negotiations, the purchase price was reduced by $1,500, with Mark and Angela fixing up the problem themselves after closing.

When Harold and Roberta learned that their prospective house had a roof that leaked, they were able to knock $1,000 off the purchase price.

Never select a home inspector who is a home renovator. Inspectors in this category may overemphasize deficiencies and defects, hoping to generate business repairing or improving the property. To ensure objectivity, stick to an independent home inspector.

No standards or criteria govern home inspectors because they are not licensed at the present time by any government agency. Anyone, with any qualifications, can call himself a "home inspector." All the more reason to hire an inspector (or avoid one if necessary) that others have dealt with previously.

An excellent book on the topic of home inspectors is *Inspecting A House: A Guide For Buyers, Owners and Renovators*, written by Alan Carson and Robert Dunlop, and published by Stoddart.

Using the chart below as a guide, list those home inspectors who you contact, the price they charge for a home inspection, the nature of the report, and other pertinent information.

Name
Phone #
Price of Report
How Long to Complete
Does Report Include:
  1) Present Condition of Property
  2) Anticipated Life Expectancies
  3) Preventive Maintenance Program

Let's now turn our attention to the third member of the real estate trio — the lawyer. He or she will actually close the transaction for the house with which the agent found, and which the home inspector found to be sound!

# 14

## Selecting a Lawyer —
## The Modern Approach

Much too often, the selection of a lawyer to process the purchase transaction is left until the offer is signed and accepted. Truly this is unfortunate as a good real estate lawyer can provide invaluable assistance to buyers of resale homes *if he or she is contacted early*. As in finding a home inspector, make inquiries, have preliminary discussions and *choose your lawyer well before an offer is ever submitted*. In a proper home-buying strategy, the selection of a lawyer is done early. *It is never left until after the offer is accepted*.

Many people feel intimidated by lawyers. First-time home buyers have often never required the services of a lawyer. Quite a few years may have passed since those "seasoned veterans" already owning a house used a lawyer. Yet developing a working relationship with a lawyer, especially before the offer is signed, will greatly benefit you as a buyer. How, then, to select a lawyer?

The legal profession is a service industry. Personal contacts are the cornerstone of any legal firm establishing a clientele. With limited forms of advertising open to lawyers, satisfied clients and referral business are the very lifeblood of a legal practice.

Start compiling a list of names by seeking personal recommendations from friends, relatives and neighbors. What type of dealings did they have and what was their opinion of the lawyer? Have other people such as real estate agents, mortgage brokers and mortgage lenders heard of or dealt with the lawyer? Do they have any recommendations? What is the lawyer's reputation, both professionally and in the community at large? Does he or she have a particular degree of expertise that other people have recognized? If you are "lawyer-less," get the names of three or four recommended lawyers. Give yourself a choice. More importantly, though, request these names well ahead of time. Waiting until the deal is struck before considering who will represent you adds unnecessary pressure to a buyer who may already be nervous and anxious. A lawyer has to be selected. Why not do it early, before the offer is signed, so he or she can have input into the transaction?

Encouraging buyers to contact lawyers early is part of the different but modern attitude the public should have when dealing with lawyers. In retaining any professional, the client should be concerned firstly with his or her level of expertise and experience, and secondly with the comfort and reassurance the professional provides to the client. While some provincial Law Societies downplay use of the term "specialist," it is a fact of life in the legal profession that some lawyers carry on a much more extensive real estate and mortgage practice. When selecting your lawyer, make sure he or she is experienced in real estate conveyancing.

Yet it is equally important for buyers to feel comfortable when dealing with their lawyer. Since a home purchase is an extremely important event for most people, the lawyer selected must demonstrate a genuine, sincere interest in his client. The lawyer's role is part advisor, part devil's advocate, part confidant, and part nurse-maid. The lawyer must be prepared to answer directly the routine questions all buyers consider of vital importance. A conveyancer can handle the simple transfer of title. A lawyer, on the other hand, can provide invaluable information and guidance on mortgage financing, pre-qualification, and the numerous creative schemes presently available. He or she must be able to reassure buyers when minor problems arise that they are not imsurmountable. He or she must be prepared to educate clients, clearly explaining all aspects of the transaction so they are clearly understood. By retaining a lawyer, you are paying him or her to attend to many of the details associated with purchasing a home.

Carefully analyze the list of names being compiled. Perhaps one or two names from different sources keep reappearing. If so, that's as good a place to start as any! Now, take several minutes and call the lawyers to discuss both the proposed transaction as well as the possibility of retaining them to act for you.

Fees are a very sensitive issue in the legal profession. Some lawyers will not discuss fees on the telephone, while many others will. Since legal fees are only one part of the overall costs that buyers incur, it is important to know early not only the amount of the lawyer's fees, but more importantly the overall costs in the transaction. These are the charges that are constant no matter which lawyer is used — disbursements, transfer tax, adjustments and deductions. See chapter 22 for more details on these hidden costs.

When they are contacted for an estimate of their fees, very few lawyers go further and volunteer information on how much money should be set aside — the approximate "overall charges" to be incurred — to close the transaction. This attitude on the part of most lawyers is unfortunate, for it leaves buyers totally in the dark as to how to allocate their financial resources. To simply quote fees, and not advise buyers of the total amount needed to close, touches on misrepresentation to the public.

Experienced real estate lawyers know what these hidden costs are and should be prepared to inform buyers at an early stage. Any lawyer who volunteers this information when asked for a price quote should be seriously considered as your lawyer, for that reason alone. Obviously only he or she is prepared willingly to give you a straight bill of goods, a reasonable estimate at the outset of the true cost of closing the transaction. Last-minute surprises can be eliminated if the total amount needed to close is discussed and planned for. If none of the lawyers contacted offers this information, then ask them for the details. Make sure you find out both what the lawyer's fees will be — and what the overall closing costs will be.

As most of the closing charges are fixed and non-negotiable, a lawyer who quotes a substantially reduced figure simply is baiting the hook. You are being told what you want to hear now, with the unpleasant news to be sprung later. Don't penalize a lawyer who has been honest and candid with you by dealing with someone else who is deliberately "low-balling" you.

The lawyer Rodney and Micki retained was the only one who was prepared to discuss both fees and overall closing costs. Were they ever glad he did! Although the legal fees totalled $550, the overall amount needed to close was closer to $2,000 when the other charges were added in. Armed with this information before signing their offer, Rodney and Micki could budget much better for closing, and applied for a mortgage that was just the right size.

To accurately advise you about the overall closing costs, a lawyer will have to ask many questions about the proposed transaction. What is the purchase price for the resale home? How is it to be financed (one mortgage or two; assumed, vendor-take-back, or new mortgage)? How is it heated (oil, gas or electric)? Is there a survey? When is it closing? The answers to these and other questions will help the lawyer gauge the amount of these "hidden" costs."

While lawyers in other areas charge for their time on an hourly basis, block fees are the norm in a real estate transaction. The fee that is charged usually is based on the amount of work involved. A cash transaction (no mortgage) involves less work than a deal with one new mortgage. That, in turn, is easier to process and cheaper than a purchaser arranging two new mortgages. A vendor-take-back mortgage, where the vendor holds the mortgage on closing, involves less work than a new mortgage with an outside lender. Even easier than both is the situation where the purchaser assumes an existing mortgage. The quoted fee should be broken down this way so the purchaser knows the amount being charged for each component. By knowing more about the transaction, the lawyer can set his fee appropriately. Unusual or unexpected problems obviously will require an adjustment of the fee quoted.

The value of the property should not determine absolutely the size of the lawyer's fee, although it is a factor. In terms of actual work involved, a purchase transaction with one new mortgage is the same if the purchase price is $50,000 and the mortgage is $35,000, or if the purchase price is $500,000 financed by a $350,000 mortgage. Of course, a lawyer's professional liability is that much greater, the more expensive the property.

Where the same lawyer acts on both the purchase and the mortgaging of the property (which usually is the case), it would be very unfair to charge the buyer double the purchase fee. Although additional time is spent on the mortgage component of the transaction, much of the work from the purchase applies equally to the mortgage transaction. The additional fee to be charged for the mortgage segment should reflect this fact.

In most areas of Canada, legal fees in real estate transactions are negotiable. Although local law associations publish suggested fee schedules ("tariffs") for real estate transactions, many lawyers honor them in the breach, charging less than tariff as their fee. The legal profession is a competitive business. Disbursements are always extra.

As a purchaser, you should shop around and compare various price quotations for legal fees. However, there is more to selecting a lawyer than his or her fees. *Never let price be the deciding factor in choosing a lawyer.* Like any professional, a lawyer specializing in real estate work, proficient in his field, will charge a premium for his services. But it's worth the extra expense. Buyers get what they pay for. A savings of $25 or $50 is nominal indeed, perhaps only one or two percent of the overall closing costs that a buyer will pay to close a transaction. When dealing with professional services, quality is the key, not price. Rejecting a highly recommended lawyer, an acknowledged expert in his field, to save a small sum of money, is being penny wise and pound foolish.

Once you have decided which lawyer to retain, make an appointment to see him or her. At the first meeting, finalize the question of fees and discuss when and how they are to be paid. Expect to pay the lawyer's fee in a real estate transaction in full on closing. On request, some lawyers will make other arrangements, if settled early. More and more lawyers are asking clients for retainers in real estate transactions to cover the cost of initial disbursements. Be prepared for this as well.

Inquire how the lawyer's office operates. The delegation of responsibility is essential to make any legal office operate efficiently. Learn at the outset the name of the secretary assisting with the file. No one, though, should find himself dealing with a lawyer's office, but never seeing or talking to the lawyer! Some lawyers operate real estate factories, where client contact with the lawyer is often nonexistent. Despite any nominal cost savings, this type of law firm should be rejected. The ultimate responsibility rests with the lawyer. As a purchaser, you are paying your hard-earned money to retain *a lawyer*; you have a right to communicate with him or her.

As is the case with the home inspector, have the lawyer available "on standby." This way, once an offer is prepared, the lawyer can be contacted *to review the offer before it is signed.* This is critical, and is discussed in chapter 26.

One final word about lawyers acting in real estate transactions: it is acceptable for one lawyer to represent both the buyer and a lender in a purchase transaction, their interests being compatible at this stage. One lawyer never should represent both the buyer and the seller in the same transaction. This is the classic conflict-of-interest situation, where each side needs separate representation.

Now that the three real estate professionals have been assembled, it is time to examine in greater detail the particular property you may be buying.

# 15

## The Home Site

Home buyers following the HOBS approach will now have narrowed down their choices of location (community and neighborhood). The next stage is to zero in on a particular resale property within the neighborhood, again applying the HOBS technique. As with community and neighborhood selection, every buyer will view and rank the features raised in this chapter differently. Yet each point should be carefully considered both with the purchase and with a subsequent sale in mind. To maximize the potential resale value of a property, remember the need for objectivity. Factors unimportant to one person could be paramount to another.

### Lot Sizes

Lot sizes are usually quoted in terms of street frontage: a 25-foot lot, a 40-foot lot and so on. When considering different properties, depth should not be overlooked, for the deeper the lot, the deeper the front and back yards. Years ago, lots 120-feet deep were prevalent in older areas. This meant two cars easily could be accommodated in a driveway. In newer sub-divisions, lots are only 100-feet deep, meaning shorter front yards and driveways. Coupled with narrower lots in some areas, this results in serious on-street parking problems. Just try to find a parking space when the distance between driveways is half a car length!

With the increased use of metric measure in real estate

developments, lot sizes have shrunk even further. The "metric" 35-foot × 100-foot lot often turns out to be 10.5m × 30m. In actual fact, this is equivalent to 34.45 feet × 98.43 feet!

Lot size is important for another reason. It determines the size of the house that is permitted on the lot, a material consideration for purchasers planning to enlarge the premises. Most municipalities base the maximum permitted size of a house on the size of the lot itself. This is called "coverage." Sixty percent coverage means the size of the house (in square feet) on a lot cannot exceed 60 percent of the size of the lot itself. Eddie and Ellen bought a property recently with a lot size of 35 feet × 100 feet. The house was 1,400 square feet in size. Since the maximum allowable coverage was 60 percent, the largest house permitted on the lot was 2,100 square feet (60 percent of the total lot size of 3,500 square feet). Obviously, the bigger the lot, the bigger the house it can support. *Don't forget about depth!*

## Parking

Parking is a very important consideration to most people. While the "suburban dream" is a two-car garage, obviously it is not always available. Be practical. Is a house with a one-car garage adequate? Will a sufficiently longer driveway compensate for the lack of a second garage? If no garage is available, see if a mutual drive exists. In some older areas, the only type of available parking is on-street parking. Check with the local municipality ahead of time about any restrictions that may exist as to overnight or permit parking. If private parking is an absolute necessity, find out *now*, before an offer is submitted, if it is available.

## Mutual Drives and Rights-of-Way

Home owners are entitled to privacy. Anyone coming onto their property without consent is a trespasser, unless a legal right of access is given. Mutual drives or walkways, found in many older areas of urban communities, are typical examples of that right. The term "mutual drive" is an everyday expression explaining a legal concept — the right-of-way.

Alan and Jack are next-door neighbors who share a mutual

drive. Alan's deed says that Jack has the right to use the south four feet of Alan's property, 75 feet in from the street. Jack's deed says Alan has the right to use the north four feet of Jack's property, 75 feet in from the street. Although each person owns his own 4-foot by 75-foot strip of land, both Alan and Jack have an equal right to use this 8-foot by 75-foot right-of-way, without any interruption by the other. Due to the dual rights of ownership and usage, both parties must agree on the proper use of the right-of-way. Arrangements will have to be made for parking on the right-of-way, since neither Alan nor Jack can use it alone, excluding the other. Snow removal and maintenance also must be mutually agreed upon. Owning a house with a mutual drive or mutual walkway is a surefire way of gaining an early introduction to the next-door neighbor. As coexistence is the key, few problems normally arise with mutual drives.

## Municipal Easements

Ron and Jennie own a house where a "service corridor" of telephone and hydro wires runs across the width of their property, underground, at the rear five feet of the lot. Although Ron and Jennie own this land, the municipality has the right to maintain this equipment in its present location and to send its representatives onto that area, without being considered a trespasser. This five-foot strip of land is called a municipal easement, and is usually granted to a municipality or other utility supplier, such as the telephone, hydro, natural gas or water company.

In older areas of a community some municipal easements run across the rear of the lot, the services often being above ground. Not all municipal easements are visible to the naked eye, though. Imagine how surprised Len and Gail were to learn that a 10-foot-wide sewer easement ran across the backyard of the property they were thinking of buying, completely undetectable above ground. In newer areas, services are provided at the front of the property, and below ground in the newest of subdivisions. One easement still running across the rear of many properties, both old and new, is a drainage pipe and "catch-basin," described more fully below.

Detailed agreements registered on title state how the area affected by the easement on Ron and Jennie's property can be used. Obviously, rights of access are given to the municipality or utility company. Usually they have the right to trim and even remove trees and shrubs if these are interfering with the operation of the utility service. No permanent structures are permitted on the easement, such as extensions to the house or a swimming pool.

Buyers who have specific plans to use any portion of the rear or front yards should advise their real estate agent and lawyer of this fact before an offer is signed. Proper steps then can be taken to determine if a municipal easement exists, and if so, where. A properly drawn up-to-date survey will disclose the existence of these easements, as should the deed. Since many offers say that buyers agree to take title subject to "minor" municipal easements for utility purposes, the time to raise these concerns is now, before pen touches paper.

## Party Wall

Lorne and Miriam live in a semi-detached house. Greg and Marguerite live in a unit of row housing. In both cases the "common wall" between their property and the adjoining property is known as a party wall.

The boundary line between the properties runs directly through the middle of the party wall. As structural support is required from both sides of the wall, neither owner can remove his side of the wall without the consent of its co-owner. Owners of homes with party walls face another concern — noise from the adjoining property. To learn whether this might be a problem, ask the home inspector to check the level of sound insulation in the common wall. Inadequate soundproofing could lead to hearing much of what the neighbors do in their home — when and how they do it! Party walls, and the level of sound they allow to be transmitted, could bother some buyers but not others.

## Road Allowance

Like most home owners, Bernie and Hilary were shocked to learn that they do not own most of their front yard! In Ontario, for example, municipally owned road allowances are 66 feet wide. While the actual road is not that wide, the total area of land owned by the local municipality is 66 feet in width. The paved roadway on Bernie and Hilary's street being 26 feet wide, the municipality owns another 20 feet on either side of the asphalt. Included in this 20-foot strip of land are the boulevard, sidewalk and utility services. The remainder is land which appears to be part of Bernie and Hilary's front yard, and which they use as part of their front yard, but which is really owned by the municipality.

While Bernie and Hilary are responsible for maintaining the non-owned portion of their front yard, the trees and bushes growing on it legally belong to the municipality. Before removing or even trimming the trees or bushes on their front yard, Bernie and Hilary should check with the local municipality. Otherwise, they could face a charge of damaging or destroying municipal property!

Similarly, municipalities are responsible for their trees and bushes. One of its trees could cause damage to a house or its occupants, with roots growing into the sewer system, or by housing a hornet's nest. The municipality then would have to correct the problem at its expense, and compensate the home owner for damages.

In newer residential subdivisions, the municipality owns triangular pieces of property at all four corners of a street intersection, called "sight triangles," in addition to the road allowance. This way municipalities can ensure that the lines of vision for motorists will not be obstructed by the owners of the corner lots. Many owners of corner properties have planted shrubs or trees, only to find out later that they were placed on a municipally owned sight triangle.

To learn where the municipally owned road allowance or sight triangle begins, examine the survey for the property. Measure the distance from the building to the property/municipal boundary line. If the exact location of the lot line is extremely important, do this before an offer is submitted. If no survey is available, the offer could be made conditional on determining and being satisfied with the exact location of the boundary line, based on a new survey, within a fixed number of days after the offer is accepted.

## Zero Lot Line

Municipal zoning by-laws require that houses be a set distance from the property line. Often this set-back was four feet, meaning the area between the houses was eight feet wide. As land prices skyrocketed in the 1960s and 1970s, a new planning concept, zero lot line, was developed. To keep the cost of housing affordable, developers were permitted in some areas to build more houses per acre by reducing the gap between houses. One home is located four feet from the boundary line, while the other is built very close to it. Hence, "zero" lot line. The gap between the houses is reduced to slightly more than four feet. With four extra feet gained per lot, developers could keep house prices reasonable by increasing densities this way. Zero lot line, in effect, is a way of manufacturing land!

All houses on the following survey sketch have a zero lot line on their southern boundary. Slightly more than four feet exists between the houses to permit roof overhangs, eavestroughs and downspouts to extend from the walls. The areas between the houses (marked as Parts 5, 6, 7 and 8) are all "maintenance easements." These areas of common usage are a necessity with zero lot line properties. Maintenance easements are similar to the mutual drives and rights-of-way referred to earlier.

Felix is the owner of Lot A on the survey. Oscar owns Lot B, which includes the area marked Part 5 between the two lots. In his deed, Felix is permitted access onto Part 5 *only* of Oscar's property without interference from Oscar, in order for Felix to maintain his property. Oscar's deed confirms that Felix has this right. Practically speaking, Felix can use the area between the two homes as if he owned it, and without being considered a trespasser, to paint his house; clean the eavestroughs and downspouts; gain access to the roof; and otherwise repair and maintain his property. Oscar, in turn, has a similar right over Part 6 of Lot C owned by Theo.

Much concern has been expressed over zero lot lines in recent years. The houses are so close together that owners complain

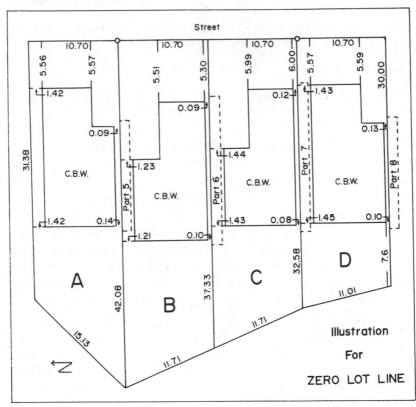

Illustration

For

ZERO LOT LINE

about the claustrophobic feeling that results. With a smaller separation between the houses, zero lot line properties are somewhat of a fire hazard. A fire in one home can spread easily to its adjoining properties, especially on a windy day. As maintenance easements are greatly shielded from the sun, rarely will grass grow there. Unless they are covered with crushed stones, patio stones or bricks, they are ugly at the best of times and muddy at the worst.

## Corner Lots

Some people love them and some people hate them! With portions of two road allowances being used by the home owner, some people desire corner lots for the feeling and look of roominess they provide. All that extra land, though, means additional grass to cut, more sidewalks to clear of snow, and more fencing to erect with no neighbor on one side to split the cost. Privacy considerations and security threats are probably the greatest deterrents to owning a corner lot. Unless the backyard is totally enclosed with a privacy fence, it is easy for anyone on the street to peer into the backyard. Personal possessions like patio furniture, lawn equipment and barbeques can be easily removed from an unenclosed area as well.

## On the Sunny Side of the Street

A popular song years ago, it still has meaning today. When selecting a house, decide whether you want to receive morning or afternoon sun. Houses on the west side of the street get morning sun at the front of the house, and afternoon sun in the backyard. Elliott and Mandy, with two young children, chose a house on the west side of the street. The afternoon and evening sunlight provides additional time for outdoor play. Of course, across the street, the reverse holds true. Home buyers also should consider the side of the house on which the master bedroom is located. People who dislike waking to bright morning sun may not wish their bedroom facing east or south.

Darryl and Michelle bought a house on the north side of the street. After one winter they discovered that the snow on their front yard and driveway melted faster than their neighbor's across the street. Yet those neighbors across the street, with the kitchen in the rear, received the nice rays of the morning sun when they ate breakfast. Those who like to sunbathe will have much more exposure from the sun in the backyard with a house on the south side of the street as well. Windows facing south also get more light, meaning lower heating bills.

In deciding on which side of the street to buy a house, carefully consider the impact of the sun on the house, both inside and outside, as well as your personal lifestyle.

## Zoning By-laws

Few buyers address their minds to the question of zoning. They automatically assume a residential neighborhood is zoned just that — residential. Yet learning more about the zoning for a particular house, its neighborhood and its community, is absolutely crucial. Home ownership is affected by zoning by-laws in three ways:

a) The use that can be made of property;
b) The restrictions they impose on the height of the building and the distance that must exist between the house and the front, side and rear yard property lines (called "setbacks"); and,
c) The different degrees of density permitted, even within a residential neighborhood.

Most zoning by-laws dealing with permitted uses are phrased in the negative — "no uses are permitted, except . . ." If a property is to be used in a particular way, check it out with the local zoning department early. Alternatively, make the offer conditional on the zoning allowing the property to be used that way. To check afterwards for the first time could be too late. Terry and Evelyn wanted a satellite dish in their backyard very badly. When they learned the zoning in the area of their proposed purchase prohibited these dishes, they decided to buy elsewhere. Duncan and Jackie planned to buy what appeared to be a triplex. Revenue from the basement apartment was needed to offset the monthly expenses. Upon inquiring at the municipal offices, they learned the property was zoned for a duplex only, and that the basement was being used illegally. No offer was even submitted. For an excluded use to become a permitted use, the property must be rezoned, usually involving an application to the local municipal council.

Yard setbacks are dealt with somewhat differently. Often a proposed alteration to the building would violate the zoning requirements, but ever so slightly. When the general intent and purpose of the zoning will not be violated, exceptions to the by-law, called "minor variances," are granted. Bucky and Pat wanted to build an addition to their home that would result in the west wall being only four feet, nine inches from the property line, instead of the required five feet. The requested minor variance was obtained. In Ontario the administrative body granting minor variances is called the Committee of Adjustment. When the proposed alteration would significantly depart from the requirements of the zoning by-law, it becomes necessary to formally rezone the property. Anyone planning changes to the external structure of a building after closing should inquire about the setback requirements as well, before proceeding overly far with a draft offer.

Municipal by-laws also regulate many other aspects of home ownership. Fences, hedges and patios are just some of the areas regulated in terms of height, setbacks and coverage.

Zoning by-laws impose different density levels permitting many different types of possible dwellings, all under the umbrella of "residential" zoning. Stewart and Nanci were shocked to learn the medium density zoning in a neighborhood they investigated would allow single or semi-detached dwellings; townhouses; multiple family dwellings; condominiums; and apartment buildings. Think about it — there isn't much else!

Zoning by-laws are not retroactive. Just because zoning standards are tightened over time does not automatically render a legal use of a property illegal. Otherwise, houses would have to be torn down and businesses would have to close every time a zoning by-law was changed. The question becomes: which came first, the cart or the horse? When a zoning by-law is passed or amended, it exempts buildings that were erected lawfully before that time, as well as lawful uses of a property prior to its passage. Only future uses are prohibited, not prior legal uses. Even though the requirements of the current zoning by-law are violated, these "legal nonconforming uses" can be continued indefinitely, without requiring any further action.

Craig erected a satellite dish in June, when the installation of dishes was not prohibited. Although Nick, the next-door neighbor, was thinking about a dish as well, he did nothing. A by-law was passed in September prohibiting satellite dishes. Now Nick cannot install a satellite dish without violating the by-law. Since Craig's dish was in place before the by-law was passed, his dish can stay forever as a legal nonconforming use.

Knowing whether a property is a legal nonconforming use is very important, especially in older areas. Properties were built and used years ago with little regard for planning and zoning standards. How else could the following appear in one block of a downtown neighborhood: a corner grocery, two houses, an auto repair shop, three more houses and a corner restaurant? How else could detached homes have only 15 inches separating them? These are perfect examples of uses and standards that could not be duplicated today. Yet these existing uses of the land in violation of the current zoning by-law are permitted, since they preceded the by-law, so long as they continue to be used for that purpose. Any interruption or discontinuance of that use will permanently destroy the protection of being legally nonconforming. In other words, Craig can keep his satellite dish in its present location forever. But if he ever removed it for an extended period of time, the dish would lose the status of being a legal nonconforming use.

Purchasing a home means investing a substantial sum of hard-earned money. Buyers should do everything they can *before submitting an offer* to ensure that an attractive residential community retains that character. To do this, call or visit the municipal offices. Discover how the immediate area is zoned and what the zoning permits. Also, check on the "official plan" for the area, which is a general statement of land use policy for a community, to be used as a guide for future development. Ask whether any rezoning or specific site development applications are pending which might affect the character of the area. Unless the proper inquiries are made *early*, a future high-density development could be an unwelcome surprise.

## Other Factors

Fire hydrants, streetlights, hydro boxes, stop signs and catch basins (grated outlets, usually at the rear of a property, where water travelling over land can enter the storm sewer system) are viewed differently by most people, depending on individual taste. Fire hydrants do not add to the esthetics of a house, and make parking in front of a house impossible. On the other hand, they are very handy to have close by in the event of a fire. A streetlamp in front of a home makes it a less inviting target for night prowlers. Yet with a bright light shining in, getting to sleep may be more difficult in those bedrooms at the front of the house. Green hydro transformer boxes appear above ground in many newer areas. Few people like them — they are clumsy looking and have their allure for dogs. Being close to a stop sign is important to some people. Traffic should be travelling slower than normal when approaching or leaving the intersection. Catch basins are unsightly, the terrain around them always sloping downward. As a catch basin is the external outlet for a sewer easement, its surrounding area must be kept clear of buildings, structures, improvements or expensive landscaping. Having a catch basin at the rear of a property substantially affects the use and enjoyment of that area.

A checklist dealing with the factors raised in this chapter appears at the end of chapter 17, "The Home Itself."

# 16

## *Be Patient!*

It's time! Yes, prospective home buyers are now ready to start looking at specific homes in earnest. The time has come to go house-hunting with your real estate agent, to locate that dream home. Before you do, though, stand back and consider what has been accomplished so far. By now, you should have your own, tailor-made home buying strategy. Both needs and wants have been carefully considered. Your financial ability to pay for and carry a home has been examined. Decisions have been made on both a community and a neighborhood, plus the factors affecting specific sites. Preliminary discussions have been held with the three key real estate professionals — the real estate agent, the home inspector and the lawyer — and all are awaiting your next move. Your adrenalin level probably is very high, and you are finding it difficult to contain your enthusiasm. You are ready to move forward, fully prepared, totally aware of where you are going. Without question, you are ready to act.

Finding an appropriate and yet affordable house will take some time, and will involve still more research. Many homes that might satisfy the needs and wants on your shopping list will be shown by your real estate agent. You may be asked to view some properties at open houses held by listing agents. There is no simple answer how long it will take, and how many houses must be viewed, before the house you *really* want is found. For that reason, *be patient!* The careful analysis applied to date in deciding what and where to buy, now must be focused on particular properties. Only this way can a proper, educated decision on a specific home be made.

On the other hand, do not procrastinate. Well-priced homes do not remain available forever. Too often, purchasers who dawdle learn the hard way that a property has already been sold. Prior development of a home-buying strategy, though, will save valuable time. It could be the difference between buying the house and missing the boat. Shortly after seeing a house, buyers with their HOBS in place will know if it adequately fills the bill.

Knowing what is included in a house is very straightforward. Learning what does not accompany a home is much harder to determine. To solve this dilemma, Don and Aline applied another HOBS idea before submitting an offer. They attended several open houses for properties outside their price range, and inquired about the features that accompanied each home. By preparing a chart listing those items, Don and Aline established a yardstick against which to compare houses in their price range. Immediately they knew when an affordable property offered good value for the money by including features normally only found in higher-priced houses. That turned out to be the home Don and Aline bought.

*Don't rush into things!* Don't be swayed by the argument often raised, that someone else is waiting to buy the property. Let them! Once the offer is accepted, it is too late to change your mind. Be absolutely certain the property satisfies your needs and as many wants as possible. Make sure your home inspector and lawyer play their important roles before the contract becomes firm and binding. Whatever the type and style of house, buyers cannot afford to be overwhelmed or intimidated. Keep your composure, and only make decisions with your head and not your heart.

Children learning how to ride a bicycle get better with each outing. Practice makes perfect. So, too, with buying a house. Do not get discouraged. Each house viewed is an opportunity to learn a little more, to gain a little more experience and confidence, and to redefine, both for yourself and your agent, what you are seeking.

Several points should be kept in mind when inspecting properties:

1. Comments, criticisms and reactions to a particular property should be kept to a minimum. You are there to inquire about a property, not to downplay it. Analysis of a home should be done in a private conversation with the agent as soon as possible after the appointment.
2. Consider a home from your own lifestyle and point of view. Ignore how it is presently being used or maintained. Don't let fancy decor or superficial features such as paint, wallpaper and a few accessories influence you. How a room or even a whole house is finished and furnished will not reflect how it will look when you move in. On the other hand, try to visualize the potential in a property. Imagine how it would look if painted or wallpapered differently, with your own furniture in the rooms. If you like what you see, then look at the house even more closely.
3. Be courteous to both the home owner and yourself. Make each visit as easy as possible on yourself. Keep distractions to a minimum. If possible, keep children and pets at home when out viewing houses.

# 17

## *The Home Itself*

Now that specific homes are going to be examined and compared, keep in mind the following questions. What makes one particular house more suitable in contrast to other houses? What factors distinguish one home from another? What features should buyers be looking for in a particular property?

When looking at prospective homes, keep your shopping list of needs and wants handy. As part of the HOBS approach, compare how many needs and wants are satisfied by each particular home. The property ultimately chosen should satisfy all of your needs and as many wants as possible, while still remaining affordable. Constantly refer back to your shopping list to refresh your memory on what is a need, and what is a want.

As in the selection of a community and neighborhood, prepare a personalized ranking system, separating key features from unimportant items. Again, be sure to carefully consider each feature, both in terms of your buying the property and your selling it to someone else in the future.

The printed form of most offers states that the buyer has inspected the property before signing it. Although a home inspector will be examining the property once the offer is accepted, buyers must still thoroughly investigate a property even before making an offer. Noticing that the paint is peeling, plaster is cracked and that the floors and carpeting are worn do not require any expertise. Yet they may dissuade you from even submitting an offer. Remember, too, that the home inspector examines the property from a structural point of view. As the purchaser, you must examine and inspect the nonstructural items in the house — the items listed in this chapter. Bring any concerns you have to the attention of the home inspector, for him to investigate further.

When considering potential homes, view them both in the daytime and at night. Certain features may only be noticeable when the sun has set, such as the exterior lighting of the house and the effect of streetlights.

When seriously considering a property, bring a friend or relative along. It never hurts to get an unbiased, reliable and objective opinion.

## YOUR CHECKLIST

Type of House
Single-family detached \_\_\_\_      Duplex (triplex) \_\_\_\_
Semi-detached \_\_\_\_              Townhouse \_\_\_\_
Link \_\_\_\_                       (freehold or condominium?)
                                Row house \_\_\_\_

Style of House
Bungalow \_\_\_\_                   Back-split \_\_\_\_
Two-storey \_\_\_\_                 Condominium apartment \_\_\_\_
Side-split \_\_\_\_                 Square feet \_\_\_\_

## Rooms

How many rooms are in the house? What are their types and sizes (bedrooms, bathrooms, kitchen, living room, dining room, other rooms such as a family room or laundry room)? What is the overall layout of the house? Is it a center hall plan? Does the layout of the rooms suit your lifestyle? Will traffic flow be difficult from room to room? Is the kitchen also a hallway? Is there adequate cupboard and counterspace in the kitchen? Is there adequate space in the kitchen for a fridge, stove and a dishwasher? Is the dining room near the kitchen? Are the dining room and living room adjoining? Is the kitchen at the rear of the house? Are there visible "high traffic areas"? Is the laundry room on the main floor or in the basement? Is a bedroom located on the main floor or in the basement? Does the master bedroom have an ensuite bathroom? How many levels of stairs are in the house?

Wise purchasers will prepare a rough sketch of all levels of the house, and then measure their furniture and appliances to ensure they will fit in the various rooms.

## Basement

Is there a basement? Is it finished? Is it high enough to be used, or is it little more than a crawl space? Are there signs of water damage? With a little work, could it be converted to additional living space?

## Storage

No house ever seems to have enough storage space. Is there ample closet space? Where is it located? Is a closet located in each bedroom? Is there a linen closet? Is there a broom closet, where cleaning materials and a vacuum cleaner can be stored? Can any changes be made inexpensively to create more storage space? Is there a pantry in the kitchen? Are there sufficient kitchen cupboards? Is the front closet large enough to hold your winter outerwear and that of your guests?

## Heating and Cooling

How is the house heated — oil, gas, or electric? Natural gas currently is the cheapest method of heating a home. Is it heated by forced air or by hot water radiators (the older style of heating)? Is there supplementary heating such as a wood stove? What about a heat pump? How old is the furnace? Is it covered by a warranty plan? Is the house air conditioned? Is there a humidifier attached to the furnace? Does it have an electronic air cleaner? When were all of these items last serviced? Have permanent electric baseboards been built onto the floor, a sure sign of a cold or drafty area or room? Ask for the furnace and air conditioner to be operated, depending on the season, to be sure both are functioning properly.

## Water Heater

Is it owner-owned, or is it a rental? How is it heated? Does it need replacing?

## Plumbing

Do the toilets flush properly? Are there any leaks? Does hot water flow from the faucets and shower heads properly? How high is the tub enclosure tiled?

Is the flow of cold water adequate? Flush the toilets, run the showers and try the faucets. Don't be dissuaded by an embarrassed agent or seller who "has never heard of such a thing." After all, it is the buyer who acknowledges that he has inspected the property, not the agent nor the seller.

Check the location of the laundry taps for the washing machine. Check the location of the main water shut-off. Check the tub, toilet and sinks for scratches, dents and marks. Are they white or coloured? Test the outside hose bibs. Note how many there are and where they are located.

See if there are any water stains on the floors, ceilings, walls or under sinks — a sure sign of water leaks, past or present.

Is there room for a dishwasher? Has the plumbing for a dishwasher even been installed or "roughed-in"?

## Electrical

Does the house have a fuse box or circuit breakers? Where is it located? What is the amperage? (100 amps is standard) Is the wiring aluminum or copper? Are there sufficient electrical outlets throughout the house? Are there sufficient electrical outlets in "high volume" rooms (bedrooms, kitchens)? Are they adequately located? Are there any outside outlets? Where? Will all the electrical light fixtures accompany the house, or will any be excluded? Are they adequately located? Is there a heavy-duty plug for a stove and dryer? Check the light switches and outlets to make sure that they work. Check the location of the main electrical shut-off switch.

## Garage and Driveway

Is there an enclosed garage? For one or two cars? Carport? Is it a private or mutual drive? Is it wide enough for two cars? Is it long enough for two cars? Is it paved or gravelled? What is the condition of the driveway? Does the garage door open properly? Is it a pull out or roll-up door? Has an automatic garage-door opener been installed?

## Landscaping

Is the grass in good condition or will it have to be replaced? Do the trees and shrubs look healthy? Will diseased ones have to be removed? Is there an area for a garden?

## General Condition of the Interior

**Walls** — Are they painted? Wallpapered? Are they badly chipped and cracked? Can they be "lived with"? Are they plaster or drywall?
**Floors** — Are they cracked, badly scuffed, marked, or scratched? Are they linoleum, tile, vinyl or wood?
**Ceilings** — Are they cracked or broken? Are there any signs of water stains?
**Carpeting** — Where is it located? Is it totally worn out? Is it worn out in places? Does it need cleaning? How good is the underpadding?
**Windows** — Are they single-pane or thermopane? Are they broken? Do they open properly and easily without excessive force? Try to open one or two windows to see. Have they been adequately caulked and weather-stripped?
**Storms and Screens** — Are they broken?
**Doors** — Do the doors open and close properly? Do the locks work properly? Do any of the locks have deadbolts? Have the doors been adequately weather-stripped?

## Outside Items

What is the visible condition of the brick and mortar? The aluminum siding? The wood panels? The stucco? The chimney? Eavestroughs and downspouts? The steps and stairs? Outside painted areas? Does it need a fresh painting? How does the roof look? Have any shingles lifted? What about the porch? Is there a television antenna or TV tower? Test the reception. Does the ground around the perimeter of the house slope away to permit proper drainage and to prevent water accumulation around foundation walls?

## Rear Yard

How large is the backyard? Is there sufficient room for children to play? Is there a patio or deck? Do they need repair? Is the backyard fenced? Is the fencing solidly erected? Wood or chain link?

## Type of Construction

Is the house solid brick or brick front? Newer homes are often brick front. Solid brick homes are supposed to represent a more solidly constructed house. A solid brick house has alternating rows of bricks facing side-out and end-out. There are five rows of bricks facing side-out and one row of bricks facing end-out.

Brick front, in comparison, has all rows of brick facing side outwards. Here the brick is an external veneer, just like aluminum siding or wood, surrounding a wood-frame construction. Brick front is very popular, to convey the impression of being a "brick" home. Is the house wood frame, with stucco or aluminum siding attached to it? Is it a combination of the above?

## Additional Items and Special Features

Is there a fireplace? Where is it? Is it a ceiling-to-floor fireplace, or only mantle height? Does it work properly? When was the chimney last swept? Will any appliances and fixtures accompany the house (fridge, stove, washer, dryer, dishwasher)? Are they in good working order? When were they last serviced? How well insulated is the house? With what type of insulation? Has any insulation been added recently? Does the property include drapes, drapery tracks and window blinds? Do the bathrooms have mirrors? Do they need repair? Is there a smoke detector? Test the door chime and see if it works. Walk on the floors and up and down the stairs, testing for squeaks and stability. Are the handrail *and* pickets made of wood, or just the rail? Is there a kitchen hood fan? Is it ducted to the outside?

In the space below, list the special features and overall impressions about specific properties of interest. Record the information on this scorecard immediately after viewing the houses. Otherwise, one property will be confused with the others very quickly. Some real estate agents prepare information or data sheets, highlighting the features of property listed for sale. Others will provide a copy of the listing to prospective buyers. Attach those sheets here as well. Don't forget to rank the properties viewed as to how successfully they satisfy your shopping list of needs and wants.

| | House #1 | House #2 | House #3 |
|---|---|---|---|
| Address | | | |
| Price | | | |
| Mortgage Arrangements | | | |
| Taxes | | | |
| Type of House | | | |
| Style of House | | | |
| Size of House | | | |
| Lot Size | | | |
| Parking | | | |
| Mutual Drive & Right-of-Way | | | |
| Municipal Easements | | | |
| Party Walls | | | |
| Road Allowance | | | |
| Zero Lot Line | | | |
| Corner Lots | | | |
| Side of the Street | | | |
| Zoning By-laws | | | |
| Other Factors | | | |
| House Layout and Rooms | | | |
|    Living Room | | | |
|    Dining Room | | | |
|    Bedrooms | | | |
|    Kitchen | | | |
|    Family Room | | | |
|    Bathroom | | | |
|    Basement | | | |
|    Layout of Rooms | | | |
| Storage Space | | | |
| Heating & Cooling | | | |
| Water Heater | | | |
| Plumbing | | | |
| Electrical | | | |
| Garage & Driveway | | | |
| Landscaping | | | |
| General Condition of Interior | | | |
| Outside Items | | | |
| Rear Yard | | | |
| Type of Construction | | | |
| Additional Items & Special Features | | | |

Have you seen a property you like? What does it have to offer compared with other homes you have seen? Would you like to own it? If so, the time may be right to consider making an offer on the property.

# 18

## *Purchasing Rural Property*

A number of additional topics must be investigated by purchasers of property in rural areas, in developing their home-buying strategy. All enquiries must be made before the offer is signed, so the necessary clauses can appear in it, drafted appropriately.

### Permit for the sewage disposal system

Rural properties rely on septic tank systems consisting of holding tanks and tile drainage fields to dispose of sewage. Compare this with the municipal sanitary sewer system available in most urban areas. Knowing the condition of this septic tank system before the offer becomes firm and binding is absolutely essential.

Learn where the septic tank and tile bed are located. Ensure they are far enough away from any well, so the quality of water will not be affected. Ask to see any maintenance records the seller has for the septic tank system, and check them carefully. Find out when the tank was last cleaned out. Most importantly, have the condition of the septic tank and tile drainage field checked, to ensure they function properly and are not under-sized.

When Rob and Ellen bought their country home, the offer was conditional on having the septic tank system inspected by a representative of the environment ministry. In addition, an unqualified certificate of approval and use permit under provincial legislation were to be issued within a set period of time; otherwise, the offer was null and void. The condition permitted access onto the property for an on-site inspection, plus the right to dig the necessary test holes. By requiring that the certificate be unqualified, Rob and Ellen had the option to proceed, terminate or renegotiate the offer, depending on the results of the inspection and the cost of bringing the system up to standards.

Larry and Wendy took a slightly less elaborate route when they bought rural property. They simply inserted several conditions into the offer. One required that there be no work orders, deficiency notices or complaints on file with either the provincial environment ministry or the local health unit. Another required that any certificate of approval or use permit issued for the construction, enlargement or alteration of the sewage disposal system be delivered to them before closing. With this information, Larry and Wendy were satisfied with the state of the septic tank system when they closed their purchase.

### Well record

Ask the seller for a copy of the report prepared by the contractor when the well was dug. It should show when the well was dug, its location on the property, the method of drilling and the bedrock materials encountered, casing and open hole information, details of the plugging and sealing, plus data on the rate of water flow from the well. As this information may be many years old, it would be wise to have the pumping rate tested again, making the offer conditional on a certain rate being achieved. Many institutional lenders will require that an up-to-date pump test be conducted, before advancing funds on a mortgage secured by rural property.

### Unregistered easements

An easement is right-of-way granted by the owner of the property to someone else. Some provincial hydro-electric commissions have rights-of-way across rural properties, without their being registered on title. The right-of-way can consist of a major transmission tower, or simply poles, wires and anchors running across the property. In either case, a visual inspection of the property should reveal if such rights-of-way exist. If the absence of a hydro right-of-way is important to you, insert a condition into the offer that none exist.

### Access to provincial highways

Entrance or access points may require a permit onto provincial highways issued by the provincial highways ministry. While David and Jan might own a property abutting a provincial highway, no access to it would be permitted, until the government grants its approval. This reverses the normal rule that access onto a property from a roadway is permitted at whatever location the owner wishes. In this manner, the government can prevent driveways from being placed in locations where the line of vision is poor — on hills or a curve, for example. When they purchased their property, David and Jan inserted a condition into the offer, that the required permit from the department of highways be delivered on closing.

### Water quality

Purchasers want to be sure the water is safe for drinking, or potable. In urban areas, this is easy. Everyone assumes the water flowing from a tap connected to a municipal water supply system is safe. On a rural property, where water is drawn from a well, the property owner must ensure the water is safe for drinking.

A sample of water taken from the well on the property can be tested to determine its potability. A bacteriological examination of that sample is conducted, often by a provincial public health laboratory, to determine the total coliform count, as well as faecal count. Total coliform bacteria are located in animal wastes, sewage, soil and vegetation. Faecal coliform bacteria are a much greater concern, as they are more likely to represent sewage contamination, their source being the intestines of warm blooded animals like humans. Less than 2 total coliforms per 100 ml and zero faecal coliforms per 100 ml are the acceptable limits, rendering the water safe for drinking. These bacteriological tests have nothing to do with the chemical quality of the water (the presence of sodium, fluoride and nitrates) which are also important.

When Peter and Ann bought a rural property, they inserted a detailed condition into the offer dealing with the potability of the water supplied by the well. The offer was made conditional on a sample taken immediately before the offer was signed, indicating that the well water was potable. A second examination was to be conducted one week before closing, requiring that the water again be bacteriologically safe for drinking. If it was not, then the seller would be obligated to install whatever chlorination system was necessary to continuously treat the water. Both tests indicated that the water was potable, and the purchase closed smoothly.

Seeing a lawyer before signing an offer is a key component of HOBS. Anyone buying rural property has all the more reason to see a lawyer early to ensure these key conditions are properly worded to protect you, the purchaser.

# 19

## *Condominiums*

As an independent small community, condominiums represent a different type of lifestyle, foreign to many people, where community interests often take precedence over individual rights. Anyone contemplating a condominium purchase, especially existing home owners, must thoroughly understand how they work and how they differ from conventional ownership of property. Only this way can a purchaser be absolutely certain his personal lifestyle and the condominium way of life are compatible.

Though relatively new to Canada, condominiums are not a new concept. This form of ownership, called Strata Titles in British Columbia and Co-ownership of Immoveables in Quebec, has been very popular over the years in Europe and in parts of the United States as a form of middle- and upper-class housing. Owners of condominium units justify the limitations on personal freedoms, noting that condominiums give them the best of both worlds — home-ownership without many of the responsibilities of maintaining a home. Payment of a monthly maintenance charge ensures these "other items" — such as cutting the grass and shovelling the snow — are properly dealt with, permitting a more independent lifestyle.

When condominiums were first introduced to Canada in the late 1960s, their historical foundation was ignored. Condominiums were promoted as a means of providing "affordable" housing for Canadians. During its formative years, the condominium developed a black eye arising from the problems encountered in selling and maintaining them as a form of low-income housing. The abuses of some builders in developing early condominium projects did not help its initial reputation either. Only in the middle 1970s, when condominiums returned to their historical roots — housing for middle- and upper-income Canadians (the so-called "luxury condominium"), did the boom in condominium development really begin. While lingering doubts remain in the minds of some people, the problems encountered in recent years in condominium ownership are pale by comparison.

Today, condominiums have a special appeal for people entering retirement — the so-called "empty nesters." Condominiums are also attracting their share of young couples who wish to live in the city core at a reasonable price, owning their home instead of renting it.

Condominiums are creatures of provincial statutes. While minor variations do exist from province to province, the following commentary applies to most condominiums across the country.

Only the purchase of a resale condominium unit will be discussed here. Just as acquiring a newly constructed home differs considerably from buying a resale property, so too with condominiums. Purchasing a unit in an unregistered condominium complex subjects buyers to a set of rules and situations no other purchasers face.

## What Is a Condominium?

While the term "condominium" is often used as an adjective for a type of building, it really describes a system of land ownership. The purchaser of a unit in a condominium, whether townhouse or apartment, acquires

a) a specific residential dwelling unit where title is registered in the buyer's name. Many of the expenses usually associated with home ownership (realty taxes, mortgage payments, maintenance and repairs to the unit) remain the buyer's responsibility.

b) a percentage interest in the remainder of the condominium property and the common areas, properly called the "common elements," which are owned by all unit owners. Included here are the hallways, stairwells, lobbies, driveways, elevators, walkways, parking garage, recreational facilities, grounds and playground, as well as the land itself upon which the building is situated.

c) some parts of the common elements fall into a third category, exclusive use common elements. Although they are owned and maintained by the condominium corporation, their use is restricted to one owner. Typical examples are balconies, parking spaces and storage lockers in condominium apartments, and lawns (front and back) in townhouse developments. More information on exclusive use common elements appears below.

Since all unit owners own the common elements, they all are responsible for paying their proportionate share to maintain it. An owner's share of total common area expenses should correspond to the percentage he or she actually owns of the common elements. By owning a three-bedroom unit, Rick and Sharon would own a larger percentage of the common elements and would pay a higher monthly common expense or maintenance charge than David and Zena, the owners of a two-bedroom unit.

Like single family homes, condominium units are bought, sold and mortgaged separately. Any unit owner who does not pay his mortgage will not jeopardize anyone else's unit in the complex.

A monthly maintenance (common expense) fee is levied against all unit owners for the expenses incurred in operating the condominium corporation. All unit owners also become members in the condominium corporation, which operates the business affairs of the condominium.

## Types of Condominiums

Most condominium developments are either high-rise apartments or townhouses. Important differences do exist between the two. Apartment condominiums have higher monthly common expense payments, due to the very nature of living in an apartment building. Maintaining and repairing a bank of elevators, internal maintenance, repair and cleaning internal common elements as well as maintaining, repairing and cleaning an underground garage are costs only high-rise condominiums will incur.

However, townhouse condominiums usually treat utility charges differently; hydro, water, gas and cable television charges often are excluded from the monthly maintenance fee, being separately billed to individual townhouse units. With condominium apartments, these charges often are bulk-metered to the condominium complex as a whole, and included in the maintenance fee. Conscientious townhouse owners can avoid having to subsidize their more extravagant neighbors this way.

## Advantages of Condominium Ownership

Convenience — that probably is the biggest advantage of condominium ownership. It is not necessary to do any maintenance outside the unit. As part of the monthly charge, a condominium owner has the grass cut, snow removed, grounds landscaped and exterior maintained. Obviously, a condominium will not appeal to the home handyman, those who want a backyard garden, or anyone who hates paying for a service he can provide himself. Yet acquired convenience is a major force behind the increased popularity of luxury condominiums amongst older people, childless couples and some career-conscious individuals.

Some buyers are attracted to condominiums by the recreational facilities they include. Swimming pools, squash and racketball courts are just some of the recreational features increasing the attractiveness of condominium ownership.

## Disadvantages of Condominium Ownership

By their very nature, condominiums place severe restrictions on the freedoms many home owners enjoy. A condominium, after all, is a hybrid — a cross between owning a home and being a tenant — whether the condominium be a townhouse or apartment complex. Anything done by one unit owner could affect others in the complex. To ensure peace and harmony, restrictions are imposed to regulate how the condominium *and its individual units* are used. Condominiums, then, are governed not only by federal, provincial and municipal laws, but also by the laws of the condominium corporation, enacted to control activities within its boundaries.

How acceptable those restrictions are will depend on the background of the buyers. Former tenants will be familiar with many of the concepts, in contrast to former owners of single-family homes. Consider Doug, who recently bought a unit in a high-rise condominium after years of owning his own home. Like a conventional home owner, Doug has control over many aspects of property ownership — how to finance his purchase, how to decorate the unit, and when to sell his property. Since the unit he owns is part of a larger complex, many other rights are shared in common with other unit owners, and can only be decided by committee. These include the use of the common elements and the operation of the condominium corporation as a small business, points Doug recognizes and accepts. What Doug is having a difficult time accepting are the regulations imposed by the condominium corporation, including restrictions on *the use of his unit*. More information on condominium rules and regulations appears later in this chapter.

## Factors to Consider When Buying a Condominium

When deciding whether to buy a resale condominium — it is important for you, as a purchaser, to develop and apply your own unique, tailor-made home-buying strategy. The same considerations described earlier about community, neighborhood and specific property location obviously apply here as well. Additional topics, unique to condominiums but similar in large part to living in an apartment, also must be considered. These include

- the adequacy and location of parking spaces, both for owners and visitors (parking spaces are explored in more detail below)
- the adequacy, location and accessibility of locker and storage space (is it inside or outside the unit)

- proximity to the elevator and the garbage chute
- how well is it lit by natural light (a great concern for people wanting to grow indoor plants)
- floor level in an apartment condominium (often a premium is paid for upper floors)
- the maintenance fee: How much is it? What does it include and exclude? Who pays the utility charges (hydro, water, gas), heating and cable television?
- the type of complex: Adult only? Are there adequate facilities for children?
- the recreational and other amenities: Swimming pool (indoor or outdoor)? Sauna? Tennis/squash/racketball courts? Meeting/multi-purpose room? Health Club?
- Is twenty-four hour security provided for the residents?
- Is there adequate sound insulation to ensure proper sound-proofing? Buyers of resale units have the advantage of being able to actually hear the level of sound being transmitted through walls, ceilings and floors. If noise is a concern, make sure the unit is distant from garage doors, saunas, laundry rooms, elevators, garbage chutes, and heating and electrical plants.
- the Rules and Regulations: What you can and cannot do, both with your unit and within the complex.

## What Do I Own and What Can I Use?

The documents establishing the condominium, called the "Declaration" and the "Description," state precisely what is acquired when a condominium is purchased. While the boundaries are the same for the most part, some differences do exist from condominium to condominium. In layman's terms, a dwelling unit generally consists of the area from wall to wall, ceiling to floor — "a box in the sky." Legally speaking, the boundaries of the unit generally are defined to be the upper surface of the concrete floor slab, the lower surface of the concrete ceiling, and the interior surface of the unfinished walls. Everything else, including the space between the floors and the units, are common elements.

Knowing the precise boundaries of a dwelling unit is very important, as it determines who is responsible for repairing damage. Individual unit owners like Arnold and Hyla must repair and maintain their unit. The obligation to maintain and repair the common elements rests with the condominium corporation. Recently a leaky pipe damaged the walls in Arnold and Hyla's fourth-floor unit, as well as the hallway outside their apartment. The condominium corporation would have to repair the wall itself and repaint its surface in the hallway (common elements). As Arnold and Hyla own the surface of the wall in their unit, they would be responsible for repainting or wallpapering it.

Parking spaces provide an interesting example of the different ways a condominium purchaser acquires an interest in the property. A buyer of a condominium unit can acquire a parking (and often a locker) space in one of four ways, depending on the specific condominium project: a) freehold; b) leasehold; c) exclusive use and d) allocated. A freehold unit is best for a buyer, the allocation method being the least advantageous. While all entitle a unit owner to use a specific parking space, the legal interest acquired differs greatly.

Norm bought a freehold parking unit. He owns it outright, just like his dwelling unit, a deed to the parking unit being registered in his name. Since he also bought a second parking unit, he can use it, lease it or sell it to anyone else in the condominium complex, depending on his particular situation. If a freehold unit is not available, a leasehold parking unit is the second best choice. Leasehold units are owned by the condominium corporation as part of the common elements, but are leased to the people like John, the owner of a specific dwelling unit, on a long-term basis, perhaps as long as 99 years. The dwelling unit and the leased parking unit go hand in hand for the term of the lease. On a sale by John of his dwelling unit, the lease automatically is transferred to the new owner of the dwelling unit. Exclusive use common element parking spaces are probably the most common method of distributing them among unit owners. Like leasing, the condominium corporation owns the parking spaces as part of the common elements. Instead of leasing them to individual unit owners, the Condominium Declaration specifies who has the exclusive right to use which parking space.

For example, the owner of dwelling unit 4, level 11, has the exclusive use over parking space 160. If Julie sells that dwelling unit to Alex, he automatically has the exclusive right to use parking space 160. This exclusive right of use is nontransferable, unless the dwelling unit is being conveyed. With exclusive use parking spaces, a specific parking unit is guaranteed to a specific unit owner, without a deed ever being registered. The worst way of acquiring a parking unit, from a purchaser's point of view, is the allocation method. Although each unit is entitled to a parking space, the directors of the condominium corporation determine its precise location. Who gets what parking space then becomes a political issue. As properties are sold, "prime" parking spaces, closer to the elevator, are reallocated to long-term residents and those on the board of directors. Newer occupants wind up with the less advantageous locations.

Most condominium owners are surprised to learn they do not own the backyard patio or front and rear yards of townhouses, or the balconies of apartment condominiums adjacent to their dwelling units. All of these comprise parts of the common elements owned by the condominium corporation. What owners have is the exclusive right to use those parts of the common elements to the exclusion of other people, identical to the exclusive use common element parking space. Often the condominium corporation will repair and maintain those areas, although occasionally the responsibility rests with the unit owner.

Before signing any offer for a condominium unit, purchasers applying HOBS will learn exactly what the unit includes, the nature of the parking unit, and those areas which are exclusive use common areas.

## Rules and Regulations

As a mini-community, every condominium corporation imposes restrictions on certain activities of its residents. Probably the best-known restrictions are incorporated in a document called the Rules and Regulations which are passed by the board of directors of the condominium corporation. Many Rules and Regulations are practical and make good sense.

Similar to house rules in apartment buildings, they promote the safety, security and welfare of the unit owners. Condominium rules also should strike a balance among the unit owners, to prevent unreasonable interference with an owner's use and enjoyment of his property.

Most house rules do not simply place restrictions on the use of the common elements. *They also regulate and restrict the manner in which individual units are used.* This is the feature of the house rules that some people dislike. Typical clauses deal with pets, or may require that certain areas in an apartment unit be carpeted, to keep noise levels low for the floor below.

Without question, Rules and Regulations affect a unit owner's unrestricted use and enjoyment of his property. Yet that is the very nature of condominium ownership — the different lifestyle discussed earlier — where regulations are placed on some personal freedoms, to provide the greatest protection for the greatest number of residents.

The role of Rules and Regulations in townhouse condominiums is often questioned. In actual fact, a townhouse complex resembles a small subdivision. Builders often impose restrictions in a new subdivision to control how it is developed and maintained; for example, the prohibition of clotheslines and TV antennaes will add to the esthetic beauty of a subdivision. So too with the Rules and Regulations affecting a townhouse complex.

Only in the rarest of cases can a conventional home owner be forced to spend money when he does not wish to. Not so in a condominium. Consider the situation a unit owner like Joey faces, where a major expenditure such as the construction of new recreational facilities is approved. All unit owners, even those like Joey who are opposed to the project, then become obligated to pay their proportionate share of the expense incurred. Many condominium owners, especially former owners of conventional homes, are uncomfortable with this arrangement.

Representatives of most condominium corporations are permitted to enter a unit at any time in an emergency situation without notice to repair the unit or to correct any condition which could cause damage or loss to the unit or the common elements. This power parallels that given to landlords in most leases. To ensure proper access is possible, the condominium corporation retains a key to all locks in each unit. While this type of emergency access clause can be justified to protect the overall interest of all unit owners, it certainly differs from the privacy and security of a conventional home. Former tenants may feel quite comfortable with this arrangement, while the idea may be foreign to long-time traditional home owners.

Before signing any offer, learn more about *all* the restrictions and house rules imposed by that condominium corporation. Are any of them unacceptable, or inconsistent with your intended use of the unit? The question of pets is a classic example. Different condominiums have different rules on the keeping of pets. Some prohibit them altogether while others restrict the type of pet allowed, and where they are permitted.

Learning more about the condominium's Rules and Regulations in the pre-contract stage is very important. Knowing where to find *all* the house rules is much more difficult than buyers think. Not all restrictions on the use and occupation of common elements appear in the Rules and Regulations. Some restrictions — and in particular those dealing with pets — are buried in the condominium constitution, the Declaration. This way the rule is virtually unalterable, requiring unanimous consent of both owners and lenders before it can be changed! Rules and Regulations, on the other hand, can be easily changed by the directors of the condominium corporation.

Aaron and Sharon wanted to keep their French Poodle when they moved to a condominium. Upon asking the real estate agent about keeping pets, before the offer was signed, he pointed out that the Rules and Regulations were silent on the point, implying that pets were permitted. When they asked a friend who lived in the same building about this, she noted that the prohibition against pets *only* appeared in the Declaration to the condominium, and not the Rules and Regulations. Luckily for Aaron and Sharon, this confusion was clarified at the pre-offer stage.

If keeping a pet like a dog is important, buyers in Aaron and Sharon's situation should do either or both of two things:

a) Ask the seller for and review the Rules and Regulations *and* the other condominium documents before entering into any agreement. To avoid future problems, do not simply rely on the information provided to you. Ask questions about areas of specific concerns, and independently verify the answers given before signing anything. Remember, not all rules and regulations appear in the Rules and Regulations. To be absolutely certain, take the condominium documents to a lawyer for his or her opinion as well.

b) Add a condition (not a warranty) to the offer, that a dog is permitted in the unit and on the common elements. This way, if no dogs are allowed, buyers like Aaron and Sharon could cancel the contract, as the condition had been breached.

If the condominium documents are not available when an offer is to be signed, don't be afraid to make the offer conditional on the seller providing you with them by a specified date, and upon your being satisfied with the contents of those documents within a set number of days after that. Otherwise, the deal becomes null and void. This gives you the time needed to get a legal opinion on any concerns you might have.

## Points to Know About Owning a Condominium

### 1. The Condominium Corporation

Once the Declaration and Description are registered, the condominium is born, together with a non-share company known as the condominium corporation to manage its affairs. All unit owners are members of the condominium corporation. Each unit has one vote, no matter how large a percentage interest is owned in the common elements.

Like any business corporation, the condominium corporation has officers and a board of directors elected by the condominium owners to manage its affairs. By-laws are passed and rules are set, provided the proper corporate procedures are followed. As running the condominium corporation on a day-to-day basis can be very time-consuming, most corporations retain the services of a management company, their fees being added to the common expenses.

The management company attends to the upkeep, maintenance and repair of the common elements and other assets of the condominium corporation, keeps the corporation's records up to date, collects and disburses the common expense funds, enters into contracts and other agreements on behalf of the corporation with dollar limits, and prepares the annual budget which forms the basis of the monthly common expense charge. Policy decisions continue to rest with the board of directors.

A common complaint of many unit owners is that decisions are being made without their input. Consider who is making those decisions: the directors. Directors are residents in the complex who have taken the time to get involved in the management and operation of the condominium corporation. Instead of complaining, participate! Become part of the decision-making process. Seek election to the board of directors. Learn first hand about condominium ownership with "on-the-job" training. Don't leave it up to someone else. As a member of the board of directors, you will know what is happening, as it happens. Your voice will be heard and your ideas will be considered. What an excellent way as well to meet your neighbors, make new friends and gain valuable experience.

## 2. Common Expenses (commonly called maintenance)

This is the monthly fee paid by unit owners for the upkeep, maintenance and repair of the common elements as well as the operation of the condominium corporation. Typical items included are utilities (if not individually metered); operating costs such as snow removal and lawn maintenance; the cost of repairs and maintenance of common elements; service contracts; personnel; supplies; insurance on the common elements; fees paid to the management company; administrative charges; and contributions to the reserve fund, discussed below. Many condominium owners rightly are upset when garbage disposal fees are included. In a sense, they are paying double for garbage pick-up, once to the condominium corporation and once to the municipality. Like unpaid realty taxes, if one unit owner does not pay his share promptly, all unit owners must bear the burden.

To ensure everyone pays his due, the condominium corporation can place a lien against a unit when common expenses are unpaid. If necessary it even can sell a unit to recoup outstanding charges. While this may prevent a particular unit owner from getting out of hand, widespread default could endanger a condominium corporation's economic health.

Prior to closing a purchase, the buyer's lawyer orders a document called an Estoppel Certificate from the condominium corporation. Estoppel is a legal term, whereby a party issuing a statement is bound to its contents, if the statement is relied upon. This certificate provides a status update on the unit and its owner, plus information about arrears for the unit. It also contains information about the condominium corporation itself, such as the amount of the reserve fund, pending lawsuits, and alterations and improvements to the common elements. Accompanying the Certificate are pertinent condominium documents such as the Rules and Regulations, Declaration, By-Laws, Certificate of Insurance, the most recent financial statements and the current budget for the corporation.

### 3. Selling/Leasing Unit

According to the provincial condominium acts, dwelling units can be freely sold, subject to any restrictions in the Declaration. Whether such restrictions on sales are enforceable is another question. In the United States, the board of directors often must approve any subsequent purchaser of a unit. In effect this gives the board a veto over who can own a unit in their complex. Though permitted by condominium legislation in some areas of Canada, these restrictions are not nearly as prevalent.

The right of a unit owner to rent his property is clear, provided he complies with the provisions of the Declaration. Again, the condominium corporation can place restrictions on the leasing of units. While this is rarely done, requiring that specific information about the tenant be given to the condominium corporation, is quite common. The tenant in turn must agree in writing to comply with the Rules and Regulations, Declaration and By-laws of the condominium corporation during his tenancy.

## 4. Insurance

The distinction between individual units and the common elements of the condominium corporation is most noticeable when dealing with insurance. Insurance coverage is arranged by the condominium corporation through a master policy on the common elements only, providing protection against loss by fire, water, smoke and other major perils on a replacement cost basis. The premium paid for this insurance coverage is included in the monthly maintenance payment. Liability coverage for the common elements also must be maintained by the corporation.

This coverage does *not* protect the unit owner, the unit, improvements made to the unit nor contents of a unit. Public liability coverage for a unit is also *not* provided by the condominium corporation's insurance. Insuring the unit remains the responsibility of the unit owner.

The insurance industry has developed what it calls "Condominium Unit Owner's Package Insurance" to provide the insurance coverage unit owners need. Coverage of this type is a hybrid, recognizing that a condominium itself is a hybrid between conventional ownership and a tenancy. In some respects this insurance coverage resembles a home owner's package as the unit itself is owned, while it parallels a tenant's package in other areas because the unit is only one in a larger complex. When arranging insurance coverage before closing, inform your insurance agent that a condominium unit is being bought. The appropriate condominium unit owner's package insurance needed for closing then can be booked.

Options to consider in addition to the basic unit owner's insurance and contents coverage include insuring improvements made to the unit; insuring on an all all-risks basis, providing much broader coverage than the standad named-perils basis; plus replacement cost coverage. Personal liability coverage which protects the unit owner if he is sued by someone suffering damage in the unit should also be included. Some insurance companies even will provide coverage at nominal cost for any loss suffered by a unit owner arising from a deficiency in the condominium corporation's insurance coverage. This could arise if the common elements are damaged, and the condominium corporation's insurance coverage is inadequate to repair the damage in full. All unit owners would have to make up the shortfall by way of a special assessment. With this additional coverage (called Loss Assessment Coverage) owners are reimbursed with the amount of the special assessment.

Two incidents at a party held in Donald and Daisy's condominium apartment illustrate the different types of insurance that must be arranged. Mickey, a guest at the party, broke his ankle when he tripped on the rug in the hallway of the apartment building. As it happened on a common element, Mickey must make a claim against the condominium corporation's personal liability insurance coverage. Minnie, on the other hand, tripped on a rug in Donald and Daisy's suite, breaking her ankle. Minnie will have to look to Donald and Daisy's personal liability insurance coverage. So too with a fire. Depending on whether it occurred on a common element or within a unit, the different insurance policies would be responsible for bearing the cost of repairing the damage.

## 5. The Reserve Fund

One of the problems early condominiums faced was a shortage of money for major repairs. As an inducement to sell units, developers pegged the amount of the monthly common expenses (maintenance) artificially low. No money was being set aside for a "rainy day." When costly repairs were needed, or major assets had to be replaced, condominium corporations lacked the necessary funds to do the work. Special assessments had to be levied against units to generate the needed cash. If unit owners refused to pay, liens were registered against their units, followed by proceedings to sell them. This exercise ended up pitting owners/neighbors against one another in their own condominium complexes. Yet who was the real author of the problem? The developer.

Reserve funds, "the money for a rainy day," now must be maintained to solve this dilemma. Each condominium corporation maintains a reserve fund to provide sufficient money to cover the cost of major repairs and the replacement of major assets which wear out, such as roofs, sidewalks, heating, electrical and plumbing systems, elevators, laundry machines, carpeting plus recreational and parking facilities. A portion of each monthly maintenance payment must be set aside as a contribution to the reserve fund. The exact amount of the reserve fund contribution is based on the expected repair, replacement cost and life expectancy of the common elements and corporate assets. In Ontario it must be at least 10 percent of the maintenance otherwise payable. Older condominiums should have larger reserve funds, as the likelihood of needing to repair and replace major assets and equipment is considerably greater.

A unit's proportionate interest in the reserve fund is easy to determine. Simply multiply the total amount in the reserve fund by the unit owner's share of the common elements. The Estoppel Certificate states the amount of money being held in the reserve fund. Per unit, the amount of money involved could be in the hundreds of dollars.

According to the Estoppel Certificate issued when Irv and Lillian purchased their condominium unit, the corporation's reserve fund amounted to $177,960. As they owned .550514% of the common elements, their proportionate interest in the reserve fund totalled $979.69. This begs the question: Does the seller get a credit for this amount when the unit is sold? Obviously, sellers feel they are entitled to be reimbursed for this money, as it represents prepaid funds, comparable to prepaid realty taxes. Buyers argue that no adjustment of the reserve fund should be made, as the money cannot be paid out according to the provincial condominium acts. The money in the reserve fund is an asset of the corporation by law, just like the bricks and mortar of the building. By acquiring a unit, the buyer should also acquire the vendor's interest in the reserve fund without adjustment.

Many offers deal with the issue, specifically stating that no adjustment of the reserve fund shall be made on closing. Even if the offer is silent on the point, this is the more accepted point of view. On the other hand, an offer could be drawn specifically requiring the amount in the reserve fund to be credited to the vendor. In that case, the buyer should be prepared to pay a sizeable sum of money on closing.

A serious problem would exist if insufficient funds were held in the reserve fund to cover the cost of unexpected major repairs. While the Estoppel Certificate provides information about the size of the reserve fund, normally it is obtained shortly before closing, too late to permit a buyer to withdraw from the transaction. Purchasers of resale condominiums might consider inserting a clause into the offer that if the proportionate share of the reserve fund for this unit did not exceed a specified amount, the vendor would credit the shortfall to the purchaser on closing. Be prepared for sellers to reject such a clause. Already incensed about not receiving a credit from the buyer for the reserve fund, they certainly are not prepared to pay any additional funds to the buyer for the same purpose.

## 6. Mortgage Clauses

Most mortgages secured against condominiums include specially tailored clauses. Typical clauses include:

- lenders are given the right to exercise the borrower's vote at any meeting of the condominium corporation, although it is usually not exercised. Lenders want this right to protect their investment.
- copies of all relevant notices and documents must be given to the lender, so it knows what is happening in the condominium.
- the borrower must agree to pay punctually all common expenses to the condominium corporation. When a borrower defaults, the lender can pay the arrears and add it to the mortgage debt. Many lenders will do this, as up to three months' unpaid maintenance fees have priority over and rank higher than a first mortgage.
- borrowers must agree to comply with, observe and perform *all* duties and obligations imposed by the provincial condominium act, the Declaration, By-laws, Rules and Regulations of the condominium corporation. Noncompliance gives the lender the right, *at its option,* to demand repayment of the mortgage in full. Taken to the limit, housing a pet in violation of the condominium's Rules and Regulations could be grounds for a lender to terminate the mortgage!

Until recently, some lenders felt that condominium mortgages were riskier investments because the borrower only owned his unit and an interest in the land. Higher interest rates were charged on condominium mortgages. While that is not the case today, the equity cushion demanded reflects this concern. Some lenders will only grant condominium mortgages for 70 percent of the value of a condominium, somewhat lower than the 75 percent financing that is granted on conventional properties.

## What a Condominium Offer Should Contain

To reflect the uniqueness of condominium ownership, several additional clauses must appear in the offer submitted. Purchasers of resale condominiums should ask the following questions and ensure the offer addresses the following.

- Find out the condominium unit and level number, plus the condominium corporation number. Many high-rise buildings have no thirteenth floor for numbering purposes, but do not ignore it as part of the legal description. Also, the unit number does not have to correspond with the apartment number. Apartment 2102 very well could be unit 5, level 20.
- Make sure the reserve fund is *not* to be adjusted in the seller's favor.
- Find out whether the parking space (and locker space) is freehold, leasehold, exclusive use or allocated. Is any additional fee payable for parking?
- Does the unit owner have an exclusive right to use any other area — patio/balcony; front yard/side yard?
- How much is the monthly maintenance (common expense) payment? Does it include hydro rates? Water rates? Heating charges? Cable television fee? When was it last raised? If a year has passed since the last increase, expect it to be raised imminently.
- Have any special assessments been made against the unit which have not been fully paid? If so, make sure the seller pays them before closing. Are any special assessments

contemplated? A unit owner would know this, since special assessments can only be levied if approved at a meeting of the condominium corporation. Has such a meeting been held recently?

- Has the seller already assigned his voting rights to a mortgagee? If so, the buyer or his new mortgagee may not be able to exercise that vote.
- Are any legal actions pending by or against the condominium corporation? This is very important, since a judgment against the condominium corporation also is a judgment against each unit owner *at the time of judgment.* No one wants to buy a lawsuit, or someone else's headache.

Perhaps someone slipped on ice outside the building, and is suing the condominium corporation. By closing the transaction, the seller dumps his potential liability unto the buyer. That is why learning this information now, not later, is so important. With sufficient advance notification, arrangements can be made to ensure the seller satisfies his proportionate interest in any judgment against the condominium. Making the seller responsible this way is only fair, since the seller was the owner of the unit when the basis for the lawsuit occurred.

Too often clauses like these are drafted in offers as warranties. As is noted in chapter 24, if a warranty is breached the buyer cannot refuse to close the transaction. He must proceed with the closing, and sue the seller for damages afterwards. If these issues are important, to the point you as a purchaser would want the right to cancel the contract if the information is incorrect, these clauses should be framed as conditions, and not as warranties.

- Are there any restrictions in the declaration or the by-laws on the sale of the unit? Learn this now, before even submitting an offer. According to the fine print in some standard form resale offers, if the written consent of the condominium corporation or its board of directors is required, the offer is conditional on obtaining that consent before closing. This is small consolation to buyers like Neil and Jane, who only learned about the approval requirement a week after their offer was accepted, and three weeks before closing. Imagine how they felt seven days later upon learning their application for consent was rejected. Here were Neil, Jane and family, two weeks before closing, with no place to live, no offer and no recourse against the seller for damages. That's right! Since the contract was conditional on obtaining that consent, the contract never was firm and binding, as the condition never was satisfied. This was disastrous for Neil and Jane, who had made numerous plans based on the anticipated purchase of this property, including the sale of their present home.

As a member of the condominium corporation, the seller should have known whether any restriction on sale existed. The real estate agent also should have independently verified this information before preparing an offer, the same as the particulars of a mortgage to be assumed must be verified. verified.

To safeguard against this happening, all buyers of resale units should do the following:

a) ask the agent and the seller whether any restrictions exist on the transfer of the unit.

b) Based on their reply, insert a CONDITION into the offer that no restrictions exist in the condominium documents on the sale of the unit. Don and Lyn did this, and were glad they did! Two weeks after the offer was signed, they learned that approval to the transfer was required, despite the assurances given by the agent and the seller, Ian. This meant the condition in the contract had been breached. Don and Lyn then had to decide whether or not to make the necessary application for consent, something they were not legally obligated to do. In saying yes, Don and Lyn did so only on clearly spelled-out terms. If the required consent was not available three weeks before closing, then Don and Lyn could withdraw from the transaction. Ian, the seller, would have to compensate them for *all* expenses incurred in finding alternative accommodations. The consent was granted on time and the deal closed as scheduled.

After almost twenty years in Canada, condominiums are no longer foreign to most people. Before purchasing a resale condominium, be sure you fully appreciate the different life-style it represents, and the different obligations it entails.

# 20

## *Mortgage Financing*

Few Canadians are fortunate enough to buy a home without the need of a mortgage. As a mortgage plays a pivotal role in the transaction, buyers should shop as prudently for a mortgage as they do for a house. While the legal concept of a mortgage, security for the repayment of a loan, is the same from lender to lender, the mortgage package may vary considerably. Different lenders offer different features today, all under the umbrella of "creative financing." With so many options available, the choice of a mortgage is all the more difficult. In this chapter, some of the key elements of mortgage financing for resale homes will be explored. Further information on mortgages — what they are, how to arrange the best possible mortgage, and then how to pay it off as quickly as possible — is available in the companion volume to this book, *Hidden Profits in Your Mortgage*.

Devotees of the HOBS approach to buying a house will not leave the question of arranging a mortgage to the end, after the offer is signed, almost as an afterthought or an appendage to the transaction. Instead, they will inquire and go mortgage shopping well *before* the offer is submitted, to know what is available in the marketplace, and those features which are most appealing. Inquiries can be made free from the pressures of time that many purchasers face. Armed with the information in this chapter, buyers even can determine that both they and the property being purchased will qualify for a mortgage before the property is even bought. Preliminary discussions also should be held with potential lenders at this pre-offer stage, to confirm that a loan will be granted if the offer is accepted. By informally pre-qualifying yourself this way, you can then formally apply for the best possible mortgage from a position of strength after the offer is signed. As you can approach various lenders head high, the usual scenario changes dramatically. Instead of asking whether a mortgage will be granted, the question now becomes who will grant that mortgage! One large real estate company has taken this informal pre-approval process one step further. It now will formally qualify buyers for a mortgage even before the offer is signed. If HOBS is properly applied, once the offer is signed, little more remains to be done with the mortgage than file the formal application and await the formal response. All the necessary questions will have been asked, the informal pre-qualifying will have been done, the right mortgage package and lender selected. To leave the mortgage until after the offer is signed can only work against a purchaser's best interests.

Many offers are submitted and accepted conditionally on obtaining satisfactory financing within a very short period of time. The purchaser inevitably accepts the first mortgage approval presented, whatever the terms. With just a little more foresight and advance planning, this type of situation, far too common amongst purchasers, easily can be avoided.

A key element of a home-buying strategy encourages purchasers to take unsigned offers to their lawyers for review and comment. More and more purchasers are doing this with unsigned mortgage commitments as well. This way, they ensure the commitment contains what it is supposed to contain, nothing unexpected being added in and nothing important being omitted. Having a lawyer do this makes good sense, and offers considerable piece of mind. Most commitments can be reviewed in a very short period of time, making the cost to the purchaser nominal.

To arrange a mortgage loan, it is necessary to know more about the nature of the beast. Some of the expressions that will be encountered are

**Equity:** the owner's interest in the property; the difference between the fair market value of a property and the outstanding mortgages. Howard and Sheila own a house worth $90,000 and owe $55,000 on their mortgage. Their equity is $35,000.

**Term:** the life of the mortgage. It could be anywhere from six months to ten years. It is *not* the same as the amortization.

**Amortization:** the period of time that it would take for the mortgage loan to be paid off in full, if all mortgage payments were made on time, with no prepayments. At the end of the amortization period, the mortgage is fully paid off. Shorter amortizations mean higher mortgage payments, but lower overall interest costs. A typical mortgage has a three-year term, 25-year amortization, meaning it matures in three years, the payments being calculated as if it would take 25 years for the loan to be retired in full.

**Blended payments:** Where the same amount of money is paid to the lender each payment during the term of the loan. However, the mix between principal and interest constantly is changing. Over time, the principal component ever is increasing, while the portion of the payment allocated to interest constantly is decreasing.

When buying a resale property, buyers can get a mortgage in one of three different ways: by assuming the existing mortgage; having the seller take back a mortgage for the unpaid balance of the purchase price; or arranging their own mortgage.

## Assuming the Existing Mortgage

Maynard is sellng his home which already has a mortgage registered against it. Dobie, the purchaser, will be taking it over on closing. This means Dobie will assume all of Maynard's rights and obligations under the mortgage. When calculating the amount payable by Maynard on closing the amount of the assumed mortgage is deducted from the purchase price. This is the situation where a purchaser pays "cash to the mortgage," the cash plus the mortgage equalling the purchase price.

Why assume an existing mortgage? It is an easy, quick and inexpensive way to find a mortgage. As the mortgage already is on title, there are no appraisal or legal fees to be paid. When the interest rate on the mortgage is less than the current mortgage interest rate, the buyer will save money with each mortgage payment. A mortgage like this could be a selling feature of the house, if assumable.

As the loan already is outstanding, its terms are nonnegotiable. If the principal is too small, the rate is too high, or the term is too short, the mortgage may not be acceptable for a purchaser to assume. Knowing all these details ahead of time, before an offer is submitted, becomes extremely important.

Mortgages automatically are assumable by a purchaser of a property, unless any restrictions appear in the mortgage itself. Many mortgages today become due and payable if the property is sold, at the lender's option. The other side of the coin means the mortgage is assumable, provided the purchaser applies to assume the mortgage, the purchaser qualifies for it, and the lender permits the purchaser to assume the mortgage, the last point being very important indeed.

If you are planning to assume an existing mortgage on closing, learn whether it is assumable, and on what terms. The listing agent should have verified this and other particulars of the mortgage (outstanding principal, interest rate, payment and maturity date) when the listing was obtained. Otherwise, you could be planning to assume a mortgage which is totally nonassumable.

## Granting a Vendor-take-back Mortgage

The seller takes back a mortgage for the unpaid balance of the purchase price, called a VTB mortgage, to help the purchaser acquire the property. Payment of part of the purchase price is deferred this way, for a number of years.

A VTB mortgage parallels assuming an existing mortgage in a number of ways. It is an easy, quick and cheap mortgage to arrange. Once the offer is accepted, the buyer has been approved for the mortgage. No credit checks, application or appraisal fees, or legal expenses for the purchaser.

The wording of the clause in the offer dealing the VTB mortgage dictates the terms of the actual mortgage. Here, the terms of the mortgage are determined *before* the offer is accepted. Key points to consider include the amount of principal; the interest rate; the amount of the payment (or the amortization period for the loan); and its term. Special clauses such as prepayment privileges and assumability on sale must appear in the offer, to be picked up in the mortgage. If the offer lacks a clause requiring the delivery of post-dated cheques, you, as borrower, are not obligated to deliver them.

Most VTB mortgages are both fully open and fully assumable. Since a VTB mortgage represents the unpaid purchase price, most sellers permit the mortgage to be prepaid before it matures. Often they are written as assumable mortgages, the seller looking to the property, his former house, rather than the buyer, as the security for the loan.

VTB mortgages are used by a home owner to sell his property. With a VTB mortgage, the offer does not have to be made conditional on financing. Upon acceptance, the offer is firm and binding, and the mortgage is committed, just like that. The interest rate probably will be one-half to one and one-half percent less than the market rate for a comparable institutional mortgage. Yet the rate also is higher than the seller would receive simply by placing his funds into a term deposit or Guaranteed Investment Certificate. Both the seller and the buyer benefit this way. If the seller needs the money, the mortgage always can be sold. Knowing the background to the sale is relevant, for it could indicate that a VTB mortgage can be arranged.

Several points about VTB mortgages should be kept in mind. First, most are short-term mortgages, one to three years. Second, a VTB mortgage never should be considered as permanent financing for a property. Few VTB mortgages are renewed at maturity, the vendor already having waited several years to receive these funds. With a seller being under no obligation to renew a VTB mortgage unless such a clause appears in it, refinancing costs will have to be incurred in the near future. These costs could have been avoided if a longer-term institutional mortgage had been arranged when the property was purchased.

## Arranging a New Mortgage

Far and away, this is the most common situation today. The purchaser negotiates his own mortgage, arranges a cash transaction with the seller, and pays the mortgage proceeds together with his own funds to the seller on closing.

Where can a purchaser get a mortgage? Obviously a number of traditional sources exist, such as banks, trust companies, insurance companies and credit unions. Mortgage brokers bring lenders and borrowers together, for a fee. Before using a mortgage broker, find out what the broker's fee will be, and what services are being provided. Many lawyers have lender clients investing funds in mortgages. Often, private lenders will offer more liberal prepayment privileges, or slightly better interest rates, to be competitive.

Lenders consider both the property and the borrower when deciding whether to grant a mortgage loan, and how much to advance. To determine the value of a property, institutional lenders will have it appraised, at a cost to the purchaser of $150 to $200, even though the purchase price should determine what the property is worth. Private lenders often will not require an appraisal, when the mortgage funds are being advanced to finance the purchase.

The rules on property qualification are quite straight-forward. A conventional mortgage cannot exceed 75 percent of the appraised value of the property. When Nick and Maria bought their home for $120,000, the conventional first mortgage could not exceed $90,000. This is the "loan-to-value" ratio that lenders use. Because of this requirement, a borrower must have at least 25 percent equity in the property. At least 25 percent of the purchase price must come from his own resources, to obtain a conventional mortgage.

Just because a buyer does not have 25 percent of the purchase price does not mean he cannot purchase a home. Mortgages can be arranged for more than 75 percent of the appraised value of the property, for a cost. These "high-ratio" loans require the buyer to arrange mortgage payment insurance on the *entire* amount of the mortgage. This type of insurance, examined in more detail in chapter 29, protects the lender if the borrower defaults. Not only is the insurance fee quite substantial, up to 2.5 percent of the amount borrowed, but it usually is added to the outstanding principal. When Jason and Kylie borrowed $60,000 on a high-ratio loan, adding the $900 insurance fee to the mortgage meant they owed more on the mortgage ($60,900) than they actually borrowed! In some cases, up to 95 percent of the appraised value of the property can be borrowed this way, although most lenders insist that the buyer have a minimum downpayment of 10 percent.

Pre-qualifying the property before submitting an offer is relatively easy. Assuming the purchase price equates to its appraised value, determine how much money you have to put down ($20,000), and multiply if by three, for a figure of $60,000. If the size of mortgage needed to complete your purchase is less than or equal to this figure, a conventional mortgage can be arranged. If more than that amount is needed, a high-ratio mortgage will be necessary. Easy, isn't it?

Besides the property, lenders consider borrowers and their ability to repay the mortgage before granting the loan. Probably the most agonizing time for buyers is the interval after acceptance, when the condition on financing has not yet been satisfied. Buyers who informally pre-qualify themselves for a mortgage, knowing what the income requirements are, can avoid all this. Leaving it until after the offer is signed results in unnecessary anguish.

Like any loan application, the lender will require detailed information about the buyer and his financial resources. Lenders then must decide if the borrower's gross income is sufficiently large and stable to support the mortgage. Usually, the combined gross incomes of both a husband and a wife are considered. The generally accepted rule is that the mortgage payment (principal and interest), taxes and maintenance for condominium mortgages should not exceed 30 percent of the borrower's gross income, before any deductions. This is the Gross Debt Service (GDS) ratio lenders use. Furthermore, lenders consider the percentage of gross annual income needed to service *all* debt payments — house, car loan, personal loan and credit card payments. Called the TDS or Total Debt Service ratio, it requires that the total debt payments not exceed 37 to 40 percent of the borrower's gross incomes. Most lenders adhere quite strictly to these rules.

An easy method exists for buyers to know early if their gross incomes will qualify to service a mortgage loan. Add together the monthly mortgage payment (principal and interest) amortized over 25 years; one-twelfth of the estimated annual taxes; and the monthly condominium maintenance payment, if applicable. Multiply the total by 40. If your gross incomes exceed this figure, the GDS requirement is satisfied, and you should qualify for the mortgage. That's all there is to pre-determine if you earn enough money to qualify for a mortgage.

Using this approach, Tony and Margaret determined that the monthly mortgage payment on a non-condominium property for the mortgage they are thinking of arranging would total $640. The annual taxes are $1,320, or $110 monthly. The gross income needed to qualify for the mortgage is ($640 + $110) times 40, or $30,000. Knowing what they now know, imagine how confidently Tony and Margaret can negotiate their mortgage.

How do borrowers know what the appropriate monthly mortgage payment will be? The chart in chapter 8 lists the monthly mortgage payment per $1,000 of mortgage loan at various interest rates, amortized over 25 years. Earlier on, the chart was used to consider how large a mortgage could be arranged, based on the borrower's gross income. Now the reverse is being considered: how large a gross income is needed to carry a specific mortgage? Once the appropriate rate is selected, multiply the figure by the amount of the mortgage, in thousands of dollars, being arranged. The result is the approximate monthly payment. In Tony and Margaret's case, they considered a $64,000 mortgage at 11.5 percent. By multiplying 9.97 by 64, and rounding it up slightly, they calculated the approximate amount of the monthly payment to be $640.

The mortgage packages offered by institutional lenders differ considerably. While rate should be a factor when shopping for a mortgage, it never should be *the* only factor in deciding which lender to choose. Proper application of your home-buying strategy requires that you inquire about and analyze these features at the precontract stage. Considering which mortgage is the most appropriate is considerably easier *before* you sign the offer.

## a) Interest Rate

The rate of interest charged on a mortgage is closely tied in with its term. A premium is paid for long-term mortgages; they bear a higher rate of interest each month during the entire mortgage term, for the security of the longer, fixed-rate commitment. While short-term mortgages of six months and a year carry lower interest rates, they subject borrowers more frequently to the volatility of the interest rate market. Where interest rates are going is virtually unpredictable; there is no easy or right answer when deciding whether to go short-term or long-term on the rate.

When obtaining quotes for interest rates, also ascertain for how long the rate is guaranteed. A 30-day guaranteed rate is of little value to a buyer with ninety days to wait until closing.

## b) Term

When considering the term of a mortgage, ask yourself how long this house will satisfy your wants and needs. Often this is difficult to answer, considering the house has not even been bought yet! Is it a starter home, to be sold in three or four years? If so, then choose a mortgage term that reflects this period of anticipated ownership. A five-year loan will mean a higher interest rate, a larger monthly payment, and a possible prepayment penalty if you want to break the mortgage before it matures. When in doubt, round the term down, not up, to avoid this penalty.

## c) Frequency of Interest Calculations

No matter how frequently a mortgage is paid, the standard way of calculating interest in Canada is semi-annually. The more frequently interest is calculated, the more expensive it is for a borrower. Stay away from mortgages calculated monthly. They will cost you money. Ensure the mortgage is *calculated* semi-annually, although it may be *payable* monthly, weekly or bi-weekly.

Mortgages in Canada are payable "not in advance." This means the payment is made at the end of the month, not at the beginning, like rent. January's rent may be paid January 1 in advance, but January's mortgage payment is made February 1, not in advance. This arrangement benefits borrowers, not lenders.

### d) Realty Tax Account

Many lenders collect 1/12th of the estimated taxes with each monthly mortgage payment, and pay the taxes as the bills are issued. The argument usually advanced by lenders is convenience, making budgeting easier. Rarely is a fair rate of interest paid on the money deposited in a tax amount. Also, to ensure funds are available when the next tax bill is issued, lenders require that borrowers prepay their realty taxes up to six months ahead of time. If at all possible, try to pay your own realty taxes.

### e) Assumability

Mortgages in Canada are automatically assumable by a subsequent purchaser of the property, without requiring the lender's consent, unless the mortgage contains a restriction to the contrary. Most mortgages today are "limited assumable," rendering the mortgage due and payable at the lender's option if the property is sold. This allows the lender to decide if an existing mortgage can be assumed when the property is sold.

Mortgages are assumed quite easily. By simply closing a resale transaction after any required approval has been given, and paying the vendor the difference between the purchase price and the outstanding mortgage (cash to the mortgage), the purchaser has assumed the mortgage. Rarely are buyers asked to sign a formal mortgage assumption agreement, creating a direct, contractual link between buyer and lender.

### f) Portability

After a number of years, home owners like Dwayne and Emma decided to buy a larger house with a larger mortgage. In the real estate business, this is known as "trading up." As the buyer of their home did not wish to assume the existing mortgage, Dwayne and Emma faced a dilemma. They will have to incur a prepayment penalty to retire the old loan, while they will need a new larger mortgage to finance the new home purchase. Some lenders allow borrowers like Dwayne and Emma to take their old mortgage to the new home, eliminating the prepayment penalty. If a larger mortgage is needed, the rate is blended, like paint, to reflect the proportions of old money (the mortgage from the old home) and new money (the additional money needed to finance the purchase). Of course, this assumes both the borrower and the property qualify for the new mortgage.

### g) Prepayment

Interest paid on mortgages in Canada generally is not deductible from other income. For this reason, it is extremely important for Canadians to retire their mortgages as quickly as possible. When a mortgage is prepaid, the borrower saves both interest and income tax on the money that had to be earned to finance the prepayment. Simply put, Joe's prepayment of $500 saved him $6,000 in interest over the term of his mortgage. Being in the $33\frac{1}{3}$% marginal tax bracket, Joe would have had to earn $9,000 in income and pay tax of $3,000, to be left with the $6,000 he saved in interest. This prepayment of $500, in effect, saved Joe $9,000 in income.

When a mortgage is amortized over 25 years, it assumes the same payment is made every month for that full period of time. Any additional money paid toward the mortgage, before it is due (called a prepayment), reduces the amortization as well as the interest cost for the loan. Fast-pay mortgages, such as weekly and bi-weekly mortgages, can also result in huge savings of interest payments.

## Hidden Costs in Mortgage Transactions

Home buyers are absolutely astounded when confronted with the cost of arranging a mortgage loan to finance a purchase. Al and Lorna booked a $50,000 mortgage with Vaughan Trust, which was registered when their purchase closed on September 11. Following HOBS, they asked about the cost of arranging a mortgage before signing the offer to purchase. Imagine how surprised they were to learn the hidden costs would be $800! Better to learn this information now, and plan for it, than immediately before closing.

Keep in mind that the buyer pays *all* the costs incurred in arranging the mortgage when purchasing a resale property. These expenses are "cash" costs, payable up front, on closing. As most of them are deducted by the lender at source from the mortgage advance, the buyer must make up the difference on closing from his own resources. In Al and Lorna's situation, the net advance was only $49,166.23, meaning they had to give their lawyer the $833.77 difference on closing from their own pocket.

Whether any of the following items are deducted will depend on the circumstances of the particular mortgage loan.

## a) Mortgage Appraisal/Application Fee

Most lenders charge a "mortgage initiation fee" to cover the administrative costs of booking the mortgage. Fees of $150 to $200 are not uncommon. Another charge incurred is the cost of obtaining the appraisal. Ask whether the mortgage application fee covers the appraisal fee, or whether they are separate charges. The combined fee to Al and Lorna was $175.

## b) Interest to the Interest Adjustment Date

Mortgages in Canada are paid in arrears, "not in advance," at the end of the payment period. This timing question accounts for the deduction made by institutional lenders under this heading. In its simplest form, it means a buyer/borrower is paying the interest for the balance of the month of closing somewhat earlier than normal. Although it is a legitimate charge, the mechanics usually are not well understood. If not properly planned for, interest to the interest adjustment date can devastate a borrower's cash flow on closing.

Most institutional mortgages are paid on the first of the month, for the month just recently completed. In Al and Lorna's case, their first mortgage payment will be November 1 for the month of October, the first full month they own the property. But what about the broken month of September? Obviously, Al and Lorna are responsible for the payment of interest for that portion of September beginning on the 11th of the month. When is it paid? October 1 is considered by the lender to be the "interest adjustment date," the day the mortgage effectively begins to run. The first payment is due one month later, November 1. To collect interest for the broken period of September, most lenders deduct it at source from the mortgage advance, calculating the interest daily. As Al and Lorna's mortgage carried a 12% interest rate, this 20-day deduction totalled $328.77. Very few lenders make a full mortgage advance and bill the borrower later for this interest.

Private lenders for the most part and the odd institutional lender make the interest adjustment date the date of closing, avoiding this problem altogether. The first payment falls due exactly one month after closing, meaning no deduction of interest is necessary on closing. A VTB mortgage can help a buyer's cash flow on closing immensely for this reason.

With this deduction being made, Al and Lorna in effect are paying on September 11th the mortgage payment otherwise due on October 1. One consolation to the cash flow crisis faced on closing is the fact that no mortgage payment is due for almost two months. This will help Al and Lorna replenish their resources.

Closing earlier in the month (i.e., September 4) would compound the problem further, as a larger amount would be deducted on closing. Closing should not be delayed until later in the month, though, just to minimize this expense. Serious problems surround late month closings, as illustrated in chapter 24. More importantly, interest to the interest adjustment date is an expense that can very easily be planned for. Simply multiply the amount of money being borrowed by the interest rate being charged, and divide that total by 365. Then multiply it by the number of days remaining in the broken month. In Al and Lorna's case, the figures looked like this: $50,000 × 12% = $6,000; divided by 365 = $16.4383; multiplying that figure by 20 days = $328.77.

### c) Establishing a Realty Tax Account

The taxes on Al and Lorna's home are estimated to be $1,320 yearly. All current year taxes are paid. With each mortgage payment, Vaughan Trust will be collecting $110, starting November 1. When the interim tax bill for half the year's taxes is issued in late January next year, Vaughan Trust wants to have approximately $660 in the tax account. With only three regular payments to be made before the bill is issued (November, December and January) the lender will be short $330. To cover this shortfall, the lender collected $330 from Al and Lorna on closing by deducting this amount from the mortgage advance.

Borrowers who are able to pay their own taxes save in several ways. First, they can avoid this lump-sum deduction on closing, which ravages a buyer's pre-closing budget. Second, they avoid prepaying taxes. By the time the tax bill is issued, Al and Lorna will have paid six months' taxes to the lender before they actually come due. Learn if the lender insists on having taxes paid this way. If so, buyers adopting HOBS can then budget for this expense on closing. Learning about the deduction for the realty tax account for the first time at the eleventh hour, can create a cash flow crisis.

### d) Mortgage Broker's Fee

Buyers who retain the services of a mortgage broker to handle the paperwork on the mortgage application will have to pay a fee to the broker. If you are in this category, know what the fee will be and plan for it, before making any final commitments.

### e) CMHC/MICC Payment Insurance Fees

High-ratio mortgages must be insured with either of these two organizations to protect the lender and ensure the mortgage is paid promptly. Current rates on resale homes run from 1.5 to 2.5 percent of the amount borrowed.

### f) Other Insurance

Besides payment insurance, both life insurance and rate insurance come under this umbrella heading. More details appear in chapter 29.

Take a copy of the accepted offer to the lender, when making a formal mortgage application. If both a sale and a purchase are involved, copies of both offers should be given to the lender, plus information about any outstanding mortgages. This information is needed to establish the equity on the existing home. Most lenders also will require an "equity letter" from your bank, confirming that you have sufficient money on deposit to pay the balance of the money on closing. A salary letter will also be needed from your employer, certifying the amount of your salary. Once the mortgage application has been filed, be patient. Approval does take time, perhaps a week or more. To most buyers, this is a period of agony and anxiety, not knowing whether the mortgage will be granted and whether the purchase can proceed. To buyers like Frank and Irene who informally pre-approved themselves as part of their home-buying strategy, the wait is much easier to endure.

Every borrower should have an amortization schedule for his mortgage loan. Inexpensive to obtain ($5 to $10), it shows how the mortgage payment is allocated between the principal and interest components, plus the outstanding balance following each payment. Amortization schedules are an invaluable tool in cutting down the high cost of mortgage financing in Canada. For a thorough explanation of how to order a schedule for a mortgage, and how to take advantage of the information it contains to save thousands of after-tax dollars, see *Hidden Profits In Your Mortgage.*

Buyers who want to close their purchase first, followed several days later by their sale, will be interested in the chapter on bridge financing. After that, as part of HOBS, it will be time to explore and understand some of the additional charges buyers will incur on closing — "The Hidden Costs."

# 21

## Bridge Financing

Anyone selling a home and buying another would be well advised to consider arranging bridge financing. Bridge financing involves closing the purchase transaction several days or weeks *before* the sale. Instead of taking the net proceeds from the sale and applying them directly to the purchase the same day, an amount equivalent to the net proceeds is borrowed from the bank as a short-term loan to close the purchase. These funds are returned to the bank, plus interest, when the sale is completed. Bridge financing considerably lessens the aggravation that accompanies most back-to-back transactions, where the sale and the purchase close the same day. Although there is a cost associated with bridge financing, the alternative often ends up being even more costly, and certainly more demanding. A key component of HOBS for existing home owners changing houses is to close the two transactions on two separate days by arranging bridge financing or, as it is sometimes called, interim financing.

Jerry and Linda sold their old home on Dinky Drive and bought a new home on Cyclops Crescent. Both deals were scheduled to close May 30th. Obviously, the Dinky Drive sale had to close first, as Jerry and Linda needed those funds to close the Cyclops Crescent purchase. Luckily, Doug and Aline, the purchasers of their old home, were moving from an apartment. This meant their closing the Dinky Drive property was not dependant on any other deal closing, as is often the case.

Still, the lender financing Doug and Aline's purchase would not release the mortgage funds until 10:00 A.M. on May 30th. Those funds had to be delivered to Doug and Aline's lawyer, who in turn would use them to close the Dinky Drive purchase from Jerry and Linda. Only then could Jerry and Linda's lawyer close their purchase on Cyclops Crescent. Any similarity to dominoes is purely intentional!

The time spent in waiting for the Dinky Drive deal to close, coupled with the volume of business at the registry office, delayed the closing of the Cyclops Crescent property until 4:00 P.M. Being on pins and needles the whole day was only part of Jerry and Linda's problem. More importantly, the movers, who had started loading their truck at 8:00 A.M., and were finished at noon, had nothing to do but sit around for over four hours, time totally wasted, at Jerry and Linda's expense. Even after the Cyclops Crescent deal closed at 4:00 P.M., Jerry and Linda still had to get the keys from their lawyer to gain access to the property. Only at 6:00 P.M. did Jerry and Linda open the door to their new home. Imagine — six hours down the drain, with a moving crew being paid. This delay in closing the two deals cost Jerry and Linda over $300 in extra moving costs.

Lewis and Lily did things differently. Knowing that closing both transactions the same day often means costly delays, they scheduled their Bebop Road sale to close that same May 30th, but their Jazz Avenue purchase for May 27th. Since they would own two houses over that three-day period, a weekend as it turns out, it was necessary for them to arrange bridge financing for the purchase.

Much to their pleasant surprise, Lewis and Lily learned it was not necessary to bridge finance the entire $100,000 purchase price for their new home. All they had to borrow by way of bridge financing was their equity in their Bebop Road home. The remainder of the funds for the purchase on Jazz Avenue, whatever the source, would be available no matter when the closing of the purchase transaction took place. Of the $100,000 purchase price, a new $60,000 first mortgage was being arranged, with the vendor taking back a $10,000 second mortgage. The equity in their old home amounted to $22,000, the remaining $8,000 coming from Lewis and Lily's own savings. This meant that of the $100,000 purchase price, everything except the $22,000 equity in their old home would be available for closing, whenever that was — May 27th, May 30th, any day before, after or in between. All they would have to bridge finance was $22,000.

Having made prior arrangements to bridge finance their purchase, $22,000 of the bank's money was applied to Lewis and Lily's purchase on Jazz Avenue on May 27th. When the sale of Bebop Road closed on May 30th, $22,000 of the sale proceeds plus interest was returned to the bank to retire the bridge financing.

What did Lewis and Lily gain from the bridge financing? First, they found that May 27th was not a wasted day. Both of them put in a full day at work, picking up the keys to their new home from their lawyer after hours. That evening, they moved several delicate and fragile items into the house, and gave it a once-over cleaning. One bedroom, badly needing a paint job, was done that night. When the movers came to the old house at 8:00 A.M. the following morning, they loaded up the truck, travelled to the new property and immediately began unloading. By 3:00 P.M., the job was completed. Saturday night and all day Sunday were dedicated to unpacking, unpacking and unpacking, making the new home "habitable." A quick trip to clean up the old house, reminisce and say goodbye to Bebop Road was made early Sunday evening. Monday, while they continued unpacking, the Bebop Road sale was closed, and the bridge financing was paid off. Total cost for the bridge financing: approximately $200. Life was back to normal by Tuesday, with barely a disruption. By arranging bridge financing, Lewis and Lily were able to move from one home to the other, like a king and queen. In doing so, they even saved money, compared to Jerry and Linda.

As a very short-term unsecured loan, bridge financing is not cheap, but it is not overly expensive either. Most financial institutions levy an administrative fee (perhaps in the $150 range) plus interest, a common charge being a floating rate of prime plus 2%. Of course, these charges will vary amongst financial institutions. Before granting the bridge financing, your bank manager will want to see copies of the firm (not conditional) offers on both properties. Additional data may have to be provided, of the amount outstanding on any existing mortgages, plus any amount being borrowed on any new mortgages. All this information is used to verify the net equity in your old home, the maximum amount a bank is prepared to advance unsecured in this fashion. As the transactions are processed, assurances may be required from your lawyer that no problems have been encountered, or were foreseeable in either transaction. You would also have to consent to having the bridge financing secured immediately against either or both properties, if the purchase transaction closed but the sale did not, for any reason.

As Jerry and Linda learned the hard way, the cost of bridge financing is money well spent, compared against the additional charges incurred when two transactions are closed the same day. Staggering the closings this way allows a more leisurely move, with less anguish and anxiety. Often, as Lewis and Lily learned, money even can be saved by arranging bridge financing. Even where that is not the case, the nonmonetary benefits that bridge financing brings — the extra time it allows to clean the house, paint a room, lay some carpet and unpack, coupled with the aggravation it eliminates — makes the decision an easy one. Learn from experience. Too often after the turmoil of a back-to-back move, people wish they had arranged bridge financing.

With the loan being unsecured, the lending institution wants some assurance that the funds will be repaid as scheduled. The last thing it wants to do is chase after the borrower for the money after both deals are closed. To get first claim on the sale proceeds, buyers like Jack and Elaine sign what is called a Letter of Direction addressed to their lawyer. In it, Jack and Elaine authorize their lawyer to pay to the bank from the sale proceeds the amount borrowed plus all accruing interest and administrative charges *before* any money is paid to them. Besides directing their lawyer in writing this way, their bank required that the lawyer acknowledge in writing that he would honor the terms of the Letter of Direction, forthwith, after the sale closes. Only by being assured that the funds will be short-circuited to the bank this way, would it release the bridge financing funds needed for Jack and Elaine's purchase.

Bridge financing poses a "chicken and egg" dilemma. Banks will not grant bridge financing loans until two firm offers exist. On the other hand, a buyer like Vince cannot make both transactions firm, with two different closing dates, unless he knows that bridge financing will be available. To resolve the question, Vince should make preliminary inquiries and seek informal assurance that a bridge financing loan will be granted, before signing the offers and setting the closing dates. Any snags encountered even at this early stage probably would force him to close both transactions on the same day, against his better judgment. If a financial institution is prepared to grant the loan, provided both offers are firmed up, Vince should learn what the interest rate and administrative costs will be. If they are acceptable, Vince can proceed to firm up both offers, with staggered closing dates, knowing the bridge financing will be in place for closing.

Most financial institutions are reluctant to grant unsecured loans as bridge financing unless the purchaser is an established and well-known customer. This is one situation where shopping for a loan may not be overly helpful. Since lenders are under no obligation to grant bridge financing loans, the best source may well be the bank or trust company you deal with regularly. Often what tips the scale is the customer himself — his past dealings with the branch, and his reputation. Another excellent source to contact is the lending institution providing the mortgage on the home purchase. The better the loan package, the more likely the bridge financing will be granted. When Carey and Sharon met with their bank manager, they discussed bridge financing as well as the terms of the mortgage they needed to close the purchase. Both loans ultimately were approved.

Once the two contracts are signed and the two closings are scheduled to close the same day, it is very difficult to reschedule one, and then consider bridge financing. As part of a HOBS, existing home owners should seriously consider bridge financing the transactions. This could be one of those rare situations, where borrowing money ends up being the cheaper alternative!

# 22

# How Much Money Is Needed To Close?

Most buyers are genuinely shocked when told how much money is needed to close the transaction. No one wants to find himself facing a cash-flow crisis on closing because he did not know how large the hidden costs of closing would be. Imagine the anxiety and concern a buyer would then face. Most of the so-called "hidden costs" are known with reasonable accuracy well in advance of closing. Obviously, they will be revealed eventually. Unfortunately, the overall amount needed to close a real estate purchase, including legal fees, disbursements and other closing charges, traditionally has been disclosed for the first time immediately prior to closing.

Frankly, there should be no hidden costs in any real estate transaction. By asking the right questions of the right person as early as possible, buyers subscribing to the HOBS approach will learn how much money to set aside for closing the deal *before* signing and submitting the offer to purchase. Last-minute surprises can be totally eliminated this way. Buyers can budget and plan their finances for closing as educated consumers, knowing how much they can afford to spend on the purchase, and how large a mortgage to arrange. Having the overall charges disclosed at this stage, before making any commitment, is the only way to approach the situation.

Who should provide this information to a buyer? Very rarely will a real estate agent in a resale transaction volunteer this information. The financial news not being pleasant, they are fearful of losing a prospective purchaser by telling him or her too much too soon. An excellent opportunity to learn this information, though, is in your preliminary discussions with a lawyer. This can be done either when obtaining price quotes or, more appropriately, when the content of the draft, unsigned offer is being reviewed with your lawyer. Face to face, you can learn about, review and expect the unexpected — the expenses most buyers know nothing about until the last minute — and plan your cash flow on closing accordingly.

Hidden closing costs fall into six categories: a) legal fees; b) disbursements; c) provincial taxes; d) adjustments; e) deductions on the mortgage; f) miscellaneous. When determining how much money a buyer requires to close, the legal fees, disbursements, provincial taxes, adjustments and miscellaneous fees are added to the purchase price to determine the gross amount needed to close. Deducted from this figure is the deposit and the amount of money coming from other sources, such as a new first mortgage (net of any deductions made by the lender), a vendor-take-back or assumed mortgage, or the sale of an existing home (after expenses). The difference is the net amount of money the buyer must bring to his or her lawyer by certified cheque to close the purchase transaction. Remember that closing costs, including the lawyer's fee, are cash costs, payable up front, before closing.

Ed and Joyce are planning to buy a $100,000 home, with a $5,000 deposit. The new mortgage they are arranging will be $75,000, an additional $20,000 being paid on closing. Meeting with their lawyer before the offer was signed, they learned the legal fees will be approximately $500, disbursements $150, transfer tax $725 and adjustments approximately $450. The gross amount needed to close, then, is $101,825. Deducted from this amount are the net advance on the mortgage ($74,725) and the $5,000 deposit for a total of $79,725. This leaves a net amount payable on closing of $22,100. As Ed and Joyce expected to pay, in raw numbers, $20,000 on closing, the "hidden costs" in this transaction total $2,100.

To avoid being too close to the line, and to avoid any last-minute contingencies, Ed and Joyce were told to set aside another $250, for a total of $2,350. In their own minds, these funds were already committed and spent on the closing. If the actual amount needed to close was around $2050, Ed and Joyce would be left with $300 of found money to spend on paint and wallpaper for the house.

To give a reasonable estimate of what the closing costs will be, a lawyer will need to know much about the proposed transaction. If the figure quoted by a lawyer seems high, remember one very important fact — he does not earn all that money! Many other closing costs are included in that figure as well.

What are these hidden costs that buyers must know about and properly budget for, prior to closing?

## Legal Fees

What the lawyer takes home varies greatly from province to province, region to region within a province, within a small geographical area like a city and from lawyer to lawyer. For more information on the setting of lawyer's fees, see chapter 14.

## Disbursements

These are out-of-pocket expenses lawyers incur on behalf of clients. Many disbursements are paid to obtain clearances and reports needed for the title opinion. The actual disbursements and amount charged for each item will differ both from file to file and from municipality to municipality. Typical disbursements include:

*By-law/zoning and work order report* — That the property complies with all zoning and other by-laws, and that no work orders are outstanding. Usual charge — $25.
*Tax certificate* — That no realty taxes are outstanding. Normal charge — $10.
*Utilities certificates* — That no public utility charges are outstanding — $10.

*Search of title* — The cost of ordering deeds, mortgages and other agreements on title, which are then reviewed and summarized. This cost is usually at least $25, depending on the complexity of the state of title.

*Registration costs* — The cost of registering each instrument on title. In Ontario, the minimum charge to register a document is $16. Registering a deed and two mortgages would cost $48.

*Transportation and courier charge* — Timing is crucial in a real estate transaction. Couriers are absolutely necessary to deliver time-sensitive items to and from a lawyer's office (i.e., the net mortgage advance from a lender). Typically budget $25 for this, plus the cost of two trips to an out-of-town registry office, if applicable (once to search the title, and once to close the transaction).

*Execution certificate* — This is issued by the local sheriff or land registrar, indicating that there are no outstanding judgments on file against the purchaser, the vendor and previous owners of the land. Depending on the number of prior owners of the property, this charge easily could be upwards of $25.

*Amortization schedule* — It shows the allocation of the mortgage payment between principal and interest, and the balance outstanding after each payment is made. A normal charge is $5 for each mortgage.

*Estoppel certificate* — Issued by a condominium corporation, it provides relevant information about the status of the unit as well as any outstanding arrears affecting it. Cost: $25.

*Personal Property Security Act searches* — In the $10 range, based on a charge of $2 per name search in Ontario. This shows the existence of liens against any personal property being acquired.

*Subdivision agreement report* — This represents the cost of obtaining a report from the municipality that all the terms of any subdivision agreement have been complied with, and that occupancy is permitted. Normal charge is around $25.

*Long-distance telephone charges,* if applicable. $10 and up.

*Photostatic/miscellaneous charges* — $15 and up depending on the exact work done in the transaction.

## Provincial Taxes

### i) Transfer tax

Depending on the province involved, an additional charge is levied whenever title changes hands, in addition to the cost of registration. This special one-time tax must be paid, or else the deed will not be registered. In Ontario, for example, Land Transfer Tax is assessed against all properties, virtually without exception, whether it be residential, commercial, industrial, agricultural or recreational. Inter-spousal transfers of title are exempt.

Land Transfer Tax in Ontario is applied on an escalating scale — $5 per $1,000 of purchase price for the first $55,000, and $10 per $1,000 on the balance of the purchase price. Where the property is a single parcel of land containing one or two single-family residences, a further $5 per $1,000 of purchase price is imposed on that portion exceeding $250,000.

On Moe's $100,000 purchase, the land transfer tax payable in Ontario was $725. It was calculated as follows: ($5 × $55,000) plus ($10 × $45,000) = $275 + $450 equals $725.

### ii) Retail Sales Tax

Very often the purchase price includes items of personal property called chattels, most often appliances. If Eli and Karen bought them new or used in a store, retail sales tax would be payable to the provincial government through the merchant. When they are included in the purchase price of a house, retail sales tax should be paid as well.

To avoid problems arising in the future, the buyer should agree with the seller on the amount of the purchase price being allocated to the chattels. As retail sales tax rates are high (in Ontario, $70 per $1,000), the buyer will want to purchase these chattels as inexpensively as possible.

Although the offer may contain a list of personal property being acquired as part of the purchase price, the payment of retail sales tax is often overlooked. When used appliances are being purchased, they really have only nominal value. That the payment of retail sales tax often is ignored does not mean it is not properly payable. It is simply a statement of reality.

## Adjustments

One of the documents to be reviewed with your lawyer before closing is the Statement of Adjustments. It "fine-tunes" the transaction, so numerous charges are allocated between the buyer and the seller, right up to the day of closing.

The Statement of Adjustments reflects the transaction between the seller and the buyer *only.* Mortgages arranged with anyone other than the seller do not appear on the Statement of Adjustments. When Diane bought Peter's house in an all-cash transaction for $80,000, it meant Diane would be paying Peter $80,000 on closing. The fact Diane arranged a $50,000 mortgage to finance the purchase was irrelevant to Peter. He did not care how Diane came up with the money — all Peter wanted to see was $80,000 cash on closing.

Examine the Statement of Adjustments on the following page. Joseph bought this house from Daniel for $100,000, with $5,000 down. According to the offer, Joseph was to assume a first mortgage of approximately $49,500. Part of the difference will be paid by Joseph granting a vendor-take-back second mortgage to Daniel for $25,000. The remaining $20,500 will be paid in cash on closing. This last figure is the "unadjusted" balance due on closing. It always is "subject to the usual adjustments," described in this chapter.

When told that a further $461.56 was payable for adjustments on closing, Joseph rightfully wanted an explanation. To understand why, the contents of the Statement of Adjustments must be examined.

Prepared by the seller's lawyer, the Statement of Adjustments shows how the final balance owing to the seller — the "adjusted" balance due on closing — was calculated. When examining the Statement of Adjustments, remember that everything in the right-hand column is a credit to the seller, while everything in the left-hand column is a credit to the buyer.

All figures are calculated on a daily (or per diem) basis. Changing the closing date means all figures must be recalculated. Joseph, the buyer, is responsible for the payment of all items on the day of closing, even though he does not own it the entire 24-hour period.

## STATEMENT OF ADJUSTMENTS

VENDOR:                     **DANIEL**
PURCHASER:                  **JOSEPH**
ADDRESS OF PROPERTY: 18 Shimshone Road, Thornhill
CLOSING DATE:            April 11 (100 days)

|  | *Credit Purchaser* | *Credit Vendor* |
|---|---|---|
| SALE PRICE | | $100,000.00 |
| DEPOSIT | $ 5,000.00 | |
| FIRST MORTGAGE: Assumed with Vaughan Trust | | |
| i) Principal as of April 1 Credit Purchaser | 49,645.26 | |
| ii) Interest to April 10 (9 days) at 13% Credit Purchaser | 157.14 | |
| iii) Credit in tax account Credit Vendor | | 87.18 |
| SECOND MORTGAGE: Taken back by Vendor Credit Purchaser | 25,000.00 | |
| TAXES: based on previous year's taxes of $1,464.82 | | |
| i) Paid by Vendor — $733.00 | | |
| ii) Vendor's share — $401.32 | | |
| Credit Vendor | | 331.68 |
| OIL: 200 gallon tank at $1.613/gal. | | |
| Credit Vendor | | 322.20 |
| WATER: for the period January 1 to June 30 — $51.17 | | |
| i) Vendor has paid — $51.17 | | |
| ii) Vendor's share — $28.27 | | |

| | | |
|---|---:|---:|
| Credit Vendor | 22.90 | |
| ADJUSTED BALANCE DUE ON CLOSING payable to O'Really & O'Reilly or as they may further direct | $ 20,961.56 | |
| TOTAL | $100,763.96 | $100,763.96 |

As any accountant would say, both columns must add up to the identical figure. When both columns are totalled, the amount of the adjusted balance due on closing is a "plugged" figure (the figure that is inserted to make both columns match). The difference between the adjusted balance due on closing and the unadjusted balance due on closing ($461.56 here) represents the net amount of the adjustments.

Changing one component on the statement affects the balance due on closing and nothing else. If a seller's credit (i.e., taxes) is increased by $50, the balance due on closing must be increased by $50, for everything to balance. If a purchaser's credit (i.e., mortgage) is increased by $100, the balance due on closing falls by $100, for everything to continue to balance. The buyer's lawyer must verify independently each item on the Statement of Adjustments by obtaining written statements confirming the information.

### i) Sale Price

Always credited to the seller. It is the starting point for the entire transaction.

### ii) Deposit

The money paid by Joseph when the offer was signed. Even though the listing agent may be holding the deposit, the buyer is always credited with it. Interest on the deposit, if agreed upon, usually is not credited to the buyer on the Statement of Adjustments. It should be forwarded directly to the purchaser by the real estate agent shortly after closing.

## iii)  First Mortgage Assumed

### a) Principal

According to the mortgage assumption statement Joseph's lawyer received from the first mortgagee, Vaughan Trust, $49,645.25 is outstanding on the first mortgage after the April 1 payment was made. The first mortgage is the first of the adjusted amounts, as it exceeds by more than $145 the amount of the first mortgage as stated in the offer. Most offers require that the buyer assume a mortgage for "approximately" a certain sum of money, preventing a minor difference like this from threatening the transaction. Assuming the existing mortgage is part of the consideration Joseph, the buyer, is giving to Daniel, the seller, on closing. The outstanding principal on the mortgage is credited to the buyer, reducing the balance due on closing, as the buyer is taking over and assuming the seller's obligation to pay that mortgage.

### b) Interest

As mortgages in Canada are paid in arrears and not in advance, Daniel's mortgage payment of April 1 represented the payment due for the month of March. Following that payment, the slate was clean. No interest was owing to the lender, and no interest had been paid in advance to the lender.

When Joseph makes the May 1 mortgage payment, he will be paying interest for the entire month of April, together with the principal component. Why, he asks? He bought the property on April 10. Shouldn't Daniel be responsible for nine days' interest? The lender really does not care whether Daniel or Joseph makes the May 1 mortgage payment, provided it is made on time. The question of who makes that payment, rests solely with Daniel and Joseph.

Joseph is 100 percent correct with his concern. One way to ensure Daniel pays his fair share of the May 1 mortgage payment is to collect a cheque from Daniel on closing for $157.14. What if the cheque bounced? To simplify matters, Daniel gives Joseph a credit on the Statement of Adjustments instead of a cheque for the amount of interest that was Daniel's responsibility — $157.14. If no other adjustments were made, Joseph would be paying Daniel $157.14 less than anticipated on closing. When the May 1 mortgage instalment is made, Joseph will be paying the amount normally due that day, in full. This consists of interest from April 10 to May 1 (his responsibility), plus interest to April 10 (Daniel's responsibility), for which Joseph already has been reimbursed. Now Joseph is happy.

### c) Credit in the Tax Account

Like many institutional lenders, Vaughan Trust collects one-twelfth of the estimated annual taxes from the borrower with each monthly mortgage payment. These funds are kept in a tax account from which the tax bills are paid as issued. After the April 1 payment was made, Vaughan Trust held $87.18 of Daniel's money in this account. Vaughan Trust does not want to get involved in refunding this money to Daniel now that the property is sold, and collecting a similar amount from Joseph. To short-circuit this, Joseph buys the credit from Daniel by crediting Daniel with that amount on the Statement of Adjustments.

### iv) Second Mortgage Back

Besides assuming the existing first mortgage, Joseph is giving Daniel a $25,000 VTB second mortgage. Representing an unpaid portion of the sale price, payment of which is postponed, Joseph is credited with it on closing. After all, if the transaction between the parties had been structured without any second mortgage, the adjusted balance due on closing would be $25,000 higher.

### v) Realty Taxes

How property taxes are adjusted on closing depends on a number of factors. When in the year the deal closes is important. Here, the taxes payable for the year have not yet been determined. This is quite common when the transaction closes in the first few months of a calendar year. The most up-to-date figure on which to base taxes is the previous years' bill. Calculated on a daily basis, Daniel is responsible for 100/365ths of the taxes, or $401.32. Yet he has already paid, through the lender, the full interim tax bill of $733. Having overpaid the taxes by $331.68, Daniel is reimbursed with this amount by being credited with it on the Statement of Adjustments.

If the final bill has not yet been issued, some lawyers representing sellers will estimate the current year's taxes by increasing the prior year's taxes by an inflation factor of 3 to 8 percent. What appears on the adjustments then more accurately reflects the tax situation for the current year.

Sellers agree in writing to recalculate the realty taxes once the final bill is issued, and to reimburse any money owing to the purchaser. Assume the taxes rose by 6.9 percent, to $1,565.89. Daniel's share would increase to $429.01, meaning he should have been credited with only $303.99 ($733 paid less $429.01 actually owing). Having been credited with $331.68 on the Statement of Adjustments for taxes, Daniel owes Joseph $27.69.

When taxes are adjusted based on last year's taxes, a readjustment of taxes after the final bill is issued often benefits the purchaser, as is the case here. Once the final tax bill is received, Joseph should contact his lawyer to determine the amount to be refunded. So should you. Mark down on your calendar to contact your lawyer during the summer about the possible readjustment of taxes in your favor. Money may be owing to you. Make sure you receive it!

If the transaction closed in the second half of the year, the adjustment for taxes would have been based on the final tax bill. Then, the amount to be adjusted for taxes depends on a) whether the vendor paid, and b) whether you will be paying realty taxes directly, or through the mortgage lender. Most home owners who pay their own taxes do so as the instalments come due. If the taxes are paid through the mortgage lender, the lender will pay the *entire* final bill when it is issued, ignoring the instalment payment plan.

Taxes on Al's home totalled $1,200 for the year, and were paid in full by the lender from the tax account it maintained. Anyone closing a purchase from Al at the end of July will have to come up with an additional $500 on closing. Why? As Al, through his lender, has paid the entire $1,200 tax bill, Al will be credited with 5/12ths of those taxes, or $500, on closing.

George recently purchased a house where the taxes are $1,200 annually as well. Closing is scheduled for the end of July. Only $700 in taxes had been paid prior to closing. George's lender will be maintaining a tax account. Here, the lender will be deducting at source $500 from the mortgage advance to pay the balance of the year's taxes on closing. With the net advance on the mortgage being reduced by $500, George will have to come up with an additional $500 on closing. In this case, the $500 is not an adjustment to the vendor on closing as in Al's situation; it is a deduction on the mortgage. Either way, it is money out of the purchaser's pocket on closing, affecting an already tight cash flow.

### vi) Oil

The only type of home heating energy that is included on the Statement of Adjustments is fuel oil. Gas and electric charges are metered, not requiring adjustment. Only by topping-up the oil tank can the amount in it accurately be determined. Daniel will do this, and pay the oil company for the amount of the final delivery. Joseph in turn will reimburse Daniel for the value of the full tank of home heating oil on the Statement of Adjustments.

Many homes have 200-gallon oil tanks. With home heating oil now costing approximately $1.75 per gallon (909 litres and 38.5¢ per litre in metric) buyers of homes heated by oil can expect to pay close to $350 as an adjustment on closing.

What if Joseph will be converting his heating system off oil immediately after closing? Why pay for a full tank of oil he will never use? Joseph then should insert a clause into the draft offer that no adjustment for fuel oil will be made on closing. Often the decision to convert is made after the offer is signed. Where a good rapport exists between seller and buyer, some sellers co-operate by agreeing to "split the difference" — taking a credit for half a tank only, regardless of its actual contents on closing. While the seller does not have to do this, many will.

### vii) Water

Most utility accounts are not adjusted, as they are metered. The final bill is sent to the seller, with a new account being established on the day of closing in the buyer's name. Where a utility is billed on a flat-rate basis, such as the water account in some large metropolitan centers, an adjustment is necessary. Here, the total water bill for the 181-day period from January 1 to June 30 is divided into the buyer's share (81 days) and the seller's share (100 days). As Daniel has overpaid his share by $22.90, he is credited with that amount on the Statement of Adjustments.

No adjustment of utility charges is necessary in condominium transactions. Either the charges are calculated on consumption as measured by meter, or are bulk-metered to the condominium corporation, and paid as part of the maintenance fee.

### viii) Other Adjustments

Other adjustable items include insurance premiums, rent and related sums for tenant-occupied properties, and condominium maintenance (common expense) payments. Few insurance policies are transferred from seller to buyer in resale transactions, meaning they are rarely adjusted. Where tenants are involved, the buyer should get a credit for the balance of the rent collected by the landlord in advance for the month of closing, plus any last month's rent or security deposit held by the seller/landlord. If interest is to be paid on the last month's rent, either by contract or provincial law, it should be credited to the buyer as well, calculated from the last day it was paid. Condominium maintenance charges usually are payable monthly, in advance. Sellers will get a credit on the adjustments for any amount overpaid for the month of closing. Condominium reserve funds only are adjusted if the offer specifically provides for it.

### Deductions on the Mortgage

Enough is enough! What more can there be? Costs associated with a new mortgage a buyer is arranging, that's what! Most of these must be paid by the purchaser on closing, causing absolute havoc with a buyer's cash flow.

Whether any particular item applies depends on the circumstances of the specific loan. These are discussed in more detail in chapter 20.

## Miscellaneous Expenses

Five charges fall into this category — survey; insurance; home inspection; moving; and bridge financing.

### Survey

The buyer may have to order a new survey if none exists, or if it is not acceptable to the mortgage lender. See chapter 23.

### Fire Insurance

What will be the cost of the new fire insurance policy the buyer must arrange on closing? See chapter 29.

### Home Inspection

How much will the home inspector's fee be? See chapter 13.

### Mover

Whether you move yourself in a rented truck or hire a mover, some expense will be incurred. How large will it be?

### Bridge Financing

For buyers who close the purchase now and the sale later, what will be the bridge financing cost? See chapter 21.

Two points now should be self-evident. First, when asking a lawyer for a fee quote, learn what the overall closing costs will be as well. Second, *learn this information before signing any offer.* Know what your financial commitments will be, early. Waiting until after the offer is signed could cause unnecessary grief and anxiety, when it is least desired.

In the space below, prepare both a preliminary Statement of Adjustments as well as a preliminary Statement of Closing Costs. This will help immensely in budgeting for a purchase, before committing yourself to a property. Ask as many questions as necessary of as many people as necessary — real estate agent, lawyer, insurance agent, mortgage broker or lender, and home inspector — to get the needed answers.

## STATEMENT OF ADJUSTMENTS

|  | | PURCHASER | SELLER |
|---|---|---|---|
| Sale price | | | $ |
| Deposit | | $ | |
| First mortgage | – principal | $ | |
| | – interest | $ | |
| | – taxes | | $ |
| Second mortgage | – principal | $ | |
| | – interest | $ | |
| Taxes | | | $ |
| Oil | | | $ |
| Water | | | $ |
| Other adjustments | | $ | |
| — rent and related sums | | | |
| — condominium maintenance | | | |
| Adjusted balance due on closing | | _____ | _____ |
| TOTAL | | $_____ | $_____ |


## STATEMENT OF CLOSING COSTS

| | | | |
|---|---|---|---|
| I | Fees | - purchase | $ |
| | | - mortgage | $_____ |
| | | | $_____ |
| II | Disbursements | - by-laws/zoning and work order report | $ |
| | | - tax certificate | $ |
| | | - utilities certificate | $ |
| | | - search of title | $ |
| | | - registration costs | $ |
| | | - transportation and courier charge | $ |
| | | - execution certificate | $ |
| | | - amortization schedule | $ |
| | | - estoppel certificate (condominiums only) | $ |
| | | - Personal Property Security Act searches | $ |

- subdivision agreement report $
- long distance telephone
  charges $
- photocopy/miscellaneous
  charges $_____
  $_____

III Provincial taxes - land transfer tax $
                           - retail sales tax $

IV Adjusted balance due on closing (from Statement
    of Adjustments) $
    TOTAL GROSS AMOUNT NEEDED TO CLOSE $_____

V  Mortgage       Amount of new first
   Considerations  mortgage applied for $
                   Less: deductions on the
                   mortgage
                   - mortgage appraisal/
                     application fee $
                   - interest to the interest
                     adjustment date $
                   - establishing realty tax
                     account $
                   - mortgage broker's fee $
                   - CMHC/MICC
                     insurance fee $
                   - life and rate insurance
                     fee $_____ $_____
                   NET ADVANCE ON NEW
                   MORTGAGE $_____

### SUMMARY:

TOTAL GROSS AMOUNT NEEDED
TO CLOSE $_____
LESS: net advance on new
       mortgage ($_____)
DIFFERENCE: approximate net
amount needed by purchaser to
close transaction $_____

The miscellaneous charges also should be added to this net amount to learn the overall amount of money needed to close.

|  |  |
|---|---|
| - survey | $ |
| - fire insurance | $ |
| - home inspection | $ |
| - mover | $ |
| - bridge financing | $_____ |
| OVERALL AMOUNT OF MONEY NEEDED TO CLOSE | $_____ |

# 23

## *Survey*

Surveys do more than simply show the location of a building and other structures (fences, garages, decks) on a property. A survey is a graphic description of the extent of the seller's property. It indicates the size of the lot, its dimensions, the exact location of its boundaries, plus items affecting the property such as fences, hedges, easements, rights-of-way, mutual drives and road widenings. Only with an up-to-date survey can a buyer know whether the structures on the property are located wholly within the lot lines, and whether there are any encroachments onto the property, or onto an adjoining property. Municipalities require a survey to confirm that the location of a building on a property complies with the applicable zoning by-laws. For the buyer, only with a survey can he know the full legal extent of the seller's property.

According to the fine print in standard form resale offers, a seller is simply obligated to deliver to the buyer, before the title search period expires, whatever survey is in his possession. If the seller does not have a survey, that is the end of the matter. He is not obligated to obtain one. Yet the purchaser most likely will need one, especially since having a survey is a condition appearing in most mortgage loan approvals. *Knowing whether a survey exists, before the offer is signed, becomes crucial.* To ensure a survey is delivered to the buyer, the offer specifically must require it.

No survey need be located in a condominium transaction as a copy of the survey for the complex is filed in the registry office.

One of the first questions a buyer's lawyer will ask when reviewing the offer, centers on the existence of a survey. Anticipating this, buyers should ask the real estate agent if a survey exists, even before the offer is prepared. Any agent who knows the buyer will require mortgage financing, should have made inquiries about the survey in advance. If no survey is available, the buyer must be alerted to this possible expense before making any commitment.

Learning whether a survey exists is only the first hurdle. Of greater importance is knowing whether an existing survey is acceptable to the buyer, and more importantly, the mortgage lender. If a survey, however ancient, is located, it should accompany the offer, so the buyer's lawyer can review it together with the offer. If a mortgage is being arranged, the lender should be given the same opportunity to determine, at the outset, if it is satisfactory. If the survey is unacceptable, the buyer stil has time to deal with the issue, before the contract is signed.

Until recently, any survey, no matter how old, was considered acceptable. The key was to find a survey, and not be concerned with its age or accuracy. Yet a survey is like an X-ray of the property, taken as of a certain date. No doctor would dare treat a patient with X-rays that are 20 years old. Yet in many transactions, surveys that old or even older were considered acceptable. This is no longer automatically the case.

To be of any real value to a buyer, a survey should be up-to-date and reflect current conditions. Age has nothing to do with the issue. A 40-year old survey could be up-to-date, if nothing has changed since the date the survey was prepared. A two-year old survey, on the other hand, will be out of date if changes have been made to the property in the interim. These include an addition to the house, the construction of a carport, the erection of a fence or the construction of a deck. While sellers may argue that an old survey is up-to-date, surveyors counter by saying that only they, and not sellers, can accurately determine if any changes have been made to the property.

Close scrutiny can determine whether a survey is out of date. Consider the survey that is given in chapter 15. Prepared for a newly constructed home, this survey was out of date when the purchase transaction for which it was prepared, closed! The initials C.B.W. (sometimes called C.B.F.) means the survey was prepared at the concrete block wall or foundation stage. Others boldly state "dwelling incomplete" or "D.U.C." (dwelling under construction). This type of document is prepared once construction of the house begins above grade level, so the builder can get his first mortgage advance. Much has happened since then of course. A house has been built! Once even the first bricks are laid, the survey becomes out of date. Obviously the survey does not show what has been added to the property after the C.B.W. stage — the dwelling itself, eavestroughs, downspouts, a driveway, sidewalk, deck or carport.

Locating an existing survey which reflects the current state of the buildings and other structures is critical. As having a new survey drawn is expensive, most mortgage lenders, and therefore most buyers and their lawyers, are taking a more flexible position. They are prepared to accept and rely upon an existing survey, even though it may not be technically up-to-date, with one very big IF. Does it accurately describe the property, the building and the other structures currently on the property? If there have been no changes, alterations or additions to the external structure of the building from those shown on the survey, most mortgage lenders consider an existing survey to be acceptable. To verify this, the lender will want an affidavit from either the buyer, the seller, or both, before the mortgage funds are advanced. Any other buildings, decks, swimming pools, outbuildings or other structures on the property which are not shown on the survey, will necessitate having a new survey drawn. If a fence was erected after the survey was prepared, most institutional lenders still will accept it.

Sometimes it is not clear whether an old survey will be acceptable to a mortgage lender. The seller says yes, the buyer says no, and the agent says I hope so. A compromise is to insert a clause into the offer, provided it is still unsigned, allowing the lender to decide whether the existing survey is acceptable. Yes means the buyer is satisfied as well. No means a new survey will have to be drawn. The rest of the clause determines who bears the cost, and in what proportion.

Obtaining a new survey, if none can be located or if the

existing survey is unacceptable, can be an expensive proposition. The cost is upwards of $500. Valuable time between acceptance and closing may be lost as well in obtaining a survey. Research, field work and drafting the document will take at least ten days to two weeks. Even updating an existing survey does not come cheaply. Both field work and research are necessary, resulting in very little savings. Agents who claim an existing survey can be updated for a nominal sum are fooling both the purchaser and themselves.

Assume a new survey has to be drawn for a property because changes had been made to the external structure of the building. Who will pay for it? Knowing no acceptable survey was available, before signing the offer a buyer could do the following: a) insert a clause into the offer, requiring the parties to split the cost of having a new survey drawn; or b) adjust downwards the purchase price to reflect the fact the buyer will be bearing the cost of obtaining a new survey.

Norman faced the problem of a survey when he bought a home from Bill. Obviously, Bill had little to gain by having a new survey prepared. In fact, a new survey might show problems that could jeopardize the transaction, such as encroachments, a boundary inconsistent with the registered title, or structures not wholly within the lot lines. Norman too was reluctant to bear the cost of a new survey, upwards of $500. At this stage, the survey became a matter to be negotiated. Only by inserting a clause in the offer can a buyer like Norman force a seller such as Bill to bear any part of the cost for a new survey.

Surveys, though, are one of those areas where "trade-offs" are possible to strike a deal. An anxious seller may agree in the offer to pay half the cost, a fixed dollar amount or even the entire cost of ordering a new survey, simply to have the offer accepted. Occasionally the real estate agent will contribute money towards the cost of a new survey to avoid losing a sale. Yet buyers keen on a particular property may decide not to push the issue overly hard, knowing what the additional cost will be if they concede the point. By the way, Norman and Bill went 50/50 on the cost of the survey, after some coaxing by the real estate agent.

Buyers creating and applying HOBS are prudent buyers. They will know whether a survey exists, and whether it is acceptable to both lender and buyer, before the offer itself is accepted.

# 24

# *The Offer*

In this chapter, the contents of an offer on a resale home, also known as an Offer to Purchase, or an Agreement of Purchase and Sale, will be analyzed. Other concerns, arising from buying a condominium unit, are explored in the chapter "Condominiums."

Many offers are drawn as conditional offers, the contract not being firm and binding until one or more items are satisfied. Conditional offers are discussed in chapter 25.

This chapter does not provide a series of precedent clauses to be inserted into offers buyers prepare themselves. Rather, it provides food for thought, examining topics buyers will want both included and excluded from the offer prepared by their agent or lawyer, to best protect their interests.

Plain and simple, the document submitted to buy a house is a contract, meaning basic contract principles apply. For a binding contract to exist, a written offer is needed, followed by acceptance and communication of that acceptance. Few offers are accepted unscathed the first time out. Most are amended by sellers, with counter-amendments following before agreeable terms are attained. Very often an offer resembles a colorful chicken scrawl by the time it becomes firm and binding.

No document is more important to a real estate transaction than the offer. What it contains governs the relationship between the parties up to closing. For that reason, be precise and specific. Leave no room for misunderstandings or dif-

ferences of opinion. If an item is important to you, the purchaser, it must appear in the offer for the parties to be bound by
it. Otherwise, the seller is under no obligation to comply with
the request. If Eli and Karen want to buy the seller's fridge and
stove as part of the purchase price, that request must appear in
the offer. "If it's not in the offer, it's not in the deal."

Negotiating through offers is not for the faint of heart. The
interval between submitting an offer and receiving word of the
seller's response is extremely nerve-wracking for most buyers,
especially first-time buyers. Was it accepted? If not, what
changes have been made by the seller in his counter-offer? The
anxiety, tension and uncertainty over what is happening, and
whether the time interval will be days or hours, are extremely
hard on all but the most seasoned purchasers. In this period,
the best thing a buyer can do is forget about the transaction,
and keep busy with other activities. Little can be done anyways,
since the negotiations rest strictly with the agents and the seller.
Worry certainly will not make a seller accept an otherwise
unacceptable offer. So buyers should relax by putting the deal
out of their minds completely. The excitement of a house
purchase never should be overshadowed by needless concern
about events over which you have no control.

What is the scenario when an offer is submitted on a resale
home? The selling agent, if two agents are involved (or the
listing agent if there is only one agent), prepares the offer
without charge. Most real estate boards and associations have
their own standard form offers, which most agents use. Despite
what agents say, the fine print in these standard form documents have a distinct "pro-seller" bias. A number of clauses
obligate and commit buyers in ways they would never imagine.
In addition, many real estate offices use standard "John Doe"
precedent clauses which are added to the blank offer, depending on the circumstances. *Once the offer is drawn, and before it
is signed and submitted, it should be taken to your lawyer for
review, comment and revision. Buyers applying their home-
buying strategy will not sign any documents until reading the
chapter entitled "Do Not Sign On The Dotted Line Until..."*.
The reasoning is simple. It is important for your lawyer to see
the offer, when he still can do something with it, before it is

etched in stone. Many of the ideas suggested in this chapter will
not appear in the offer as originally prepared by the agent. It
will be up to your lawyer to insert them into the offer before it
is submitted for the seller's approval.

Where no agent is involved in the transaction, the buyer's
lawyer will have to draft the offer, usually on a legal stationer's
standard form offer, *at the buyer's expense.*

Negotiating a contract is an art. Experience is the greatest
teacher on how to negotiate effectively. All the more reason,
then, for buyers to retain an experienced real estate agent. It
goes without saying that buyers want to pay the lowest possible
price for a property, while sellers want the highest possible
price. Skillful negotiations by an agent will encourage each
side to re-evaluate his position, if necessary, so common
ground can be reached. When a meeting of the minds takes
place, the parties have a deal.

Try to avoid late night negotiating sessions. Every agent has
many personal recollections of negotiations continuing into
the wee small hours of the morning. By that point, the parties
are tired, especially after a full day at work. Thinking with a
clear head becomes increasingly difficult. In addition, when
negotiating an offer, try to be cool, calm and collected, to
maintain your objectivity. Otherwise, something important
could easily be missed.

### What happens when the offer is submitted?

Once the offer is signed by the purchaser, the listing agent
presents it to the seller. Where an agent is involved, the purchaser will not necessarily end up meeting directly with the
seller. Negotiations are often more successful if they are not
conducted face to face. Instead, the agent plays the role of
go-between. When the offer is presented to the seller, he or she
has three options: accept it, reject it, or make a counter-offer.

Phil wants to buy Marla's property. If Marla accepts Phil's
offer as submitted, the contract becomes binding on the parties
once Phil is notified, subject to any conditions which still must
be satisfied. Notification is usually done by a telephone call
followed by delivery of the accepted offer to the purchaser. If
Marla rejects the offer, that's it. No deal. In most cases, a vendor

who is not completely satisfied with the terms of an offer will make a counter-offer, also called a "sign back." That is what happened here. In the counter-offer, Marla changes the one unacceptable term, increasing the purchase price by $5,000, and initials the change. All other terms are left the same. For a binding contract to result, the changes now must be initialled by the purchaser, Phil. Considering that Marla, the seller, had a limited time in which to make up her mind when the offer was originally submitted, she now returns the favor by giving Phil a very short time to decide what to do!

If Phil agrees to pay the additional $5,000, he initials the change to the offer that Marla previously had initialled. The offer *now* becomes a binding contract, subject to any outstanding conditions. If Phil will pay only $3,000 more, he will change the $5,000 to $3,000, initial the change, and re-submit the offer. Now it is technically known as a counter-counter-offer. The initialling done by Phil at this stage often will be in a different color of ink, to distinguish the initials of Marla's counter-offer from those of Phil's counter-counter-offer. If the offer becomes very messy, a new offer should be prepared. This volley of papers between Phil and Marla continues until either all the proposed changes are acceptable and are initialled by both sides, or no agreement can be reached and the negotiations terminate. Pins and needles time for Phil and Marla!

Once the offer is accepted, even if one or more conditions remain outstanding, a copy is sent to each party's lawyer. Any amendments or waivers of conditions also are delivered, when they are available.

Once the offer is accepted, the transaction takes on a divine quality. "There shall be a binding Agreement of Purchase and Sale between the purchaser and the vendor." Ominous words. For this reason, buyers must be acquainted with some of the key elements of an offer. The typed-in clauses distinguish one offer from another, yet the wording of the printed form should not be ignored. Remember that the printed form clauses are not unalterable. They can, should and must be changed if they do not protect a buyer's interests.

Most offers go on to say that there is "no representation, warranty, collateral agreement or condition" affecting either the property or the contract. Plain and simple, this means "what you see is what you get!" All the more reason for a lawyer to independently verify that important statements and points appear in the document before it becomes a binding contract.

## The Purchaser (Buyer)

The buyer is the person who signs the offer, and is the person obligated to close the transaction. Determining who the buyer should be is not always a simple matter.

Gary and Judy, a married couple, are buying a house. For business reasons, title is to be registered in Judy's name alone. This way, Gary's creditors cannot seize the property if his business fails, since Gary does not own it. Only Judy, therefore, should sign the offer as purchaser. If Gary signs the offer either alone or with Judy, and the seller is taking back a mortgage, Gary would have to sign that mortgage either as owner or as guarantor, as the seller dealt with Gary as one of the purchasers. Obviously this would defeat Gary's intentions. If only Judy signs the offer as purchaser, the seller cannot force Gary to sign the mortgage because he was not a party to the original contract.

Occasionally one spouse is not available to sign the offer when it is prepared. Charley was out of town when the offer was signed by Lucy, his wife. Before closing, she can direct in writing that title be taken in her name alone in accordance with the offer, in Charley's name or in both her name and Charley's name. Written directions of this sort are very common.

## The Vendor (Seller)

The vendor is the person selling the property. Occasionally an agent is unaware whether the husband or wife or both are the registered owners of the property. Where a matrimonial home is involved, most provincial family law legislation prevents one spouse from selling it without the written consent of the other spouse. To avoid any problems from arising in the future, both the husband and the wife should sign the offer, whether or not both own the property, if it is or ever has been the matrimonial home. If a non-owner spouse signs an offer, signifying consent to the transaction, there is less likelihood that he or she will refuse to sign the deed and other papers for closing.

## The Property

The property should be described in as much detail as possible. The municipal address should be inserted, as well as the legal description for the property. This will help your lawyer to begin the search of title as soon as possible after acceptance. Any rights-of-way or easements affecting the property must be stated, as well as the dimensions of the property as verified by the survey or deed. Do not place much reliance on the expression "more or less" that appears in most printed form offers. If the boundaries of the property are clearly marked, courts usually hold that "what you see is what you get," even if the dimensions are not precisely stated in the offer.

## The Purchase Price

The "package" a buyer will pay to acquire a property is the purchase price. If Moe buys Larry's house for $100,000, Moe must give Larry $100,000 of "consideration" on closing. Cash is only one of the three types of consideration a buyer can give a seller on closing. This consideration could consist of cash (payment now); giving Larry a vendor-take-back or VTB mortgage, representing a deferred payment of the purchase price (payment later); or the assumption of Larry's obligations on an outstanding mortgage (a "cash to mortgage" transaction). Of course, it could be a combination of all three as well. If a buyer arranges his own mortgage, the transaction between the buyer and seller becomes an all cash transaction. Several examples will give a better idea of how the $100,000 purchase price can be paid in different ways with different types of consideration.

Alan and Hannah bought a house for $100,000. They will be assuming the existing mortgage for $65,000. As the deposit is $5,000, Alan and Hannah must pay the balance on closing of $30,000. Their total interest in the property is $35,000 and the total received by the seller is $35,000.

Aron and Frieda are buying a house for $100,000 as well.

They will be taking over the existing mortgage of $55,000 and are arranging a $10,000 second mortgage with a bank. Having already paid a $5,000 deposit, Aron and Frieda will be paying $40,000 to the seller on closing (the $100,000 purchase price less the $55,000 mortgage assumed less the $5,000 deposit). Of this $40,000, $10,000 is coming from the new second mortgage, and $30,000 from their own funds. Note that Aron and Frieda's total equity in the property is $35,000 as well (the $30,000 of their own money paid on closing plus the $5,000 deposit paid when the offer was signed). The total received by the seller: $45,000 ($100,000 purchase price less $55,000 mortgage assumed).

Elliott and Michelle also paid $100,000 for a home. They arranged a new first mortgage for $65,000. With a $5,000 deposit already paid to the seller, Elliott and Michelle will be paying a further $95,000 to the seller on closing ($65,000 from the mortgage and $30,000 from their own funds). Their total equity in the property: $35,000. The total received by the seller: $100,000. To him, it was an all cash deal, although Elliott and Michelle borrowed money to accomplish that.

The amount of cash paid is adjusted right down to the date of closing on the Statement of Adjustments. More information on this topic appears in chapter 22.

### What is the proper price to put in an offer?

After consultation with the real estate agent, the price inserted should be anywhere from 5 to 10 percent below the expected ultimate purchase price. Most reasonably priced houses are sold for slightly less than their asking price. Remember that buyers want to pay the lowest possible price, while sellers want to receive the highest possible price. If the price in the offer is too high, the vendor might accept the offer immediately, leaving the buyer to wonder how much lower a price could have been attained. To go in too low could insult the seller, to the point he will not entertain any further offers. Generally speaking, if the offer is reasonable, and "within the ballpark," the offers and counter-offers begin to fly until either a deal is struck or negotiations break off.

The purchase price in your first offer never should be the maximum price you are prepared to pay. As it probably will be necessary to adjust your price upwards, leave yourself ample negotiating room within your maximum price range.

When no agent is involved (a private sale), determining how much to offer for a house is difficult. Unless you have done extensive homework such as comparing real estate listings, it is not likely that you will know the true market value for a property. As it is human nature to set a high price on property, the vendor probably will value his property at the high end of the price range. Without the benefit of an agent to advise on property values, a buyer easily could end up paying more than the market price for the home. To deal with this situation, buyers in private sale transactions sometimes have a real estate appraiser value the property. The cost of an appraisal report is small, generally in the two-hundred dollar range. Armed with this information, a buyer has a much better idea of what a property is worth, and the price to offer for the property.

If *you want interest on the deposit, you must specifically ask for it in the offer. Otherwise, no interest is payable.* Two criteria usually must be met for interest to be paid on the deposit. First, the deposit must be at least $5,000; and second, the interval from acceptance to closing must be at least 30 days. This allows the agent sufficient time to buy an interest-bearing term deposit at a bank or trust company to mature on the date of closing. Technically speaking, the agent is not a party to the offer, as he or she does not sign it. This means the purchaser has no legal recourse against the agent if the request is not honored. Still, most agents do honor the clause in the offer, if these two criteria are satisfied.

In a private sale situation, the vendor's lawyer should be holding the deposit in trust in place of the listing agent. If the lawyer does not purchase a term deposit, the buyer has no recourse against him either. To ensure that interest is paid, buyers in private sale situations should consider inserting a clause into the offer, that they will be paid interest on the deposit at, say, 12% per annum from the date of acceptance to the date of closing if the deposit is not invested in a term deposit. This way, a purchaser is guaranteed interest on the deposit paid, either from a term deposit or from the vendor's pocket. A similar clause could be used in a resale offer where a real estate agent was involved, if necessary.

## Deposit

Most people equate the deposit with the down payment (i.e., $1,000 on acceptance and the balance on closing). However, the deposit is only the money paid by the purchaser at the time the offer is submitted. Deposits serve two purposes. If the deal closes, the deposit is credited as a part payment of the purchase price. Since a deposit can be lost if the deal does not close, the deposit is a guarantee that the buyer is serious about proceeding with the transaction.

### What happens to the deposit?

When an agent is involved, the purchaser's *uncertified* cheque payable to the listing agent accompanies the offer. Once the offer is accepted, the agent will have the cheque certified and will hold the deposit in trust pending completion of the transaction.

In a private sale situation, the cheque *never* should be made payable to the vendor. Find out who the vendor's lawyer is, and make the uncertified cheque payable to that lawyer, in trust. To make the cheque payable directly to the seller is like playing with fire. Try to get your money back from a seller if the deal falls through, where it has already been spent!

Buyers who earn interest on a deposit will receive a T5 Supplementary from the agent or lawyer holding the deposit, either with the interest cheque or before February 28th the following year. Interest earned this way is taxable income, and must be declared when filing your next income tax return.

As purchasers, Aaron and Naomi paid a $7,500 deposit when they signed their offer. After closing, the deposit, which is now the seller's money, was removed from trust. Accruing interest of $178.57 was paid to Aaron and Naomi. The $6,000 commission was deducted from the deposit, with the remaining $1,500 being forwarded to the seller. What if the deposit had been only $5,000? Since the $6,000 commission would exceed the $5,000 deposit, the agent would take the entire deposit (after paying the accrued interest), billing the seller for the balance. If the transaction does not close, the deposit can be tied up for years in litigation.

### How large a deposit should be submitted with an offer?

Whether the deposit earns interest or not, buyers like to pay the smallest deposit possible. Once the deposit leaves their hands, buyers feel they lose control of the funds. Sellers naturally like the largest possible deposit. Too small a deposit is unsatisfactory to the vendor, as the buyer has put little of his own money at risk — little to prevent him from simply walking away from the deal. Larger deposits indicate a greater willingness to proceed with the transaction, while giving the seller a bigger fund from which to claim, if the transaction is aborted.

Not surprisingly, agents also have a stake in getting a large deposit. Getting paid on closing is much easier if the commission, or a large part of it, is held in trust by the listing agent. When deposits are placed in income-bearing investments, larger deposits are possible, agents argue, because buyers do not suffer any loss of interest. With most commissions in the 5 to 6 percent range, agents will recommend that the deposit be at least 5 percent of the purchase price, rounding the figure upwards where appropriate. On a purchase of $91,500, the deposit inevitably is $5,000.

If you are in a back-to-back transaction, where one property is being sold and another purchased, be sure the amount of the deposit paid on your sale does not exceed the amount of commission payable. Otherwise, you could find yourself short of funds for the purchase transaction.

Glen sold his house for $100,000, as did Donna. The commission payable on both was 6% of the purchase price, meaning that each would net $94,000 from the sale. Accompanying Glen's offer was a deposit cheque for $7,500. On closing the sale, Glen would receive $92,500 from the purchaser, while the additional $1,500 would be forwarded to him sometime *after* closing by the real estate agent. As that $1500 would not be available immediately, Glen could lack sufficient funds to close the purchase. By comparison, the deposit paid on Donna's sale was only $5,000. This means she would receive $95,000 on closing, and would pay $1,000 to the real estate agent immediately after closing. This way, the full $94,000 she expected to receive on closing her sale would be available at that time, ready to be used on her purchase.

While there is no "right" amount for a deposit, generally it should not be less than 2 percent nor should it exceed 5 percent of the purchase price.

## Irrevocable Date

Peter and Angela signed an offer on December 2. This offer had an irrevocable date of 11:59 p.m. on December 5. This meant the seller had until one minute before midnight on December 5 to decide whether or not to accept their offer. During the period from December 2 to the irrevocable date, Peter and Angela were not allowed to revoke or cancel their offer. It remains outstanding, and ready for acceptance. Technically, though, unless the offer is signed and a red wafer seal is affixed next to the buyer's signature, the buyer can still revoke the offer during this irrevocable period, prior to acceptance. If the irrevocable date passes and the buyer is not advised that the offer has been accepted, there is no deal. If the seller wishes to make a counter-offer the irrevocable date should be changed as well. Once the irrevocable date passes, and no deal is reached, there is no obligation on either party to continue negotiations.

### How much time should a buyer give a seller to make up his mind?

Again, no right "answer" exists. Usually no more than two or three day's time is given, which should be more than ample for a seller to review the offer, consult a lawyer, and decide what to do. The time given by sellers to buyers on sign-backs is much less — often as short as a few hours, as little remains to be decided to strike a deal.

## Completion Date/Closing Date

This is the date the deal closes, the seller gets his money, and the buyer becomes the owner of the property.

A closing date should be set after careful thought. Sufficient time must be given to the buyer's lawyer to search the title and obtain the clearances essential for any complete title opinion. With too short a time to closing, oral replies rather than written clearances will have to be relied upon. To properly process a transaction, allow at least thirty days between acceptance and closing.

Be sure the scheduled closing date is not a weekend or a holiday. Occasionally an agent relies on a previous year's calendar, or forgets about a holiday, and schedules closing for a date when the registry office is closed. Unless the closing date is changed by mutual consent, closing is moved to the last business day *before* the scheduled date, not afterwards.

Don't let the agent automatically schedule closing for either the last day of the month or the last Friday of the month. While they may feel they are doing both parties a favor, the agent really is causing more harm than good! After all, there is no magic in closing a deal on either of those two days. A transaction can be closed just as easily, and probably faster, on a Tuesday than on a Friday, or on the 9th or 19th of the month than the 29th.

Many agents suggest an end-of-the-month closing because they think it is most convenient. Nothing could be further from the truth. Closing at the end of the month does not save buyers any money, since adjustments are calculated on a daily basis anyway. Obtaining mortgage proceeds any other day is not a problem either, because mortgage lenders do advance funds every day of the month, even though the mortgage may be payable on the first of the month. Most lawyers who have the opportunity to review an offer before it is signed, will suggest a change in the closing dates away from Fridays and the concluding days of the month.

There are other good reasons why buyers should not close their transactions at these peak periods. Many movers charge a premium, upwards of 10 percent, at the beginning and end of each month. It's the law of supply and demand at work. "Do-it-yourselfers" do not always get a break either. Rental trucks are always in heavy demand on weekends and at the end of the month. In either situation, remember to book a mover or van early.

Fridays and month-ends also are high-volume days at the registry office, where line-ups to register instruments are much longer than usual. Jim and Tammy found this out the hard way. Their purchase closed on the last Friday of the month, the busiest day that month. Although the movers were fully loaded and ready to move everything into the new house at twelve noon, Jim and Tammy could not get the keys to their new home until 4:30 P.M. that night. There was little their movers could do for over four hours, except sit and wait at Jim and Tammy's expense — several hundred dollars. Ironically, they could have closed the deal and moved two days earlier, but decided against it, as it would have cost them another $75. Talk about being penny wise and pound foolish!

Whenever possible, *all* buyers — those presently owing a home and those presently tenants — should try and close their purchase transaction at least a week before vacating their old premises. This provides a valuable "overlap" period, an opportunity at a nominal cost to clean up, fix up, repair or paint the new home before moving in. Buyers moving from an existing home who wish to benefit from this "overlap" period will have to arrange bridge financing Further information on bridge financing appears in chapter 21. The additional cost to apartment dwellers of having two residences for a short period of time is not all that high, either. If the apartment rented for $600 a month, the cost of carrying both places is only another $20 per day. Think of it. That's a small price to pay to avoid the "rush act" on closing. Whether moving from an apartment or from a house, having two residences for a very short period of time allows buyers to move into their new home with dignity. That's the way it should be.

## Title Search Period

This is the period of time the buyer's lawyer is given to search the seller's title, and to raise any defects that are uncovered, such as outstanding liens. Usually it is a blank on the offer that must be filled in either with a number or a fixed date. The standard amount of time given to search title is 30 days. If the offer was silent on the point, by law the buyer's lawyer would have 30 days from acceptance to search title. Why, then, do agents representing buyers continue to limit the amount of time for searching the title? Don't they realize that doing so prejudices the purchaser? Yet title search periods of 15 or 20 days are not uncommon. *Be sure the title search period is a minimum of 30 days.*

Conditional offers must be dealt with somewhat differently. By taking the offer to your lawyer for his consideration before signature, you can ensure the title search clock does not run when the offer is still conditional. Fred and Shirley signed an offer September 1, with a title search period of 21 days. The condition of arranging financing by September 15 was satisfied and waived that day. This meant Harry, their lawyer, now only had six days to search title and raise any defects. Fred and Shirley's agent should have inserted a clause into the offer that the title search period began to run *after all conditions were removed*, and not simply after the offer was accepted. Harry wished the agent had done so, too.

Unless buyers give firm instructions, few lawyers do anything with an offer while it is still conditional. This way, the lawyer does not run up a huge legal bill if the condition is not satisfied. When a conditional offer is signed, clearly state if your lawyer should do any work before the condition is satisfied and waived.

## Warranty and Condition

Two words that often are wrongly interchanged in offers are "warranty" and "condition." Do not confuse a condition in an offer with a conditional offer, examined in the next chapter. Buyers must remember that an important legal distinction exists between a warranty and a condition. Depending on the particular issue, buyers must instruct whether it is to be phrased as a warranty, or a condition.

*A warranty* is a minor promise that does not go to the heart of the contract. If a warranty is breached, the buyer cannot simply cancel the contract and get out of the deal. All he or she can do is close the transaction, and sue the seller after closing for damages. When Sid bought his house, the seller, Gordon, warranted that the appliances would be in good working order on closing. Even though the stove did not operate properly, Sid was obligated to close the transaction. The stove was repaired and the bill was paid by Gordon, after closing.

By contrast, a *condition* is a promise which is fundamental to the very existence of the offer. A breach of a condition allows the buyer to back out of the deal before closing, and to recover his deposit. It was the condition in Perry's offer that the property be zoned for duplexes, which allowed him to terminate the transaction when he learned the zoning only permitted single-family residences.

Anything of great importance, so important that you might want to cancel the contract if the statement is not correct, should be stated as a condition, and not as a warranty. Too often, though, matters of great concern, such as urea formaldehyde foam insulation, are included in offers as warranties. This places severe limits on a buyer's remedies if a breach is discovered. Remember, *to back out of a deal, the issue in question must be a condition, and not a warranty.*

## Chattels and Fixtures

Chattels are items of personal property, such as appliances. Fixtures are items of personal property that become part of the dwelling itself, such as doors, windows, and electric light fixtures. An area rug is a chattel, while wall-to-wall carpeting securely attached to the floor is a fixture. To simply say that "floor coverings" are included in the purchase price is ambiguous. While the distinction between chattels and fixtures often is black and white, a huge grey area exists between them.

Chattels a buyer wishes to acquire when purchasing a home must be specifically included and listed in the offer. Otherwise, the buyer does not get them. On the other hand, because they are already part of the house, all fixtures automatically accompany the house, whether or not they are listed in the offer, unless they are specifically excluded in it. This means that *all* electric light fixtures in the house automatically are included in the purchase price, unless the seller specifies in the offer which fixtures are to be removed.

Space is left in most blank standard form offers to list those chattels which are included, and those fixtures which are *not* included, in the purchase price. To avoid any misunderstandings on what is a chattel and what is a fixture, what the buyer is acquiring and what the seller can take, prudent buyers leave nothing to chance. Everything that is included in the purchase price — both chattels and fixtures — is clearly listed in the offer. Nothing can be worse for a buyer than learning that an item he thought was a fixture has properly been removed by the seller as a chattel. A word to the wise: if in doubt, spell it out. This way, the risk of being wrong is eliminated.

Too often, insufficient attention is given to the chattel clause. To simply state that the fridge, stove, washer, dryer, and dishwasher are included is not enough. Be specific. For equipment, list the make and model number plus serial number, if available. Other items like window coverings should be described by color, style, design and location to avoid future confusion.

In the offer, the seller should warrant that the personal property being acquired will be free of liens and encumbrances on closing. No one wants to buy appliances, a furnace or an air-conditioning system if a finance company has a lien on them for unpaid money.

The seller also should warrant that the personal property as well as the plumbing, heating, electrical and mechanical equipment will be in good working order on the day of closing. A warranty to this effect also should be delivered on closing. Most people assume these items will be in good working order on closing. An implied warranty of fitness forms part of every contract as well. That being the case, no seller should object to delivering this warranty. More importantly, this type of clause clearly reinforces the obligation on the seller to repair anything that breaks down between acceptance and closing. Headaches should not be included in the purchase price.

Some equipment may still be governed by guarantees or warranty plans. If so, insert a clause into the offer requiring the seller to assign or transfer them on closing.

Sometimes fixtures are to be removed, with replacements being substituted. A common example is the chandelier in the dining room that the vendor wishes to take to the new house. Sometimes the vendor will agree to install a new light fixture in its place. If this is the case, state clearly and completely what is to be done. Describe what the replacement fixture should look like. Leave nothing to the sellers's discretion. Otherwise, if nothing is said in the offer about a replacement, the purchaser will find a hole in the ceiling where the fixture used to be. Retail sales tax may be payable on the used appliances being acquired from the seller of the house. See chapter 22.

Appendix A is a list of the items of personal property most often appearing in a resale offer. Use this checklist to help decide which chattels and fixtures to include when submitting your offer.

## Surveys

The topic of surveys is examined in more detail in chapter 23.

## Utility Charges

Final utility accounts can be a problem when they are left unpaid by sellers. The buyer's lawyer should ensure that all "regular" bills issued before closing are paid by the seller on or before closing. When a property is sold, though, a special request is made by the buyer's lawyer for a final meter reading on the date of closing. It is this bill, based on consumption from the last regular meter reading to the date of closing, that causes all problems. The biggest problem is the fact it is not issued until after closing.

Matt and Ruth faced this dilemma when they bought a house from Tom on March 28th. The last regular hydro meter reading was taken on February 15th; the next one was scheduled for April 15th. The final hydro bill for $76.31 was issued April 12, and covered the period from February 15th to March 28th, the date of the final meter reading. It remained unpaid for months. Although Tom had agreed in writing to pay all utility charges to the date of closing, it was a toothless commitment. Tom had left the country and had given no forwarding address.

Why should Matt and Ruth even be concerned about Tom's unpaid account? Simply because public utilities have the legal right to place a lien against a property for unpaid utility charges. These unpaid bills can be collected as taxes, no matter who incurred the expense, and no matter who now owns the property. Remaining unpaid for many months, the munici-pality added the $76.31 to Matt and Ruth's tax bill. They ended up paying an expense which rightfully belonged to Tom.

If all previous bills have been paid to date, the amount out-standing on this final bill should not be large. To best deal with this potential problem, insert a clause into the offer that requires the seller's lawyer to hold back sufficient funds after closing to pay these final utility accounts, when issued. The buyer would be notified when they had been paid in full. Buyers like Matt and Ruth then can rest assured that the account based on the final meter reading will be honored, either by the seller or the seller's lawyer. Any clause requiring a holdback of funds must appear right in the offer.

## Urea Formaldehyde Foam Insulation (UFFI)

To give the purchaser the maximum possible protection, it should be a condition of the offer that the property never has been insulated with urea-formaldehyde foam insulation. This is different from a conditional offer described in the next chapter. By being a condition or essential term of the offer, buyers who learn the property is (or was) insulated with UFFI can back out of the transaction before closing. More informa-tion on UFFI appears in chapter 33.

## Work Orders and Zoning

Municipalities prescribe standards for the maintenance and occupation of properties. Where these standards are not met, a deficiency notice is sent to the owner, followed by a formal work order. While sellers are supposed to disclose whether any deficiency notices or work orders have been issued, this is not always done. Too often, the purchaser learns of these violations for the first time when a work order report is requested from the municipality. Understandably, buyers do not want to bear the cost of bringing the property up to municipal standards, unless this was a term of the offer, where property is bought "as is."

To protect buyers, offers should contain the seller's warranty that there are no deficiency notices or work orders against the property when it is signed, and that this will be the case on the date of closing. Any violations that exist or arise before closing must be complied with at the seller's expense. As few agents include this clause in their offer, it remains for the buyer's lawyer to add it, when the offer is still unsigned. Only by clearly spelling out the seller's obligation to comply with any violations can a buyer avoid being saddled with unexpected additional costs after closing.

Besides work orders, a buyer's lawyer is also very concerned about the zoning of the property. How the property is zoned, whether the location of the building and other structures on the property comply with the zoning requirements, and whether its current use may lawfully be continued, all must be confirmed. Municipalities are notoriously slow in providing these reports to lawyers. Buyers can do themselves a favor by giving their lawyers until closing in which to raise outstanding work order and zoning violations.

An offer should state how the property is presently being used (residential) and whether this is a permitted or a legal nonconforming use. By comparing this with the municipal zoning report, a buyer's lawyer can ensure whether the present use can be continued. If a minor change of use is planned, the future intended use should appear in the offer, so the buyer's lawyer can confirm whether the existing zoning will accommodate the proposed use. Where the property is to be used in a substantially different way, the offer should be made conditional on having the property rezoned before closing. Otherwise the purchaser must close the transaction, although he cannot legally use the property in the anticipated manner.

## Registered Restrictions

While municipalities regulate the use of land through zoning by-laws, many subdividers when developing an area often impose their own, tighter restrictions on land use. What is called a "building scheme" is registered against the title to the subdivision, containing a series of building and use restrictions. Most restrictions are imposed to improve the esthetic appearance of the subdivision — no external TV antennae; no clotheslines; no permanent parking of campers, vans, and trucks on the driveway; and no repairs of automobiles on the driveway. The local municipality may not have a by-law prohibiting satellite dishes, but the building scheme may disallow them. Most building schemes only run for a fixed period of time (10 or 20 years) after which they automatically expire.

The standard form offer says that a buyer will accept title to the property subject to any registered restrictions, provided they have been complied with. This clause could prove to be a mine field, especially where the buyer does not know if any restrictions exist. Steve and Anita found this out the hard way. They signed their offer without taking it to their lawyer first. All along they wanted to install a TV satellite dish in their backyard, but said nothing about it to anyone. Just before closing, they learned that the installation of a satellite dish was prohibited by a registered restriction on title. As Herb, the present owner of the house, did not have a dish, he was complying with the restrictions. This meant Steve and Anita were obligated to close the deal and accept title subject to the registered restrictions, since Herb had not violated them prior to closing! By not properly spelling out this future intended use in the offer, Steve and Anita had no grounds on which to back out of the deal. Literally, they were caught by the fine print.

If a proposed use of the property is important, buyers like Steve and Anita should do one (or more) of three things:

a) insert a condition into the offer that no restrictions are registered on title, or delete the printed form wording by which they agreed to take title subject to registered restrictions, provided they were complied with.
b) ask whether important proposed uses like satellite dishes are prohibited either by by-law or registered restriction. Then, to protect yourself further, add a condition (not a warranty) to the offer, that the specific use is not prohibited in either manner. This way, if you suddenly learn before closing that the proposed use in fact is not permitted, you can refuse to close the purchase, without jeopardy. The time to raise these concerns is before the offer is signed, not afterwards. Let the agent do some digging, if necessary, to determine whether the desired use is permitted.
c) obtain and review a copy of the restrictions ahead of time, to determine whether or not the proposed use is excluded. Practically speaking, very few buyers do this.

It is unfortunate that sellers do not disclose the existence of these registered restrictions in an offer. The way most printed form offers are worded, sellers need not even provide information about registered restrictions to a purchaser, unless they are being violated. This is extremely unfair to buyers. Remember, too, that not all homes are subject to registered restrictions. They usually affect homes less than 20 years old.

Although registered restrictions are established by developers, rarely are they policed after all the lots are sold. Few sanctions exist to punish violators. Furthermore, where the subdivider can pick and choose which properties will be exempted from the restrictions, the building scheme may not even be enforceable. Still, most buyers honor building schemes without question, because they greatly enhance the appearance of the subdivision. Registered restrictions are a trap for the unwary. Practically speaking, the best way to deal with them is to consult a lawyer before the offer is signed.

## Rights of Access and Inspection

As strange as it sounds, once the offer is accepted, the buyer has no further right to inspect or even enter the home unless specifically permitted in the offer. (Making the offer conditional on having it inspected by a professional home inspector is discussed in chapter 13.) Most buyers want to enter the house at some point between acceptance and closing, to measure windows for drapes and window coverings, the kitchen when purchasing appliances, and room sizes for carpeting, paint and wallpaper. Also, most buyers would like to see the house a day or two before closing, to ensure everything is "okay." Most sellers are reluctant to give buyers unlimited access to the property, fearing they will find fault with the home that could jeopardize the transaction. While many sellers voluntarily permit reasonable access to buyers, this is no assurance that a right of entry will be granted. To avoid this problem, the offer should contain a clause giving the buyer the right to enter the premises a set number of times, in the presence of the vendor, at mutually agreeable hours, *for specified purposes only*, such as taking measurements. Sincerity and friendliness may result in further rights of access despite what the offer says.

## Clear Title

Virtually all offers say that the seller must discharge all mortgages, charges, liens and other encumbrances (except those specifically being assumed) from title on or before closing, at his own expense. An obvious statement, since no buyer wishes to inherit someone else's obligations. Sellers, though, face a real dilemma with this clause. How can they get a mortgage off title for closing? Few lenders provide a discharge of mortgage before the mortgage is paid in full. "Cash on the barrelhead" is their motto. In almost all cases, the mortgage will not be discharged "on or before closing." Although it is paid off on closing, the formal discharge is registered shortly afterwards.

Normal conveyancing practice is for the seller's lawyer to receive the funds to retire the mortgage, pay them to the lender, and give a "personal undertaking" to obtain and register a discharge of that mortgage as soon as possible after closing. This is the only way a deal can close when a mortgage has to be discharged and the discharge is unavailable for closing. Keep in mind, though, that in accepting such an undertaking, buyers are waiving their strict contractual rights because the offer says these items are to be discharged "on or before closing." If this can only be done after closing, technically the seller has breached the contract, as he is not conveying on closing what was bargained for in the offer — namely clear title, free of liens and mortgages. As amazing as it sounds, an undischarged mortgage on closing gives the buyer the legal right to terminate the transaction if he wishes! That's right; if a seller does not have a discharge available on closing that he was obligated contractually to provide, the buyer can walk away from the deal and get his deposit back, with impunity.

To reduce the possibility of the deal aborting, agents often insert a clause into the offer, forcing buyers to accept the seller's lawyer's personal undertaking to discharge the mortgage, if it is not available on closing. Buyers looking to maximize their options should delete these words from the unsigned offer. Granted, the only way the deal can ever close is by accepting this undertaking from the seller's lawyer. But why make that decision now? What if circumstances were to change between acceptance and closing, requiring that the buyer get out of the transaction? What if one of the spouses was to die, or was laid off from work? The prudent buyer will delete those words now, and consent to this arrangement just prior to closing.

## Balance Due on Closing

This is the amount of money paid by the buyer to the seller on closing. Where the buyer assumes the mortgage or the seller takes back a mortgage, the balance due on closing is the purchase price less the deposit, less the amount of the mortgage. If the buyer is arranging his own mortgage financing, the balance due on closing between the buyer and seller is the purchase price less the deposit *only*. After all, between the buyer and the seller, the contract is an "all cash" deal requiring the balance of the purchase price to be paid to the seller in cash on closing.

The different ways in which the balance due on closing can be paid appear earlier in this chapter, under the heading "The Purchase Price."

## Special Clauses

Particular circumstances may require the drafting of special clauses to meet the situation. The precise wording of the clause is absolutely crucial, as it is intended to deal with a specific concern. For this reason, it is usually better that the clause be prepared by a lawyer, properly trained in drafting contracts, rather than a real estate agent.

Mark and Lee noticed water stains on the walls and ceilings of the resale home they were thinking of buying. Bob, the seller, assured them the problem had been repaired years ago. In addition to the conventional home inspection clause, their lawyer added a clause allowing a roofer to investigate and test the soundness of the roof. Knowing they had left nothing to chance, Mark and Lee felt quite relieved when no problem was found.

Whenever special clauses are needed, tell your lawyer about them as early as possible, giving him or her ample time to think about and prepare the appropriate wording.

### Is It Still "Never On Sunday?"

Sunday is the most popular day of the week to view and attend open houses. Many real estate agents would have preferred that buyers seeing a home they liked on a Sunday submit an offer that day, while the iron was hot. Rarely was an offer submitted on a Sunday, though, as the Lord's Day Act of Canada invalidated any contract made on a Sunday.

In April 1985, the Supreme Court of Canada unanimously held that the Lords Day Act infringed upon the freedoms that were guaranteed in the Canadian Charter of Rights and Freedoms. Based on this case, it is now generally accepted that any real estate offer that was made, submitted or accepted on a Sunday would be valid. No longer is it necessary for a seller and buyer to anxiously await the stroke of midnight, with pens and paper at the ready, before signing an offer to purchase.

With this legal obstacle out of the way, agents now may try to encourage buyers to submit an offer the same day they view a house. Of course, buyers applying HOBS will refrain from doing this. Instead, they will wait until their lawyer has had a chance to see the draft offer the following morning. Remember, there is no "cooling off" period that permits buyers to change their minds within a limited period of time after the offer is accepted, and cancel the deal. Therefore, buyers must avoid getting caught up in the hoopla and enthusiasm of buying a house. Sufficient time is needed to think things through, carefully. If necessary, play dumb and say "never on Sunday." No one wants to go too far on a Sunday, and wake up with regrets on the Monday. Be absolutely sure before making that commitment. Once the die is cast, there is no turning back.

# 25

## *Conditional Offers*

When an unconditional offer is signed by the buyer and accepted by the seller, it becomes "firm and binding." Quite often, while a meeting of the minds is possible on the terms of the contract, several loose ends remain to be tidied up before the buyer is ready to proceed with the offer. If these points cannot be resolved, then the buyer wants the right to back out of the deal. Other people, not parties to the contract, usually are involved in satisfying these outstanding items.

Purchasers following the home-buying strategy approach and finding themselves in this situation, will insist that a conditional offer be prepared. Despite the fact that the deal has been struck, the contract is in suspense until the conditions have been satisfied and waived. If and only if this is completed within a set period of time, does the piece of paper become a legally binding and enforceable contract. Otherwise, neither party has any right or obligations under it.

Two or more conditions may appear in an offer, depending on the particular transaction. Whenever a conditional offer is drawn, and whatever the condition may be, buyers must be certain they fully understand what the condition says and how it works, for not all conditions are alike. Noncompliance with the exact terms of a condition can have disastrous consequences.

Stan and Marlene's situation is typical of how a conditional offer works, and when it is used. Without too much difficulty, they were able to negotiate the terms to buy George and Rochelle's house. However, they had a problem; how were they going to finance the purchase, since George and Rochelle wanted all cash on closing? Stan and Marlene might have submitted an unconditional offer, gambling they could obtain a mortgage. If no mortgage could be arranged, though, Stan and Marlene still would have to close the deal! To eliminate this risk, their offer was made conditional on obtaining satisfactory mortgage financing within 14 days after the offer was accepted. If a mortgage could not be arranged, then the deal that never was really a deal would not be off. Once Stan and Marlene arranged a mortgage and took care of any paperwork to remove the condition, the contract became firm and binding. Conditional offers, then, give buyers time after an offer is accepted to straighten out and satisfy these loose ends.

A typical conditional clause (this one dealing with arranging mortgage financing) will read:

"This offer is conditional on the purchaser arranging satisfactory financing on or before June 30th, 198_, and so notifying the vendor or his agent in writing before that date. Otherwise, this offer shall become null and void, with the deposit being returned to the purchaser without interest or deduction. This condition has been inserted for the sole benefit of the purchaser who reserves the sole right to waive it at any time at his option."

Here, the offer is not "firm and binding" until satisfactory financing is arranged within a specified time, and the vendor or his agent is given written notice of this fact. Usually this is done by the purchaser waiving the condition in writing, within the specified time.

A properly drafted conditional clause should state the following:

1. The condition to be satisifed.
2. How long the buyer has to satisfy the condition. Fix a specific date by which time the condition must be satisfied, rather than simply saying that the buyer has 7, 10 or 15

banking or business days after acceptance to waive the condition. This old-fashioned approach leads to confusion when there are intervening weekends and holidays.

3. What happens if the condition is not met, and what steps have to be taken (if anything) to kill the offer. Two different kinds of conditions can be inserted into an offer: self-destructing and self-fulfilling. In this clause, if the buyer cannot, for example, arrange financing, the condition would self-destruct, the offer becoming null and void. The buyer is permitted to let the offer die a natural death. Nothing else has to be done for the contract to end, and for the purchaser to get his deposit back. By contrast, in a self-fulfilling condition, the contract does not die, but automatically becomes firm and binding, unless the buyer does something to cancel the deal. If the buyer is unable to arrange financing, the buyer must notify the vendor of that fact to kill the contract. Failure to notify the buyer does not extinguish the offer; it validates the contract! With a self-fulfilling condition, doing nothing would render the contract automatically firm and binding, rather than null and void! For this    reason, *always insist on a condition which is self-defeating. Self-fulfilling conditions are dangerous.* Make sure a positive step is needed to firm up a contract, rather than to destroy it.

4. What steps are necessary to fulfill (or destroy) the condition? What type of notice is required — written or oral? Even if oral notice is allowed, prudent buyers will put it in writing. To whom can it be given? The seller alone? The listing agent as well as the seller's lawyer? When? During the period when the condition is being satisfied? Is a further period given after the condition is satisfied?

5. That the buyer's deposit is to be returned to him without interest (unless otherwise agreed upon) and without deduction. Clarify this at the outset, so there is no misunderstanding.

6. For whose benefit the condition has been inserted, and who can waive it. The condition appearing earlier stated that it existed for the buyer's benefit, making it abundantly clear that only the buyer, and not the seller, could waive it.

Sometimes a buyer will want to, or need to, waive the condition and firm up the offer to obtain the property, even when the condition has not yet been satisfied. Mitch and Lucy faced this dilemma when they bought their house. The formal written mortgage commitment had not been delivered by the day the condition on financing expired, although they had received oral approval. With a competing offer more attractive to the seller waiting in the wings, Mitch and Lucy decided to waive the unsatisfied condition. Obviously they were relieved when the written commitment was delivered three days later.

Occasionally a buyer may have to waive a condition before it has been satisfied. If so, try to minimize the down-side risk by seeking additional information. Why has the condition not been satisfied yet? Is only paperwork involved? Waiving a condition based on oral representations, like Mitch and Lucy did, is risky. Yet it is better than losing the property altogether, or waiving the condition blindly.

Many real estate boards, associations and offices have their own "Joe Doe" standard form of conditions, dealing with numerous situations. The applicable clauses are ticked off on a sheet of paper, and added to the offer when it is typed. Unfortunately, this means very little thought is given to the precise wording of the condition. A conditional clause must be carefully reviewed and altered where necessary, to suit the needs of the particular transaction. Better yet, take the offer with the conditional clause to a lawyer before it is signed, for his review, comments and opinion.

When a transaction is made conditional, it is usually for one of four reasons: a) to have the property examined by a home inspector; b) to arrange financing for the purchase; c) for the buyer to be approved to assume an existing mortgage; and d) for the buyer to sell his or her existing property.

### a) Home Inspection

Without this clause, a buyer has no right to inspect the property himself (or have it inspected by a home inspector) in the period between acceptance of the offer and closing. Making the offer conditional on having a home inspector examine the property within a set period of time, is becoming increasingly common.

A properly worded inspection clause requires that the purchaser be satisfied with the contents of the home inspection report, and that the buyer notify the seller in writing of this fact. If the inspection reveals problems which cannot be resolved between the parties, the deal ultimately self-destructs.

## b) Financing

By far this is the most common conditional clause. Most buyers do not have formal approval for their mortgage financing when they submit an offer. Those buyers applying their home-buying strategy may have been able to pre-qualify both themselves and the property for a mortgage loan. Others may have been told informally by a mortgage officer in a financial institution there should be no problem in getting the mortgage loan. Still, lacking a written mortgage commitment in hand, these buyers may not want to sign an unconditional offer. If the seller and buyer can agree on the terms of sale, this is the classic situation for a conditional offer, where the firming-up of the contract depends on the actions of a third party.

Many offers are very specific on the terms of the mortgage that must be arranged by the purchaser: the principal, the maximum interest rate, the term, the payments, the additional clauses and so on. Once a mortgage is available on the stated terms, purchasers are obligated to waive the condition and close the deal, despite any second thoughts they are having. More flexibility is available to you, as a purchaser, by making the offer conditional on arranging "satisfactory financing" within a specified time. Of course, it is you who determines whether the financing arranged is satisfactory. This way, if you develop cold feet and have doubts about the transaction after signing the offer, you can easily withdraw. Since you are only obligated to firm up the offer if you are satisfied with the mortgage arrangements, simply reject all mortgage proposals out of hand as being unsatisfactory, and walk away from the transaction. This is an important point to keep in mind in times of rising interest rates. Obviously, sellers do not like "satisfactory financing" clauses in offers.

Leave at least a calendar week to obtain final written approval for the mortgage. Lenders like to advertise that mortgage approvals are available in 48 hours or so, but that is not always the case. By now, purchasers with a HOBS should know informally that they will qualify for a mortgage. Yet waiting for the formal mortgage approval in a purchase transaction seems to take forever. If the buyer had wanted to waive the condition before the approval was granted, the offer would not have been made conditional in the first place! As you have no control over when the decision will be made, leave yourself ample time to get approval for the mortgage. Don't permit anyone to convince you that an abbreviated period of time is better. It's not.

### c) Being approved to assume an existing mortgage

Traditionally, mortgages have been assumable automatically by a new buyer of a property, without having to qualify for the loan. In the early 1980s, lenders began inserting clauses into mortgages that gave the lender the option of deciding whether a buyer of a property could assume an existing mortgage. If the buyer is not allowed to assume that mortgage, then it must be paid off in full when the sale closes. Most mortgages are now drawn with "limited assumability" or "due-on-sale at the lender's option" clauses. Even if a buyer qualifies to assume the mortgage, the lender still must decide whether it will permit the buyer to assume the mortgage on closing. Permission to assume is not automatic, especially if the mortgage interest rate is considerably lower than the prevailing rate in the market-place.

Darryl and Kylie were going to buy a house, and wanted to assume a limited assumable mortgage. Their lawyer inserted several clauses into the offer before it was signed. First, the offer was made conditional on the lender approving Darryl and Kylie to assume the mortgage within a set number of days. They agreed to apply within a very short period of time to assume the mortgage, and to provide full financial information to the lender. As a self-fulfilling condition, once they were approved to assume the mortgage, the condition would be waived automatically. What would happen, though, if their application was rejected? Then Darryl and Kylie, *at their sole option*, would be given a set number of additional days to arrange satisfactory financing from an alternative source to keep the deal alive. (If they decided against exercising this option, the deal would be null and void.) Giving Darryl and Kylie this option was reasonable, considering that the lender could reject their application for any reason whatsoever. Depending on whether satisfactory alternative financing then could be arranged, the deal either would be on or off.

Here is what happened. When Darryl and Kylie applied to assume the mortgage, they were turned down. Since both the property and their incomes qualified for the mortgage, the difference in interest rates must have been the reason, the mortgage rate being 8%, while the market rate was 14%. Exercising the option, Darryl and Kylie applied elsewhere for a mortgage and were accepted. However, before waiving the condition, Darryl and Kylie insisted that the purchase price be reduced by $1,000, to compensate them for the extra financing costs they were incurring.

### d) Sale of purchaser's property

One way to resolve the sell-first/buy-first dilemma is to sign a conditional offer. A buyer with an existing property to sell often submits an offer to purchase another home, that is made conditional on selling their existing home. (Be sure the conditional clause makes it clear that "selling" means signing the offer, and not actually closing the deal.)

This is exactly what Paul and Louise did. They owned a house on Crescent Street, and were interested in buying Mickey's house on Wood Drive. The offer Paul and Louise submitted to buy the Wood Drive property was made conditional on them selling the Crescent Street property by April 30th. Otherwise, the offer on Mickey's house would be null and void. The sole benefit/right to waive clause was also inserted in the offer, in case Paul and Louise wanted to firm up the offer to purchase, before selling their existing home. Mickey was rightly concerned that the conditional offer with Paul and Louise effectively would take his property off the market until April 30th. This would prevent Mickey from even trying to sell his property to anyone else during that period, when the deal with Paul and Louise would be in a state of legal limbo — sold but not really sold. To resolve the seller's dilemma, an escape clause is commonly inserted into the conditional offer. Buyers should expect to see this when the period the condition can be outstanding is quite lengthy. According to this clause, Mickey could continue to list his house for sale during the conditional period. If he is presented with another offer that would be acceptable, Mickey must advise Paul and Louise of this fact. The ball is then in Paul and Louise's court, to decide in a very short period of time (48 hours) whether or not to waive the condition. If they waive it, then they have agreed to buy Mickey's house without first having sold their own property. If Paul and Louise decide not to waive the condition, then Mickey is free to sign the other contract, and their offer to purchase Mickey's house is null and void.

How long should Paul and Louise be given in the conditional clause to sell their existing home? Obviously, from a buyer's point of view, the longer the better, while for Mickey, the shorter the better. He does not want to tie his hands for too long, even though he does have an escape clause in the offer. The norm is 30 to 60 days.

Where a property is sold conditional on the buyer selling his existing home, the involvement of the real estate agent intensifies. The selling agent on Mickey's house (Mr. Elliott, or the listing agent if only one agent was involved) will insist on getting the listing to sell Paul and Louise's house. Real estate agents adore this situation, called a back-to-back or double-ender transaction. Mr. Elliott not only is the selling agent on Mickey's house, but he also becomes the listing agent on Paul and Louise's house. If he can sell their home within the allotted time, Mr. Elliott stands to win big, for he makes two commissions! To sell Paul and Louise's house, Mr. Elliott will ask them for a long listing period, at least as long as the conditional period in the contract with Mickey, say 60 to 90 days. Then he tries like mad to sell their house.

Occasionally, sellers like Paul and Louise in this situation face additional pressure to sign a sale contract. After all, if Mr. Elliott can sell their Crescent Street property, the whole picture is complete, and he has earned his two commissions. If not, Paul and Louise are left with their old house and Mr. Elliott earns nothing. See why selling first has its advantages? See, too, why choosing a real estate agent when buying a house is so important! The agent Paul and Louise used to buy their new house turned out to be the agent they had to use to sell their old house! For this reason, buyers applying their HOBS are cautiously advised to consider all the consequences of submitting an offer conditional on selling an existing house, before proceeding any further.

Having to retain Mr. Elliott as the listing agent for the Crescent Street property could have its pitfalls for Paul and Louise as well. While he may be well acquainted with the real estate market in Mickey's community, that may not be the case for Paul and Louise's area. Lack of familiarity with comparable market values there could result in his selling the house for less than it actually is worth.

Some agents working for large firms avoid this type of problem simply by transferring the listing to a local office near Paul and Louise's home. This way, an agent more familiar with the area can service the listing, eliminating most of these concerns.

## Other Conditions

Obviously these will depend on the circumstances of the particular transaction. Sometimes the seller has to do something to the property before closing, such as cleaning the furnace, painting the exterior or repairing the shower. If so, it must be clearly spelled out in the offer. Also, because the right to re-attend on the premises between acceptance and closing must appear in the offer, be sure to give yourself the right to determine that the required work has been done, properly, before closing. Otherwise, as the offer boldly states: "This Agreement shall constitute the entire Agreement between the purchaser and vendor, and there is no representation warranty, collateral agreement or condition affecting this Agreement or the property supported hereby other than is expressed herein in writing." Shortly stated, what's in the offer you get, whatever is lacking — *nyet*.

While conditional offers provide buyers with the maximum in flexibility, there is a trade-off. Unconditional offers are bound to receive a better reception, because the seller is not concerned about external events determining whether or not the deal is on. An unconditional offer becomes firm and binding by signature alone. Agents often recommend that an unconditional offer be presented, as it looks better, cleaner, and is more inviting to a seller. Buyers who are confident they can sell their present house or arrange financing might decide to proceed unconditionally, using this to their advantage in negotiating other concessions from the seller — price, appliances, survey and so on when going in firm. Remember that you must be absolutely certain about selling your house or arranging financing. Otherwise, submitting an unconditional offer could be like playing with matches. If the financing falls through, the contract still is legally binding and enforceable.

If the seller and the buyer can agree on all the key points between them, a seller should not be reluctant to sign a conditional offer, giving the buyer a reasonable amount of time to satisfy a condition. In fact, conditional offers sometimes even benefit a seller. No one wants to be in the situation Sheldon and Bernie found themselves in. Bernie signed an unconditional offer to buy Sheldon's house. The offer should have been, but was not, made conditional on Bernie arranging satisfactory financing, the agent talking Bernie out of the condition. As Bernie could not get the necessary financing, the deal did not close, and the matter ended up in the courts. Both parties (plus the agent) then faced years of expensive litigation. Better to be safe than sorry. Unless you, as a buyer, are absolutely and positively certain that a would-be condition can be satisfied, go for the conditional offer. It is better to lose that particular property than to have signed a contract which cannot be completed.

# 26

# *Do Not Sign on the Dotted Line, Until . . .*

Signing an offer is serious business. Like any contract, it becomes a firm and binding legal document once it is accepted, (unless there are outstanding conditions) with rights, duties and obligations to be performed by both parties on a specific date. Well before signing it, buyers must be certain they can and will live up to these obligations.

When buying a resale property, there is no cooling-off period which allows buyers to simply walk away from a transaction within a specified time after the offer is accepted. One of the key features of HOBS is the need to take the offer to your lawyer for his review and comments, *before* it is signed.

Many real estate agents claim that it is unnecessary for a buyer to see a lawyer before signing the offer. After all, they argue, the offer is a standard form agreement with "boiler-plate" clauses. The typed-in clauses which supposedly distinguish one offer from another, themselves are standard "John Doe" clauses used in many real estate offices. What more could a lawyer possibly add?

Realistically, nothing could be further from the truth. The standard form offer has its own shortcomings for buyers, slanted as it is in favour of sellers. While the clauses added by the real estate agent may deal with the specific issues raised by a buyer, too often they fail to adequately protect a purchaser. Of greater concern from a legal point of view is not what the offer includes, but rather what it omits. While real estate agents, aided by the John Doe forms can prepare acceptable offers, few have had the same intensive training and experience in legal drafting as lawyers. Granted, if the deal closes as scheduled, any inadequacies in drafting become academic. However, if problems do arise, everyone will regret that a lawyer did not have the opportunity to comment on the offer ahead of time. When the potential consequences of an improperly drawn offer are coupled with the dollar amounts involved, it is essential that purchasers be encouraged to have the draft offer reviewed by a lawyer.

The fact that fewer than 10 percent of all buyers of residential real estate take offers to lawyers before they are signed, is both surprising and distressing. Only that small minority can benefit from the unique three-pronged opportunity that seeing a lawyer at this stage presents:

1. To ensure the contract adequately protects the buyer, properly incorporating both his wishes and his intentions. Often a buyer will raise an issue in discussions with his lawyer that was previously overlooked. Or the lawyer may make suggestions, based on his experience, which will save buyers money. A prime example is the need for a survey, required in virtually all mortgage transactions.
2. To ensure the buyer fully understands what the offer says, and the obligations flowing from it. Frank and Joyce were glad their lawyer explained in detail the "conditional on financing" clause in the offer that the agent prepared. Drafted as a self-fulfilling and not a self-defeating condition, Frank and Joyce now knew for the first time what had to be done if the mortgage could not be arranged.
3. To review and have explained the basics of mortgage financing, as well as the hidden costs involved in a real estate transaction. This allows buyers to properly budget for these items now, rather than under pressure immediately before closing.

Sometimes it is said that lawyers want to review unexecuted offers, as it provides an excellent opportunity for them to pump up their fees. This is an unfair comment. Without question, consulting with a lawyer before the offer is signed does cost money, but far less than buyers might think. A lawyer acting for the buyer of a resale property must read the offer in its entirety before processing it. Time wise, it makes no difference whether the offer reviewed is in draft or executed form. No additional fee, therefore, should be charged for reviewing the draft offer (assuming it is later signed and the deal closed). Why not then, give the lawyer this opportunity before the offer is signed, before the terms of the contract are set? When the offer is still in draft form, a lawyer can review it, revise it, suggest additions or deletions, and generally comment on it. Once the ink is dry, this opportunity for input is gone forever. The only additional time involved when a lawyer sees a draft offer, and the only time for which a buyer should be billed, is the con-sultation time — the time the lawyer spends in a meeting with the buyer before the contract is signed. In large part this is determined by the client anyway, depending on how much time is spent in consultation. When the amount of money at stake is compared to this cost of consultation, it is incon-ceivable that all buyers do not contact lawyers before signing offers. This could be the best investment the buyer makes in the property.

To save time, arrange to deliver the offer to your lawyer in advance. This gives him or her the opportunity of reviewing it without your being there. When the appointment is held, it's right down to business! The alternative is to sit and watch your lawyer read an offer for 20 minutes or so — not terribly exciting. Where a real estate agent is involved let him or her take the draft offer to your lawyer. Why should you, as a purchaser, have to deliver it, often losing time off work? The agent stands to make several thousand dollars when the deal goes through. With that much money at stake, surely the agent can find the time to get the draft offer into your lawyer's hands as quickly as possible.

Some real estate agents are apprehensive about lawyers seeing buyers and discussing the terms of the offer before it is signed. Pressure is exerted on buyers to sign the offer now, as is, fearing the lawyer will "blow the deal." This is an unfortunate misconception about the legal profession. A competent real estate lawyer acting reasonably will only be raising and amending clauses that are not in the buyer's best interests. Few lawyers are retained at this stage to talk buyers out of deals. A lawyer's role is to ensure the prospective purchaser is fully appraised of his legal rights and obligations, that he understands them, and that he knows the financial commitment he will be making on signing the contract.

Occasionally a buyer does withdraw from negotiations at this stage. Sometimes the offer is deficient as a contract. More often a buyer realizes the financial difficulties he would have faced, either in closing the transaction or in maintaining the property afterwards. Inevitably, though, the lawyer is fingered as the culprit for the deal falling through.

With no financial stake in the transaction, a lawyer can provide a buyer with unbiased objectivity. Seeing a lawyer at this stage helps plant a buyer's feet back on the ground, rather than allowing emotions to carry the decision. Genuinely sincere real estate agents will offer no resistance when a buyer wishes to have the offer reviewed by his lawyer before it is signed.

Do not expect your lawyer to pass judgement on two questions: the purchase price and the ultimate decision whether to proceed with the transaction. Real estate agents know the market in an area much more intimately. It is their role, based on the resources available to them, to advise buyers on the purchase price and market values. Nevertheless, an experienced real estate lawyer often can tell if an offer is "in the ball park" for other properties in the area. Similarly, your lawyer can provide assistance on mortgage financing and whether you as a purchaser and the property will qualify for a mortgage loan. Nevertheless, the final decision to sign the offer must rest with you, and only you.

If a private sale is involved, the offer normally drawn by the real estate agent must be prepared by the buyer's lawyer, at the buyer's expense. The cost incurred, usually upwards of $100, could end up being a blessing in disguise. This need for an offer forces the buyer and his or her lawyer to come together early, to discuss all aspects of the transaction.

Without question, time is crucial in submitting an offer. Obviously, not every lawyer will be available to review a client's offer when he or she is needed. If that is the case, insert the following condition into the offer, to give your lawyer ample time to protect your interests:

> "This offer is conditional on the purchaser's lawyer, Alan G. Silverstein, having an opportunity to review this offer, to determine that it is satisfactory, and to approve it in full, without requiring any changes whatsoever. To satisfy this condition, a letter to this effect shall be delivered to the seller's agent on or before 11:59 p.m. on May 22nd, 1986. Otherwise, this offer shall become null and void, with the deposit being returned to the purchaser without interest or deduction."

Few sellers will deny a buyer this opportunity, provided the time given is reasonable — 48 hours or less.

By including this clause in their offer, Bobby and Jenna accomplished two things. First, it gave their lawyer ample time to pass judgment on the contents of the offer, exactly what Bobby and Jenna wanted. Second, it gave them, in effect, a short cooling-off period they otherwise would not have had, to think through, reconsider and possibly even cancel the contract after it had been signed. After all, if Bobby and Jenna had changed their minds, and decided not to proceed with the transaction, it would have been very easy for them to back out, although the contract was already signed. Only one change — any one clause found to be unsatisfactory — would nullify the entire contract.

CARDINAL RULE — Despite any pressures brought to bear, do not sign any offer to purchase until it has been thoroughly reviewed by your lawyer.

# 27

# *The Buyer's Role between Acceptance and Closing*

Congratulations! The offer has been accepted. Now while you may think that much of the work shifts to the lawyer, in reality there is much for a buyer to do, besides packing. To make the transition as smooth as possible, a buyer must do the following in the interval between acceptance and closing.

1. Contact your lawyer and arrange for him or her to get a copy of the accepted offer as soon as possible. A photocopy will suffice if you only have, and want to retain, the one original copy. While the real estate agent also will be delivering the offer to your lawyer, your extra effort can get the lawyer working for you that much sooner.

   If for some reason the lawyer is seeing the offer for the first time, arrange for an appointment with your lawyer, during which the offer will be discussed, deficiencies noted (such as the need for a survey) and instructions given concerning these matters. Be sure to review with your lawyer the anticipated closing costs, fees and disbursements, mortgage deductions and estimated adjustments, explored in chapter 22.

   Also advise your lawyer how you wish to be registered on the title to the property. (See chapter 32 for more information.) Full names, birthdates and spousal status of all persons to be registered as owners are required, depending on the province involved. If in doubt, review this information with your lawyer as well.

2. If any conditions are still outstanding, such as arranging a mortgage, being approved to assume an existing mortgage, selling an existing house or conducting a home inspection, attend to them *immediately,* and in the manner set out in the offer. Very short limitation periods usually apply to these conditions, and the clock is running. Be absolutely certain whether the condition is self-defeating or self-fulfilling and the time allotted for compliance. Know what must be done within what period of time either to keep the transaction alive or to kill it. Be sure you strictly comply with your contractual obligations.

   Individual conditions can be deleted from the offer, either by amending the offer or by waiving that specific condition. Once *all* conditions have been satisfied, assuming the conditions are self-defeating, the agent must prepare a waiver of the conditions, to be signed and delivered to the seller before the prescribed time expires. Be sure this is done promptly, and without any slip-ups. When this is done, the offer is "firmed-up" — the contract becoming "firm and binding."

   Most buyers at this stage, like Joe and Tilly, will say they have bought a house. Legally speaking, that is not the case. With an unconditional offer, all Joe and Tilly have really acquired is a legal interest in that property. They will not own the property until the transaction formally closes.

3. Buyers who presently are tenants must either cancel their lease or transfer their tenancy/sub-lease their apartment, if permitted. To avoid problems, be sure to give the landlord the amount of notice required in the applicable residential tenancy legislation. If in doubt, check it out with your lawyer. Try to arrange an overlap, so the lease terminates after the date of closing. This will make moving considerably easier.

4. Local gas, hydro and water departments are contacted by your lawyer for final meter readings the day of closing. New accounts are also to be established in your name on closing. Occasionally, slip-ups do occur especially on busy closing days or month ends. To ensure continuation of service after closing, telephone the local utilities several days before

closing. It is better to be told the matter is being attended to than to find yourself without utility service following closing.

Buyers are responsible for contacting the telephone and cable television systems. Lawyers do not contact these companies, as their outstanding charges cannot be registered as liens against the property.

For homes heated by oil, the seller arranges to fill the oil tank on closing. The seller is credited with the cost of a full tank of home heating oil on the Statement of Adjustments. Enquire whether an extended warranty or service contract is in effect on the oil furnace, and if it is assignable. With the name of the company previously servicing the furnace and supplying oil to the property, the buyer can arrange for the continued supply of oil, plus the maintenance of the furnace, after closing. No one, especially in the dead of winter, wants to find their oil tank dry, because the wheels were not set in motion for a regular "drop" of oil in the days following closing.

5. Unless the offer specifically requires delivery of a survey, there is no assurance the seller will provide one to you. Even if a survey can be located, will it be acceptable to the lender? If you have not discussed the question of a survey with your lawyer, do so immediately.

6. Arrange fire insurance coverage as soon as possible, effective the date of closing. Ensure, as a minimum, an insurance "binder" letter is available for closing. The premises should be insured for its full insurable value at all times.

7. Make the necessary arrangements for your move early. Packing takes an enormous amount of time. Get quotes from movers or a moving truck soon. Demand is highest in the middle and at the end of the month, on Fridays (especially the last Friday of the month) and the week before each of Canada Day and Labour Day.

8. Meet with your lawyer several days before closing, and give him the necessary closing proceeds no later than the day before closing.

**Checklist for things buyers should do between acceptance and closing:**

1. Review the transaction with your lawyer.
2. Satisfy all conditions — quickly and completely.
3. Tenants must give notice to terminate their tenancies or assign/sublease their apartment.
4. Double-check with the public utilities to ensure that service is not cut off on closing.
5. Determine if a survey exists, and if it will be accessible.
6. Arrange fire insurance coverage.
7. Make arrangements for the move.
8. Plan the pre-closing meeting with your lawyer no later than the day before closing.

# 28

# *The Lawyer's Role between Acceptance and Closing*

Selecting the lawyer to handle your purchase, according to your home-buying strategy, is one of the first decisions you make, never the last. With full knowledge of its contents, once the offer is accepted your lawyer can start work immediately on processing it.

Exactly what a lawyer does every step of the way is not of great concern to most purchasers. What they really want to know are the end results: where do I sign; exactly how much do I bring in; and when will the deed be registered and the keys be available?

Usually, the first step in processing a purchase is the search of title to the property. Most offers give the buyer's lawyer a very short time to examine the title and to raise title deficiencies. As the title search period generally is 30 days or less, even if closing is months in the future, getting the search underway quickly is extremely important. If the legal description appeared in the draft offer your lawyer reviewed, all it will take is your phone call, advising that the deal is firm, for him to start the search. Receipt of the accepted offer can come later. Most lawyers wait for all conditions to be removed before searching title, to keep expenses down in case a condition is not satisfied or waived. The need to consult a lawyer prior to signature again becomes self-evident. Consider the case of the buyer who makes initial contact with a lawyer several days after the offer was accepted. Precious time on that title search clock has been lost forever, to the buyer's disadvantage.

The search of title is a historical investigation of previous ownership and prior dealings with the property. Depending on the province and the land registration system involved, this could involve examining all registered instruments affecting the title for 40 years or more, to ensure an unbroken "chain of title." A lawyer's title report is based on the information appearing in the search of title.

A formal engagement contract between a lawyer and his client is rare in real estate transactions. Despite this, it is clearly understood that a lawyer must give a formal legal opinion that the buyer becomes the registered owner of the property on closing, with what is called a "good and marketable" title. Good means appropriate for the buyer's purposes, while marketable indicates that it is adequate to be conveyed to someone else, now or in the future. To do this, a lawyer must investigate the title in the prescribed manner. Following a careful review of the title search, a letter will be sent to the seller's lawyer (called a letter of requisition) setting out matters that must be dealt with, on or before closing.

Probably the most common requisition raised is the need for the seller's existing mortgage to be discharged, if the buyer is not assuming it on closing. Many other requisitions involve outstanding monetary expenses: — taxes, utility charges, condominium expenses and mortgage payments. These are easily satisfied on closing, the seller simply paying the amount owing to the appropriate creditor. Often, to ensure these sums are paid promptly, the buyer obtains a credit from the seller on the Statement of Adjustments for the amount outstanding. After closing the buyer pays the money owing on the seller's behalf.

Occasionally, a search of title reveals other outstanding and unexpected matters, such as a utility easement, a right-of-way or mutual drive, or registered restrictions. All of these detract from the "perfect" title buyers expect to receive, legally known as "fee simple" (the most extensive, unrestricted and unconditional interest in land a person can enjoy).

A properly drawn offer will disclose these qualifications on title at the outset, so a buyer and his lawyer know precisely what to anticipate from the search of title. Some of these situations are dealt with in the fine print in many standard form offers. For example, the buyer may agree to take title subject to minor easements to public utilities for the supply of domestic utility service, or the buyer may agree to take title subject to registered restrictions, provided they have been complied with.

Occasionally, the search reveals a serious title deficiency that was not disclosed in the offer. Nothing in Fred and Wilma's offer indicated that a 25-foot sewer easement ran diagonally across the property they were buying! Only from the search of title was its existence revealed. As a lawyer must implement the terms of the deal reached by his clients, Fred and Wilma's lawyer immediately contacted them about this matter. After advising Fred and Wilma of the legal implications, and discussing the situation with them thoroughly, their lawyer also recommended the course of action to follow. A reduction in the purchase price should be sought, he argued, since the affected area would interfere substantially with their use and enjoyment of the property. Fred and Wilma gave their lawyer written instructions to proceed on this basis, since the terms of the contract would have to be altered. Ultimately the deal did close, with a reduction in the purchase price.

Some lawyers obtain a written acknowledgement from their purchaser clients prior to closing, listing *all* items that title will be subject to, even those originally disclosed in the offer. This way, everything qualifying the "fee simple" title is noted, discussed and approved before title changes hands.

Numerous clearances, reports and certificates are ordered, usually a month or so before closing. A certificate is ordered to ensure all realty taxes have been paid to the date of closing and to learn whether any additional charges such as local improvements have been levied against the property. The local municipality is contacted, to ensure compliance with all zoning by-laws, and to learn if any work orders or deficiency notices are outstanding. A check is made with the local utilities — hydro, water and gas — to see if any of their charges are outstanding. At the same time they are notified that the property has been sold, and who the new owner will be. A request is made for a final meter reading on the day of closing, with the final bill to be forwarded to the seller's lawyer. Compliance letters are sought from any municipality which registered an agreement on title. A search is conducted for outstanding judgments and executions against the seller and prior owners. Personal property security records also are checked, to see if any liens, encumbrances or chattel mortgages affect any of the personal property being acquired.

In condominium transactions, an Estoppel Certificate is ordered from the condominium corporation, containing information about arrears of common expenses for the unit, and whether actions are pending by or against the condominium corporation.

Where rural property is being acquired, a number of additional searches are made. These include searching for well water records, and learning whether the sewage disposal system (septic tank) has been approved by the provincial environment ministry.

The purpose behind all of these searches is to ensure no liens or other deficiencies are outstanding against the property. Buyers are paying their lawyers to ensure all accounts are up-to-date, and that they take over the property with a clean slate effective the date of closing.

Nominal amounts are charged for most of these searches and reports. The cost of obtaining this information represents the out-of-pocket disbursements buyers incur when purchasing property.

Surveys were discussed in detail in chapter 23. If no survey can be located, or if the existing survey is unacceptable, arrangements must be made early to have a new one drawn. Several weeks are needed to obtain the new survey. Further time is needed as well, since the survey accompanies the request for a by-law and work order report. If the contents in (or the lack of) a survey are likely to be a problem, order a new survey as soon as possible. Your lawyer will arrange to order it for you, on request.

Once received, the survey should be carefully reviewed to ensure the dimensions of the property, the size of the lot and the extent of title correspond with the particulars stated in the offer. Any encroachments onto this property by adjoining properties, or by this property onto adjoining properties, should be carefully noted. Written instructions from buyers to their lawyers to close the transaction despite these encroachments (some of which may have been long in existance) is customary. Some lawyers also require written instructions from the purchaser to close, if no survey exists or if the survey is old but acceptable. Any qualifications to the title opinion, by relying on the old survey, are indicated here as well. For example, the survey for the house Sam and Roz are buying was prepared in 1973. It is proper for their lawyer's title opinion to be subject to any changes to the property that occurred between 1973 and the date of closing, that a new survey would have revealed. Not only has full disclosure been made to the purchaser about these matters before closing, but written instructions to proceed on this basis have also been delivered. The likelihood for misunderstanding has been reduced considerably.

The draft deed, Statement of Adjustments and other closing documents are reviewed by the buyer's lawyer upon receipt. To ensure its accuracy, a buyer's lawyer will independently verify the contents of the Statement of Adjustments. Any discrepancies should be raised and resolved as soon as possible.

The lawyer's role in the mortgage transaction depends on how the purchase is being financed. Three different ways exist to finance a purchase: assuming an existing mortgage; granting a new mortgage to a lender; and the vendor taking back a new mortgage.

Where an existing mortgage is to be assumed, a mortgage assumption statement is requested from the lender. Particulars sought include the outstanding principal as of the last payment; the interest rate, the amount of the payment; the maturity date; the status of any tax account; whether the mortgage is assumable; plus any prepayment privileges. This information is then compared against the clauses in the offer dealing with the mortgage as well as the mortgage as registered on title.

Where a new mortgage is arranged by the purchaser, the lender's instructions list the many documents which must be prepared before the funds will be released. Usually the buyer's lawyer is allowed to act for an institutional lender as well, saving the buyer money. Draft documents are sent to the lender for approval, and arrangements are made to have the net mortgage advance available for closing. In a vendor-take-back mortgage situation, the buyer's lawyer prepares the draft mortgage, which is sent to the seller's lawyer for approval.

Never fear discussing matters with your lawyer, or asking questions that concern you. Your lawyer has been hired for that very purpose! Also buyers, especially first-time home buyers, must never be concerned that their questions are too basic or too straightforward. Although your lawyer may have been asked the question innumerable times, *you* don't know the answer. Otherwise, you would not be asking the question. To assist buyers, some lawyers provide their clients with instruction sheets, answering many of the questions most commonly raised by purchasers. They also explain what each side will be doing in the interval until closing. Never leave questions for the final meeting either. Ask them as they arise. An unanswered question could become an unresolvable problem, if not dealt with promptly.

Plan on meeting with your lawyer to review and sign the closing papers *several days before closing*. By that time, the exact amount needed to close should be known as well. Try to avoid signing papers on the actual closing date, unless it is absolutely necessary. Most papers can be signed well in advance of closing. Who knows what can happen the day of closing? The car could break down; the children could be sick; inclement weather could make travel impossible; or a hydro blackout, fire or robbery effectively could close off an area of the city. Then what happens? Make the date of closing your last choice to meet, never your first!

Understanding and remembering everything explained at this meeting is not easy, even if held several days before closing. Scheduling it for the day of closing makes it all the more difficult. Anyway, most buyers have something better to do on the day of closing, than sit in a lawyer's office, signing papers. They want to proceed with their move! A lawyer's office is the last place they want to be — they really want to be in their new home!

Few documents will be given to buyers at this time. With the upcoming move, no one wants to run the risk of losing important legal documents. Copies of all relevant papers will accompany the reporting letter.

Signing the papers on the day set for completion delays the actual closing of the transaction. Remember that no keys are delivered to buyers at that meeting. Before keys to the new home are available, the transaction still must be closed! How, then, can buyers like Dick and Liz, who did not meet their lawyer until 11:00 A.M. that day, expect to receive their keys early? Following that meeting, their lawyer had to deposit the funds into his trust account and certify the closing proceeds. Only then could the transaction be closed in the registry office, at which time the keys change hands! As Dick and Liz learned, closing-day meetings inevitably mean late-in-the-day closings with the seller's lawyer, and an even later delivery of keys.

The situation is even worse for buyers selling an existing house. Unless bridge financing has been arranged, the sale must be closed before the purchase, as the funds required for the purchase will only be available after the sale has closed. Obviously this delays the closing of the purchase even further. Anything, then, that will expedite the closing of the transaction, such as meeting the lawyer one or two days in advance, is encouraged.

Closing proceeds often are obtained from different sources — the buyer, a mortgage lender and the bank for bridge financing. They are assembled in the buyer's lawyer's trust account, and are disbursed on closing. Unless informed otherwise, buyers must deliver a certified cheque or bank draft to their lawyer, payable to the order of the lawyer, in trust. Arranging for a lawyer to get these funds early — known as being "in funds" — is just as important as signing the closing papers early.

Joel and Nancy were asked to bring the closing proceeds to their lawyer when they met at noon the day before closing. Already concerned about the extra cost this involved, they also wondered why the net proceeds of the new mortgage being arranged were being delivered the day before closing. Then they realized that the overall cost to them, really, was quite small. Assuming the interest cost on their own money and the mortgage for one day averaged 12%, the cost on the $100,000 Joel and Nancy needed to close was only $32.88.

Joel and Nancy applied HOBS both in meeting with their lawyer a day before closing, and in arranging for him to have the closing funds that same day. Delays in closing are usually attributable to delays with buyers — and in particular, hitches in getting the closing proceeds. By comparison, most sellers are ready to close early the day of closing. Once their paperwork is signed, seller's lawyers are simply awaiting receipt of the sale proceeds from the buyer. As everything was attended to the day before closing, including the certification of the closing cheques, Joel and Nancy's purchase was closed by 10:00 A.M. and they had their keys by 11:00 A.M.

When it comes to real estate closings, the early bird catches the worm! Buyers like Joel and Nancy have a fighting chance in most cases of completing the transaction early on the scheduled closing date and getting possession with a minimum of delay. If this saves buyers even one hour's moving time, they end up further ahead financially, despite the nominal cost originally incurred. To close as early as possible on the day of closing, meet your lawyer no later than the day before closing. In addition, make sure the closing proceeds are delivered before 3:00 P.M. the day before closing.

The lawyer's role in the real estate transaction does not end with the registering of the deed and the mortgage. Immediately after closing, the tax department and the condominium corporation (if applicable) must be given the names of the new owners of the property. Any outstanding charges credited to the buyer on the Statement of Adjustments must be paid. An amortization schedule should be ordered for any new or assumed mortgages as well.

A complete summary of the work performed by a buyer's lawyer appears in the reporting letter. As proper preparation of this letter takes time, expect it to be delivered about a month after closing. Getting registered duplicate documents from the registry office accounts for part of the delay. Certain detailed information though, is needed virtually immediately after closing. Included in this category are the mortgages (date of the first payment; the amount of the payment; where payment should be sent; the account number), taxes and maintenance payments. Coupled with the fact few buyers remember all the pertinent details from the pre-closing meeting, some lawyers send an interim report to purchasers immediately after closing. Highlighted are the payments to be made in the days and weeks following closing. Often this is the first letter buyers receive at their new home address.

Separate reporting letters, containing the title opinion, are prepared and delivered to the purchaser and any mortgage lender. Copies of all relevant documents, such as the deed; mortgages; amortization schedules; Statement of Adjustments and survey should accompany the report. A proper reporting letter is not simply a form letter with the blanks filled in. It should be specifically tailored to, and include relevant information about, this particular transaction. As most buyers are very concerned about the "money aspects" of the transaction, a proper reporting letter provides commentary explaining every item in the Statement of Adjustments. How each credit was determined should be highlighted, with a copy of the document verifying the credit accompanying the letter. Special instructions received from the client before closing should be discussed as well. Deductions made by the mortgage lender at source should be clearly explained and documented.

The lawyer's bill will indicate the amount incurred for each disbursement, as well as the fees charged. In addition, a Statement of Receipts and Disbursements will provide a complete accounting of the funds assembled in a lawyer's trust account from all sources, and where the money was applied.

Properly prepared, the detailed commentary of the reporting letter, accompanied by the relevant documents, should answer all outstanding questions a buyer may have. While it provides a permanent record of the transaction for the purchaser, the reporting letter also will form the basis for any future dealings with the property.

# 29

# *Insurance*

It is safe to say that everyone buying a house knows that fire insurance is needed. How much to arrange, the different coverages that are available, and the impact of a mortgage on insurance coverage are discussed later in this chapter.

Some buyers may encounter salesmen and institutions selling three other types of insurance. These are term life insurance; mortgage payment insurance; and mortgage rate insurance. Loosely applied, the term "mortgage insurance" can refer to any of these four categories. When asking about so-called "mortgage insurance," make sure you distinguish between insuring the property, your life, the payments to the lender and the rate on the mortgage.

## Term Life Insurance

Many institutional mortgage lenders offer term life insurance at a nominal premium. If the borrower dies while the mortgage is outstanding, the insurance proceeds are used to pay off the loan. For this reason, often it is called "mortgage insurance." All it really is, though, is declining balance term insurance, available from almost any life insurance agent.

When considering whether to buy this type of insurance coverage, stand back and ask yourself the following question: do I have sufficient life insurance in the event I die to pay off my obligations, and yet leave sufficient funds from which my family can live comfortably?

## Mortgage Payment Insurance

High-ratio mortgages, where the owner has less than 25 percent equity in the property, are considered riskier investments for lenders. For institutional lenders to grant the loan, they want some assurance that the mortgage will be repaid in the event the borrower defaults. *To protect the lender,* high-ratio loans require the borrower to arrange mortgage payment insurance on the full amount of the mortgage. This type of insurance is available from two sources: a private insurer, the Mortgage Insurance Company of Canada (MICC) or the federal government, Canada Mortgage and Housing Corporation (CMHC).

Never arrange mortgage payment insurance unless you absolutely have to. In addition to their mortgage payment each month, borrowers like Howard and Bonnie pay a charge each month to assure their lender that they (Howard and Bonnie) will be making their mortgage payments punctually!

This type of mortgage insurance does not come cheaply. Depending on the size of the mortgage in relation to the value of the property, anywhere from 1.5 to 2.5 percent of the total amount of the mortgage is charged as the insurance fee. While the one-time insurance premium can be paid up front on closing, it is usually simply added to the outstanding principal and paid off monthly. Most borrowers do not realize that a $1,000 premium on a 12% mortgage amortized over 25 years will cost them a further $10.32 a month and $2,094.20 in interest over the amortized life of the mortgage. *Unless it is absolutely necessary, stay away from mortgage payment insurance.*

Ways to restructure a mortgage, to eliminate mortgage payment insurance, are explored in detail in *Hidden Profits in Your Mortgage.*

## Mortgage Rate Insurance

In February 1984, the federal government introduced the Mortgage Rate Protection Plan. One of Ottawa's greater flops, the aim was to protect home owners against sharp rises in interest rates. Great in theory, but terrible in practice. To participate, a one-time premium of 1.5 percent of the outstanding principal is paid to CMHC. Like mortgage payment insurance, usually it is tacked onto the amount borrowed and repaid monthly. Excluded from the plan are vendor-take-back and second mortgages.

Once the initial mortgage term expires, the plan protects the interest rate on the renewal term (which is identical to the initial term). No rate protection is available if rates on the renewal term increase by 2 percent or less. Above that, the initial 2 percent increase *plus* one quarter of the difference in rates remain the borrower's responsibility. An increase in rates on renewal from 10% to 18%, for example, would mean the borrower would pay a rate of 13.5% for the renewal term (10% plus 2% plus one quarter of 6% (or 1.5%).

Premiums are not pro-rated based on the number of years in the initial term. No wonder the public has turned thumbs down on this well-intentioned scheme.

## Home Insurance

Calling this "fire insurance" is to ignore the many ways a loss could be incurred. When arranging this type of insurance, the home and its contents should be protected. Personal liability coverage is needed, as well as coverage against theft. These are available in the so-called "Home Owner's Package" offered by many insurance companies.

Most insurance policies offer standard protection against loss by fire and specified "named perils," including explosions, falling objects, vehicular impact, lightning, riots, vandalism, windstorm and smoke damage. Some insurance policies (for a higher premium) provide a more comprehensive "all-risk" coverage, protecting against more possible sources of loss, although even here certain exclusions and deductibles exist.

Like most buyers, Ian and Marie are financing their purchase with a mortgage, arranged through Punch Trust. If the building burned totally to the ground, the insurance money would replace the building as security for the loan. The lender then would want first claims to those funds. Since Punch Trust has an insurable interest in the property, Ian and Marie should ask their insurance agent to show it in the loss-payable clause of the insurance policy as first mortgagee. When the mortgage is paid off, the lender's interest in the loss-payable clause will be deleted.

Paperwork takes time. Few insurance policies are available for closing, although they take effect that day. To satisfy lenders that the required insurance is in place, insurance agents issue "binder letters," giving full particulars of the insurance coverage: the insurer, the amount covered, the policy number, the expiry date together with the names of the lenders in the loss payable clause. Except for condominium units, home buyers should arrange for the binder letter to be delivered to their lawyer as early as possible before closing, as the lawyer in turn may have to forward it to the lender for approval. Knowing adequate insurance has been arranged, and that the policy will follow, most lenders will advance the mortgage proceeds on closing.

How much insurance coverage is required? When answering this question, too often buyers only consider the amount of the outstanding mortgages. To properly determine the amount of insurance coverage needed, what should be considered first is the "full insurable value" of the building (the premises). This coverage guarantees it is insured to the maximum. Seriously consider optional coverage on a "replacement cost" basis. This ensures the cost of rebuilding the dwelling *at current prices* will be paid, without any reduction for depreciation. Despite the additional premium for full replacement cost coverage, only it guarantees that a home will be replaced with one of similar type and quality in the even of an insurable loss.

An important point to remember is that land does not have to be insured. Land does not burn. If a home was totally destroyed in a fire, the lot still exists. Only the house has to be rebuilt, not the lot. Where a mortgage lender has the property appraised, find out the separate values given to the land as well as the replacement cost of the building. This will help greatly when arranging insurance coverage.

Unfortunately, some mortgages require that the full amount of the mortgage be insured, even if it exceeds the full insurable value of the property. Clauses like these cause both headaches and extra expenses for purchasers.

Ozzie and Harriet bought a property for $100,000. Their mortgage lender appraised the lot at $30,000, and the full insurable value of the house for $70,000. Needing a $60,000 mortgage, Ozzie and Harriet need at least $60,000 insurance coverage to satisfy the lender. To be prudent, though, they should arrange $70,000 coverage.

Ward and June are buying the identical house for $100,000 but their mortgage will be $75,000. Now the problems begin. The full insurable value of the dwelling, according to the appraisal, was only $70,000. Any greater coverage, then, really is unnecessary. Nothing is being insured for that extra $5,000 except the land. Their lender, Spring Farm Trust, insisted that the full amount of the mortgage — $75,000 — be insured. Unless the lender agrees to accept only $70,000 in insurance coverage, Ward and June have little alternative but to arrange the extra $5,000 unnecessary coverage. Although the difference in premiums is small, it is small consolation, considering how blatently unnecessary the extra coverage is.

Most lenders insist that the Standard Mortgage Clause approved by the Insurance Bureau of Canada be attached to the policy. What is this and why is it so important? Insurance is arranged and paid for by borrowers, to protect lenders. Only rarely do lenders deal directly with the insurance company. In the event of a loss, could the insurer pay the insurance proceeds to the lender — someone it never dealt with directly? This clause allows insurance proceeds to be paid directly to a mortgage lender, despite the lack of a direct contractual link between lender and insurer. Lenders are also assured that coverage will not be cancelled without giving notice to the lender. Most insurance policies now contain the IBC Standard Mortgage Clause as a matter of course.

Insurance policies on resale homes are arranged for a term of one year. Unlike the situation years ago, these policies are not assignable to a new owner of the property. Therefore, don't expect the seller to transfer his insurance to you on closing. Smart buyers will start shopping for insurance early, well before closing, obtaining quotations and comparing coverage, to get the best possible terms. Use the form at the end of this chapter, to record the information provided by different insurance agents. Make sure the insurance coverage takes effect from 12:01 A.M. the date of closing.

When shopping for insurance, consider dealing with an insurance broker who deals with a number of insurance companies. A better overall package should be available from one of the many insurance companies he deals with. True insurance agents work for, market and sell the product of one insurance company only. Your options and flexibility to get the best possible deal are somewhat restricted when dealing with an insurance agent.

Insurance on condominiums, both townhouses and apartment units, is handled totally differently. Both the condominium corporation and the unit owners must arrange separate insurance coverage on the property it owns. Further information appears in the chapter on condominiums.

One final word about insurance. If a fire hits your home, or if a thief ransacks your house, would you know exactly what was lost? The more precise information you can give the insurance company, the fuller the recovery. Prudent home owners will compile a complete inventory of personal possessions, prepared on a room-by-room basis. Each item should be described in detail, including serial numbers. One copy of the list should be kept in a secure location *outside the house,* such as a safety deposit box. Many police departments also will loan engraving guns to residents at a nominal or no charge. A unique identification code, such as a Social Insurance Number, can be marked on personal property such as TV sets, stereos, VCRs, appliances, cameras, china, tools and the like. This way, if your property is stolen and later recovered, returning it to its rightful owner becomes considerably easier.

Make a list of the insurance quotations received. Don't forget — any lenders must be shown in the loss payable clause of the insurance policy.

## Insurance Agencies

| Name | | | |
|---|---|---|---|
| Address | | | |
| Phone number | | | |
| Contact person | | | |
| Amount of coverage | | | |
| Insurer | | | |
| Cost | | | |
| Replacement cost coverage? | | | |

# 30

# Closing — The Moment Everyone Has Waited For

Closing takes place at the local registry office. Many law firms use trained, para-legal personnel called conveyancers, to handle the mechanics of actually closing the deal. Meanwhile, the buyer's lawyer is in his office where he can be easily reached by his client and his conveyancer, and other buyers whose deals are closing the same day. Knowing where their lawyer will be on closing, and that he or she will be available if the need arises, is very reassuring to most buyers. Last-minute instructions can be relayed easily from client to conveyancer. Information about deeds being registered and the availability of keys can be conveyed just as easily from the registry office to the client, through the lawyer in his office. On busy closing days a lawyer's office becomes a "central command," where all communications are funnelled.

Closing a deal is not nearly as mysterious as it sounds. The closing papers should have been signed a day or two before closing. The funds from the various sources should be ready for delivery the day of closing. Where draft documents have been submitted and approved by each lawyer ahead of time, as usually is the case, the closing between seller and buyer should be smooth and quick. At the prearranged closing time, the buyer's conveyancer hands the closing proceeds, any vendor-take-back mortgage and other required closing documents to the seller's representative. In return, the seller's conveyancer delivers the deed and keys, any undertakings and any other required documents. Everything is carefully checked against the closing instructions provided by each lawyer. Once this is completed, the conveyancers await their turn to register the closing papers. Only then can each side release to his or her client the items received from the other side at closing.

Buyers with back-to-back deals must close the sale of their old home first, before the purchase of the new home can be completed the same day. This results in unavoidable delays. Chris was buying Danny's house. Before that deal could close, Chris' sale to Bob had to be completed. Some delay in closing the purchase from Danny, therefore, was expected. However, Bob in turn was selling his house to Alan. The flow of money resembled dominoes falling — looking like this.

Alan ➜ Bob ➜ Chris ➜ Danny

Poor Chris. Closing both his sale and his purchase the same day led to very lengthy delays, since another deal (Alan/Bob) had to close before either of his transactions. If Chris had arranged bridge financing, he could have avoided all of this (see chapter 21).

The system of land registration in many parts of Canada is quite primitive, and extremely labor-intensive. Insufficient computerization is in place. While the exchange of documents on a closing can be completed in a very few minutes, the problems encountered in registering them accounts for the lengthy delays at closing. On busy days, registration clerks are unable to handle the sheer volume of business. Hours can be spent in lineups, waiting to register deeds and mortgages. A good reason indeed to schedule closing for an off-day. Even on quiet days, afternoons are much busier than mornings. Another good reason to meet a day ahead of time with your lawyer, and push for an early morning closing.

Probably the biggest headache of all, and the most commonly asked question is: "When and where will the keys be available?" The delivery of keys is also the source of greatest problems on closing. Everyone knows that buyers want their keys promptly, so they can start unloading the moving van. In most resale transactions, keys are delivered to the buyer's lawyer at the registry office on closing. Meeting with your lawyer a day before closing and delivering the closing proceeds at that time are crucial, if the keys are to be available as early as possible the day of closing. Yet it is impossible to guarantee a precise time when keys will be available, since the seller's lawyer may be unable to close the transaction until later in the day. Even after closing, buyers still must await the delivery of keys to their lawyer's office from the registry office. Realistically, then, buyers should not expect keys to be available until mid-afternoon the day of closing at the earliest.

As this is inconvenient to many buyers, they are encouraged before closing to make alternative arrangements for keys. Try to keep the keys in the vicinity of the property, for pick up after closing. Sometimes buyers receive the keys directly from the seller when he has completely moved out of the house. With advance planning, the keys can be picked up from a trusting neighbor, or the real estate agent. Some buyers will even go to the registry office to get the keys from their lawyer immediately after closing. Remember to tell your lawyer about the alternative plans for keys. Arrangements like these should be made several days before closing.

Occasionally buyers receive keys to the property *before* the transaction closes. Although making alternative arrangements to get keys on closing is recommended, moving into the house prior to closing is risky, and is never recommended, no matter how annoying this may appear. By doing so, the purchaser is considered to have waived all outstanding title deficiencies which in effect forces you to close the transaction. More importantly, you, as purchaser, immediately assume liability for the house and anyone entering it. What happens if a mover injures himself before the deed is registered? The potential problems could be horrendous. Prudent buyers will never use the keys to the house until the deal has closed.

Often only one key is given to the buyer on closing. Any other keys can be found in the house, usually on the kitchen counter.

When does a seller like Sam have to vacate the property? When can the buyer like Brian move in? Immediate access to the property is a pressing concern to all buyers, except those who are bridge financing their purchase, or who are keeping their apartment for several days after closing.

Practically speaking, courtesy and cooperation is the answer. Of course, before Brian is legally entitled to possession, the deal must close and the deed to him must be registered. Rarely do either Sam or Brian know precisely the moment that this will happen. While their lawyers/conveyancers are in the registry office attending to this, Sam and Brian could be anywhere — in the process of moving, at work, in a car, even at lunch. Obviously Sam will need a certain amount of time to vacate the premises too. Despite what anyone may say, few delays by sellers on closing day are deliberate. Most sellers like Sam are just as anxious to get out of their old house and into their new house as Brian is to move into Sam's old house. Typically, sellers vacate a property by early afternoon, and the buyer can start moving in at that time, if the deal has closed by then.

Buyers do benefit, though, through courtesy and cooperation. On his lawyer's recommendation, Brian spoke to Sam the night before closing and made arrangements to get the keys directly from Sam. At 12:30 P.M., Sam was notified that the deed to Brian had been registered. On moving out at 1:15 P.M., Sam gave his keys to Brian who began moving in immediately.

Most offers say the seller shall give vacant possession of the property to the buyer on completion, without specifying the time either when the deal should close, or when vacant possession must be available. Must the seller have moved out completely by the time set for closing? Can buyers like Phil recover from sellers like Vince any additional costs incurred, especially the extra amount paid to the mover, if Vince moves out after the deed to Phil is registered? To the surprise of many buyers, the answer is no. Unless the offer contains a specific time when the deal must be completed or vacant possession must be available, technically speaking the seller can deliver vacant possession to the buyer at any time up to 11:59 P.M. the day of closing. That being the case, it would be impossible for Phil to recover damages from Vince if keys were delivered to him at any time during the day of closing. Even more reason why buyers should — no *must* — cooperate with sellers.

Communications are a two-way street. As much as clients want information from lawyers on closing, lawyers will have information to relay to, and possibly questions to ask of, their clients. Plainly put, a buyer's lawyer must be able to reach the buyer *at all times during the day of closing.* Some people remain at work, and are easy to reach. Many, though, move the actual day of closing, and will be unavailable for extended periods of time. The change-over in telephones is one reason; running errands is another. In that situation, give your lawyer the phone number of someone who can reach you, quickly, despite the day's activities. A relative, a neighbor — at the old home, the new home, or both — or even a friend at work are more than adequate. Then check in periodically with your contact, to see what is happening, or has happened! With developments at the registry office and the move happening independently, buyer and lawyer must keep in touch during the day — either directly or indirectly. Everyone wants to avoid the situation where the deal has closed, but the buyer cannot be reached! Coordination of communications is important for closing day!

# 31

## *After Closing — A Buyer's Work Is Not Yet Done*

To most buyers like Ronald and Nancy, getting into their house seemed like a titan struggle. So much has happened since they first went house-hunting several months ago. Now that they own the house, Ronald and Nancy feel it's time to sit back, relax and enjoy it. True, but not yet. Much still has to be done as part of "the move," besides simply unpacking those mountains of boxes.

Several obvious items must be attended to first. Few resale houses are in "move-in condition." Walls may have to be painted or wallpapered, while floors and carpets may need cleaning. Minor repairs may be required. The benefit of closing now and moving in later — the overlap for tenants or bridge financing for existing home owners — soon becomes apparent. Cleaning and painting a vacant home is much easier and saves an enormous amount of time, compared to moving furniture and boxes from room to room. To move in first, and then spruce it up, parallels putting the cart before the horse.

Every buyer of a resale property should change the locks (or at least the tumblers) for all doors immediately after closing. While several keys may have been delivered on closing or left in the house itself, who knows how many other keys remain in the hands of friends, neighbors, relations, in-laws, babysitters and children of the former owner? Securing your home properly should start by changing the locks. Seriously consider upgrading the system at this time by installing deadbolt locks instead.

Notify *everyone* of your change of address. Start with the post office, which charges a nominal sum to redirect mail for several months to the new address. If the redirect period is insufficient, then renew it on its expiry. Change of address cards are available at the post office as well, for friends, neighbors and relations.

Sometimes the hardest job is deciding exactly who to contact with the change of address. An easy solution is to list all mail received for at least a month before closing. Appearing on the list this way will be credit card companies, magazines, the doctor and dentist, health insurance plan and banks. A quick flip through your wallet will help add several more names to your list. *Be sure to notify the provincial department of transport of your change of address both for your car ownership and your driver's licence, within the required time, usually less than a week.* Failing to do so could lead to a fine.

Diarize two weeks after closing as the day interest on the deposit should be received, if arranged in the offer. If nothing has been received by then, contact your lawyer.

List the names and addresses of people and companies to be sent a change of address card. Every time a name is recalled, mark it down. Once notice has been mailed, tick off the completed column.

Expect to receive the formal reporting from your lawyer about a month after closing. Some lawyers will send out an interim report right after closing, containing highlights about upcoming payments. You should list the names, addresses, payment dates, amounts payable and account numbers for those expenses coming up in the first month after closing (see chart below). If no interim report is mailed, call your lawyer for this information as soon as possible after closing.

| | Payment Dates | Name | Address | Amount Payable | Account Number |
|---|---|---|---|---|---|
| First mortgage | | | | | |
| Second mortgage | | | | | |

Realty Taxes

Condominium
Maintenance

Other items

When a transaction closes in the early months of a year, the adjustment for taxes is based on the amount levied for taxes the prior year. If closing takes place before the final tax bill for the year is issued, contact your lawyer during the summer about the possible readjustment of realty taxes in your favor.

Many essential items will be needed in the days and weeks following closing, if not already owned. While this list is not exhaustive, items to acquire include garbage cans; snow shovel; lawn mower and other lawn accessories; rake; hose and nozzle; sprinkler; shears; lawn fertilizer and spreader; household tools and supplies, such as a hammer, wrench, pliers, screwdrivers, nails and screws; and rock salt or sand to remove ice. Get to know the owner of the local hardware store. You will be seeing much of him the first few months after closing!

As soon as possible after closing, obtain the following emergency numbers, especially if you have changed communities. Place them near your phone. The time to look them up is now, not when you need them.

Police

Fire

Ambulance

Hospital

# 32

# *Facts to Know About Owning a Home*

From the moment an offer is accepted, a purchaser must become an instant expert on strange new topics. Consider this chapter a primer on these points.

## Title

One of the first questions a buyer will face once the offer is accepted, is how he proposes "taking title" to the property. In everyday English, the lawyer really wants to know how the buyer will be described in the deed and on title. To simply say "co-owners" is not sufficient, as several different types of co-ownership exist. More must be known about your intentions, especially in the event of death.

### i) Joint Tenancy

The first thing to know about holding title as joint tenants is that it has absolutely nothing to do with being a tenant! Where a husband and wife decide to take title together, they usually do so as joint tenants. This provides the survivorship arrangement most married couples want. If one joint tenant dies, the property automatically goes to the surviving joint tenant. Harvey and Laura took title to their house as joint tenants. If Harvey dies, Laura automatically will own it outright, by the mere fact she survived Harvey. The house would not even be included as an asset of Harvey's estate, to be distributed according to his will. Property passes on a joint tenancy *before* the assets of the deceased's estate are distributed. If Laura were to die while Harvey is still alive, the reverse holds true. By the mere fact of death, title to the property passes automatically to the survivor. While joint tenancy is not limited to husband and wife situations, its practical use elsewhere is extremely limited.

### ii) Tenants in Common

Again, this expression has nothing to do with tenancy. Taking title as tenants in common means the named parties own equal shares of the property. Tenants in common is often used where two or more unrelated people such as common-law couples, business associates or persons living in shared accommodations own a property together. Mick and Carol are living together, unmarried, and took title as tenants in common. Automatically each owns a 50 percent share of the property, which can be sold to someone else, if desired. As the survivorship rules do not apply to a tenancy in common, on his death Mick's share of the property may go to someone other than his co-owner. On Mick's death, his share of the property passes either to the beneficiary named in his will, or to the beneficiary entitled to his estate by law if no will exists. His share does not automatically pass to Carol, as it would in a joint tenancy situation. Having named Vic as beneficiary in his will, Vic and Carol now become co-owners of the property on Mick's death, as tenants in common.

If the respective shares are not owned 50/50, then the title should reflect this fact. For example, Carol may hold a 60 percent interest in the property, while Mick owns 40 percent of it.

### iii) One Name Only

Where either a husband or wife is self-employed, title to the matrimonial home is usually registered in the name of the other spouse. That is exactly what Dave (who is self-employed) and Bonnie did when they bought their home — Bonnie became the sole registered owner of the property. The theory behind this arrangement is quite simple. If Dave's business encounters financial difficulty, the matrimonial home could not be seized and sold by his creditors, as Bonnie, not Dave, owns the home. In short, the house is protected from creditors.

### iv) Family Law Reform

In those provinces which have introduced family law reform legislation, it is very difficult for the spouse who owns the matrimonial home (the titled spouse) to sell, mortgage or even lease it without the written consent of the other spouse. In Ontario, for example, Bonnie could not sell, mortgage or lease the matrimonial home without Dave's written spousal consent. The need for Dave to consent to any dealings does not mean that Dave has any *property* rights in it. All Dave has is a *personal* right to remain in the home until he consents to any transaction affecting it. The distinction between property rights and personal rights is crucial.

Practically speaking, under family law reform legislation, when a matrimonial home is involved, no matter who the registered owner is, both spouses (both Dave and Bonnie) must sign all documents if it is to be sold, mortgaged or leased. If Dave and Bonnie both own it, both must sign the deed and convey the property. If Bonnie is the sole titled spouse, Bonnie signs the deed as owner and Dave signs the deed to grant his spousal consent, releasing his personal rights to the property. The same holds true in reverse if only Dave and not Bonnie was the sole registered owner.

Spousal consent replaced the ancient English concept of dower. While dower protected only women, spousal consent applies to both men and women. Not all properties are affected in this matter; only the matrimonial home. Therefore if Bonnie owns an investment property in her own name, she can sell it without obtaining Dave's spousal consent, provided it is not occupied by both of them as their matrimonial home.

## Squatter's Rights

A legacy inherited from the English system of land law is the notion of "adverse possession," commonly called squatter's rights. People are constantly wondering whether they can gain (or lose) title to a piece of land this way. The problem with squatter's rights arises as fences are not always erected where they should be, precisely along the boundary line. Sometimes they are located to its right or left. Occasionally a portion of a building — an eavestrough or roof overhang — encroaches onto another person's property as well. Taking the statement "possession is nine-tenths of the law" to the limit, adverse possession prevents landowners from recovering land after a fixed period of time, usually 10 years. For possessory title to be gained or lost this way, the occupation and possession by the so-called "squatter" must be continuous and undisputed, to the exclusion of the registered owner.

Consider the situation of an improperly placed fence, that is located 1 foot north of the boundary line between the properties. According to the doctrine of adverse possession, if the owner of the property to the south can establish the quality of possessory title required by law for the required period of time, he can gain title to the area between the property line and the fence.

The concept of adverse possession has been abolished in many parts of the country, where a newer land registration system has been instituted. If this is the case, the owner of the northern parcel never would lose title to the area in dispute, no matter how long the fence has existed in its present location. Only by checking with your lawyer can you learn if this is the case. Finally, only a court of law can determine possessory title. Until then, home owners may think they own property by squatter's rights, but that is not strictly the case.

## Construction Liens (Mechanics' Liens)

Practically every home owner at some time hires a tradesman to do some work on their property. Stuart and Lily might put an addition onto the house, or Frank and Josephine might finish their basement. Both the tradesmen who work on the property as well as the suppliers of material add value to property. If they are unpaid for their efforts, provincial legislation gives them the right to place a lien on the property. Where the nonpayment continues, the property can even be sold to satisfy the outstanding debt, provided the legislation is strictly complied with. This lien, previously known as a mehanics' lien but now called a construction lien, prevents owners of land from realizing a windfall, having work done and materials supplied at their request, without paying for it.

The area of construction liens is one of the most confusing and least understood areas of the law as it affects home ownership. Anyone contemplating any major work to his property would be wise to read and reread the following paragraphs until the complexities sink in. Perhaps a meeting with your lawyer would be in order to review and understand the relevant legislation. A mistake, misunderstanding, or miscalculation, however innocent or unintentional, may end up costing the home owner money.

Bruce and Sandra are having their basement finished. Total cost: $10,000. Under the construction lien legislation, when work is done or materials are supplied to a property, as home owners they are obligated to withhold a set percentage of the price of the services and materials as they are actually supplied under the contract (generally called the value of the work done) until a fixed number of days after work on the contract is substantially completed. The amount of money retained in this fashion is known as the holdback. Under the older acts, the holdback was 15 percent of the value of the work done, and the holdback period was 37 days from the date of substantial completion. The newer construction lien acts have reduced the holdback to 10 percent of the value of the work done, while extending the holdback period to 45 days. Once the holdback period expires, the holdback can be released, provided no construction liens have been registered against the title to the property.

Why the holdback? Who benefits from it? In most construction situations, a general contractor is hired by the owner of a property to do the work. The general contractor in turn hires subtrades (subs) to perform individual and specific components of the overall contract. This is the scenario in Bruce and Sandra's situation. They signed a contract with General Contractors, who in turn hired the necessary subs — drywall, electrical, plumbing and so on. While Bruce and Sandra may pay money to General Contractors on schedule, that is no assurance that General Contractors will pay the subs in a timely manner, or at all. Everyone has heard horror stories of how contractors abscond with funds, or end up going bankrupt. If all money that could be released at any point in time was paid to the general contractor, this would leave absolutely nothing for the subs. With a construction lien holdback, the subs are guaranteed of getting some money from the construction project should the general contractor default in honoring its contracts with them. Of course, the subs still can sue the general contractor for the difference owing, if it still exists and is solvent. The holdback, then, is money retained by the owner of the property by law for the benefit and protection of the subtrades.

Buyers planning home renovations after closing must be familiar with their obligations under the relevant legislation, and their potential liability for noncompliance. In Ontario, for example, payment representing only 90 percent of the value of the work done at any point in time can be released without jeopardy to a general contractor until the expiry of the 45-day holdback period. For major projects, an architect issues a certificate periodically, stating the value of the work done, facilitating the release of funds. In smaller jobs, where no architect is involved, determining the value of the work done, and whether a contract has been substantially completed, depends on the circumstances of each specific case. Complicating the situation is the fact most small contracts contain a payment schedule stating what percentage of the contract price is to be paid at various stages of construction. Often the amount payable this way exceeds the value of the work done at that point in time. The consequences and liability for a home owner could be horrendous.

When Bruce and Sandra signed their $10,000 contract, General Contractors, like most contractors, required a sizeable deposit. Five percent of the contract price was paid on signing the contract, and a further 20 percent when work started. This was needed, of course, to buy materials. According to the payment schedule, a further 35 percent was to be paid when the wood frame was erected, and a further 25 percent when the drywall went on. The final 15 percent was to be paid on completion. No mention of holdbacks appeared in the contract. Also the percentages payable were based on the contract price, *not* on the actual value of the work done. As the progress payments exceeded the value of the work done at any point in time, Bruce and Sandra placed themselves at considerable risk.

Once they had paid 25 percent of the contract price to General Contractors, Bruce and Sandra already had paid too much money by law. If the material suppliers or initial tradesmen working on the house remained unpaid, they would have the right to register a lien against the property. Although $2,500 had been paid on the contract, assume the value of the work done was only $1,000. This meant that Bruce and Sandra should have paid only 90 percent of the $1,000 or $900 to General Contractors. If the property was liened by a subtrade for nonpayment by General Contractors, Bruce and Sandra can forget about the $1,500 paid in excess of the value of the work done. They paid it at their jeopardy, and now must absorb the loss. In addition, Bruce and Sandra still are responsible for the 10 percent holdback (or $100) for the subtrades based on the value of the work done. This is money that will have to be paid, in effect, a second time. Total cost of their mistake: $1,500 overpaid plus $100 still to be paid, for a total of $1,600.

To avoid problems like these, never give the contractor a large sum of money up front as a deposit. When he states he needs considerable funds to purchase materials, only give him the amount of money needed to buy the initial materials. Alternatively, offer to pay for the initial delivery of materials yourself. Since less money is paid to the contractor directly, and since you and not the contractor own those materials, the likelihood of problems is lessened.

Double jeopardy is also possible during the course of construction. Assume the electrician registered the first lien on the project when $8,500 had been paid to General Contractors according to the payment schedule. In actual fact, the value of the work done was $6,000. General Contractors then abandoned the contract. Assuming Bruce and Sandra could get another contractor to finish the job for $4,000, the total amount they would be paying for the basement renovations is $13,100, made up as follows: a) the $8,500 paid on the old contract; b) the $4,000 to be paid on the new contract; c) the $600 that should have been, but was not, held back, for which they continue to be responsible. Granted they have legal recourse against General Contractors for the $3,100, if it can be found and if it still has any money.

Most contractors insist on being paid in full once the contract is completed. *Never pay a construction contract in full at that stage.* Contractors rarely volunteer the information that a 10 percent holdback is necessary for 45 days after the contract is substantially completed. Don't be afraid to tell a contractor what are your legal obligations, and that you will be retaining 10 percent of the contract price (which is now the value of the work done) until the holdback period expires. If Bruce and Sandra pay the full contract price on completion, and a lien is registered within the 45-day period, they would have to pay the $1,000 represented by the holdback a second time.

Full discussion and agreement on how much money will be paid, when, and the question of holdbacks is necessary *before* the contract is signed. If necessary, amend the contractor's standard form agreement to say that you shall hold back all amounts required by law, for the periods of time required by law. If the contractor objects, don't deal with him. Also, don't accept his argument that you as owner can waive your construction lien rights, and that his quotation is lower than usual because there will be no holdbacks. Plain and simple, by law owners must retain the statutory holdback for the prescribed period of time, as it benefits the subtrades and not the contractor. It is an absolute duty which cannot be waived. That bargain could cost more than expected!

To be absolutely sure no liens have been registered, and that the holdback can be paid out at no peril, title to the property should be subsearched or quickly reviewed once the lien holdback period expires. The cost involved is small, compared to the peace of mind it brings.

## Realty Taxes

Realty (or property) taxes are collected by most municipalities in two stages, an interim bill and a final bill. Jack and Jill paid realty taxes of $1,000 in 1985. The interim taxes for 1986 will be one-half of this amount, or $500. Issued early in 1986, the interim tax bill is payable in two, three or four equal instalments, depending on the municipality. Once the final taxes have been determined, usually in late spring or early summer, the final tax bill is issued, again payable over several instalments. As their taxes went up 5 percent, or $50, their total 1986 taxes will be $1,050. With $500 having been paid on account, the amount payable on the final tax bill is $550.

Until a few years ago, nonpayment of property tax was an inexpensive way to borrow money. The interest penalty charged on overdue taxes was well below the current rate for bank loans. Today overdue instalments bear interest at rates similar to those charged elsewhere in the marketplace.

Looking at the other side of the coin, some municipalities give a discount for early payment of tax instalments. It could be to your advantage, then, to prepay your taxes. Check it out.

Upon receiving their tax bill, whether interim or final, many home owners send post-dated cheques to the tax department, payable the dates the instalments fall due. Interest penalties arising from late payments can be avoided this way.

Unpaid realty taxes place a strain on a municipality, as all other taxpayers must shoulder the financial burden of not receiving anticipated revenue. To ensure that municipalities collect the money justly owing to them, unpaid property taxes are a special lien against the property, ranking even higher than a first mortgage! As they wish to remain at the top of the totem-pole at all times, many mortgage lenders collect a portion of the estimated annual realty taxes from borrowers with each mortgage payment. Taxes are then paid to the municipality by the lender as the tax bills are issued, from the realty tax account it maintains.

## Utilities

Like realty taxes, unpaid municipal hydro and water charges can be enforced as a lien against a property. This approach is fair, because if the land benefitting from the utility does not bear the burden, the cost would have to be absorbed by all other

users of the service. Lien rights do not exist in favor of telephone companies, privately owned gas companies or cable
television systems.

## Land Registry Systems

In old England, the title to property was established by delivering a deed box to buyers, containing all previous deeds to the
property. When the earliest land registry statutes were enacted
in Canada, allowing the registration and recording of deeds
and mortgages, this principle was continued with one important variation. Now the provincial government maintained a
deed box in each county, where everyone could store his
contents. To establish good title, it still was necessary to search
the historical records of title for many years. Over time, a new
land registration system was introduced, simplifying considerably the searching of titles. The older format is known as
the "registry system" while the newer scheme is called "land
titles."

The development of a new land registration system has also
resulted in changes in generally accepted terminology. Traditionally, the document by which land was transferred was
known as a deed. Money was borrowed by issuing a mortgage.
Both could easily be identified with the words "This Inden-
ture" which appeared at the top of the first page. Replacing
these terms in the newer system are the expressions "transfer"
and "charge." While the legal effect of these documents is
slightly different from their predecessors, what they represent
to the public is the same.

It is impossible, simply by looking at two adjacent properties
or two different streets, to determine which land registration
system applies. Whether a particular property is governed by
one system or the other is immaterial, although searching titles
in the land titles system is considerably easier.

Many a home owner, like Maurice and Martha, unable to
locate their deed, have grown panicky, fearing a loss of their
property. Rest easy, obtaining replacement proof of ownership
is not difficult. Two copies of every deed are signed by the seller
and delivered on closing. The buyer receives one copy, while

the second copy is filed at the registry office, where it is permanently recorded and stored or microfilmed. As the provincial government — the owner of the deed box — is the keeper of everyone's deeds, it is very easy for Maurice and Martha to obtain a copy of their deed. Practically speaking, Maurice and Martha slept much better once they had the certified copy in hand.

Most people are astonished to learn that registry offices are halls of public records. Armed with a legal description obtained from the tax office anyone can learn a world of information about a property — the price paid for it, details of mortgage financing, and even the name of the registered owner — for a nominal charge. So much for confidentiality!

# 33

# *Urea Formaldehyde Foam Insulation*

Urea formaldehyde foam insulation (UFFI) was used to re-insulate the walls of older homes, starting in Canada in the mid-1960s. Its heyday was reached in the late 1970s, when the Canadian government under the CHIP Program (Canadian Home Insulation Program) offered government grants of up to $500 as an incentive to re-insulate certain homes. One of the approved forms of insulation was UFFI. With growing reports that formaldehyde gas seepage was causing health problems, its use was permanently banned by the federal government on December 17, 1980. An estimated 80,000 homes were insulated with UFFI before its ban. (See "UFFI: Acceptance of the Unacceptable Product," by Lloyd Tataryn, *Canadian Consumer Magazine,* Vol 14, Num. 6, June, 1984, page 35.) While selling a home with UFFI is not illegal, it obviously has a substantially reduced market value. In Ontario, for example, assessments for UFFI-insulated homes have been reduced by up to 30 percent. Since few buyers of resale properties would knowingly purchase a UFFI-insulated home, it then becomes critical to discover whether or not a particular home has been insulated with UFFI.

All homes built since 1981 will not have UFFI in their walls. In most resale real estate transactions, vendors give a warranty that the property is not and never has been insulated with UFFI. Although this would appear to resolve the question, it actually creates more problems than it answers.

If the person selling the house to you owned it throughout the entire period of time when UFFI was an acceptable insulator, he knows firsthand that UFFI was never injected into the walls. Rarely, however, is this the case. What if the property sold to Archie and Edith in 1980 is being resold by them now? Do they absolutely know that the property was not insulated with UFFI? They probably are relying on what they were told by the previous owner. Was the previous owner certain? As properties continue to change hands over time, and a pile of "UFFI warranties" are built up, it will be increasingly difficult for subsequent owners to know conclusively — and warrant beyond question on a sale — whether or not UFFI was used as a home insulator in a particular property. Over time, the UFFI warranty may be worth little more than the paper it is printed on.

Furthermore, this type of warranty only may allow a buyer to sue the seller for damages after closing, and not to back out of the deal, even if it is learned before closing that the house was insulated with UFFI. Unless the buyer can show that the seller's failure to disclose the presence of UFFI was a fradulent misrepresentation (and fraud is very difficult to prove), the transaction will not be invalidated. Of course, establishing this can only be done at a trial, held long after the scheduled closing date. The buyer then faces a real dilemma and a certain lawsuit: does he refuse to close, hoping he can establish fraudulent misrepresentation when he sues the seller? Of course, the buyer also runs the risk of being sued by the seller for not closing as scheduled. Or does the buyer close the transaction for the UFFI-filled home (to avoid being sued by the seller), and sue the seller for damages after closing? A quandary indeed.

Many homes insulated with UFFI have acceptably safe levels of formaldehyde. Tests can be performed to establish the exposure limit, and whether it meets current maximum acceptable UFFI standards (0.1 parts per million for dwellings). Anyone knowingly and willingly buying a UFFI home will want to make his offer conditional on acceptably safe readings being taken immediately after the offer is signed, immediately before the deal closes, and perhaps even in the interim.

To increase their marketability, some owners of homes

insulated with UFFI are having it removed from the walls and retested for acceptably safe levels. An inspection report will be issued by a federally-approved inspector, that the home conforms with government standards. As in the case of UFFI-insulated homes, the offer should be made conditional on acceptably safe levels being attained at the same three intervals.

Remember, though, that even homes not insulated with UFFI will have formaldehyde levels when tested. Formaldehyde is released by certain building products like particle board, aerosol products, natural gas furnaces and tobacco smoke. No one can live in a formaldehyde-free environment. It is all a question of degree.

To be assured that a property does not have UFFI, it must be inspected for UFFI. Without opening up the walls of a house, a home inspector cannot tell conclusively whether UFFI is present in the walls of a house. Often, though, a visual inspection will indicate if UFFI was used as an insulator. Inspectors look for drill holes in the exterior brick work, where UFFI was injected into the walls. Evidence of foam may be found near electrical outlets, or around the foundation wall. In most cases, home inspectors can detect the presence of UFFI in a home. Yet they still qualify their reports, saying "no evidence of UFFI was noted upon visually inspecting the home."

Buyers prepared to spend extra money can have the air quality tested in the wall cavities. This requires the seller's consent, as it involves drilling directly into the wall cavities. Only this test can absolutely guarantee that UFFI has not been used as an insulator.

Buyers of properties built before 1981 who are concerned that the property is not and never has been insulated with UFFI should do the following: 1) insert a condition into the offer (not a warranty as is usually done) that the property is not and never has been insulated with UFFI. Because this is a condition and not a warranty, discovery of UFFI before closing will enable the purchaser to back out of the transaction without penalty; 2) have a home inspector independently verify that UFFI never has been used as an insulator. Be sure to tell the inspector the importance of this test and how the whole transaction may hinge on his report.

Homes insulated with UFFI still can qualify for a mortgage.

Lenders will insist that the loan be insured with Canada Mortgage and Housing Corporation, no matter how much equity the buyer has in the property. Providing this insurance to protect the lender is expensive, up to 2.5 percent of the amount borrowed.

The existence of UFFI in a home is one of those items that a vendor must disclose in an offer. Prudent buyers will ask about it, and have the appropriate clause inserted into the offer. Still, buyers applying their home buying strategy also will have the house inspected and tested for urea formaldehyde foam insulation.

# 34

# Tax and the Canadian Home Owner

Most Canadians know that an owner-occupied home is exempt from capital gains tax when sold. A number of other, less well-known provisions of the Income Tax Act (called the Act in this chapter) also could be relevant, depending on a buyer's particular circumstances. Everyone buying a home must have a basic understanding of how our tax system works, and its impact on home ownership.

## Principal Residence Exemption

Profit made on the sale of a "principal residence" is exempt from capital gains tax. The term principal residence includes a housing unit (house, apartment, duplex or triplex, condominium, cottage or mobile home), or a share of a cooperative housing corporation, whether owned personally or with another person. To be tax-exempt in any given year, it must have been "ordinarily inhabited" in that year by the taxpayer, his spouse or his dependent child who must be less than age 21, over age 21 and dependent by reason of mental or physical infirmity, or over age 21 and in full-time attendance at school or university. The taxpayer also must have been resident in Canada each year in which the exemption is claimed. Qualifying for the exemption are both the building and the land immediately surrounding the building that could reasonably be regarded as contributing to the use and enjoyment of the housing unit. The maximum amount of land allowed to qualify this way is one-half hectare (about 1.23 acres).

Technically speaking, for a home to be exempt from capital gains tax as a principal residence, it must be designated as a principal residence by the taxpayer each year. Revenue Canada Taxation, though, only requires that the designation be filed the year the property is sold, stating what years it covers.

What does the term in the Act "ordinarily inhabited" in the year mean? There is no minimum time period during which the property must be owner-occupied. To qualify, the property need not have been ordinarily inhabited for the entire year either. To meet the test, the usual and accepted signs of occupancy must have been present, involving both the property and the owner. Therefore, actual physical use and enjoyment of the property to the knowledge of others is crucial. For example, home owners normally have their mail, bills and subscriptions directed to the property, while updating the address on their driver's licence. Usually it is very easy for a person actually occupying a home to establish that he or she ordinarily inhabited it.

Starting with 1982, only one housing unit could be designated as a principal residence per family per year, even if more than one property was owned and inhabited during the year. This killed the pre-1982 scheme where married couples had separate principal residences, Carole owning the cottage and Larry owning the city home, each being exempt from capital gains tax when sold. Married couples could have had two principal residences this way, to double-up on the exemption. Yet the changes introduced in the 1985 federal budget ($500,000 capital gains exemption by 1990) have breathed new life into this type of arrangement. Properly structured, Larry would own the city home, the one principal residence allowed between them that is exempt from capital gains tax. While the cottage registered in Carole's name would be subject to capital gains tax on its sale, the capital gains (or a portion of it, depending on when the sale took place) to Carole would be exempt from tax.

If only one home was "owner-occupied" in a year, this will be the principal residence for that year. What happens when home owners sell their home and move to another during the year? The formula in the Act for calculating the principal residence exemption acknowledges this, by including a so-called "bonus year." For most taxpayers the formula is:

Exempt gain = $\dfrac{1 + \text{the number of years in which the property was a principal residence, and during which the taxpayer resided in Canada}}{\text{the number of years during which the taxpayer owned the property}} \times$ capital gain

Jeff bought a house in 1983, lived in it continuously, sold it in 1986 for a $15,000 gain, and bought another owner-occupied house that same year. According to the formula, he should designate the old home as his principal residence for the years 1983, 1984 and 1985. Although only one property can be designated as a principal residence each year, Jeff still can designate his new home as his principal residence for 1986 without incurring any capital gains tax on the sale of his old home. Jeff's formula looks like this:

Exempt gain = $\dfrac{1 + 3 \text{ (the years 1983, 1984 and 1985)}}{4} \times \$15,000$

= \$15,000

As Jeff realized, it is better to designate the new house and not the old house as the principal residence in the year of the changeover to take full advantage of the "bonus year" in the formula.

Inter-spousal transfers of property (from one spouse to the other, from both spouses to one spouse, or from one spouse to both spouses) do not trigger capital gains tax. Any tax payable is deferred until the property is sold to an outsider, following which tax is collected for the combined period of ownership. If the property always was a principal residence during that time, then no capital gains tax is payable. Peter bought a house in 1976, and transferred it to Lydia in 1982. She sold it in 1986. As it was a principal residence for the entire 10-year period, the $30,000 gain was totally exempt from tax.

Whether a transfer of property to a child triggers capital gains tax, depends on how it was used by the parent prior to its transfer. In the most common situation, a parent like Lou transfers his home to his son, Ted, who uses it as his own principal residence. No tax is payable on the transfer by Lou, it having been his principal residence. No capital gains tax will be payable by Ted either, if it continues to be his principal residence. Capital gains tax would be payable by Lou (subject to the 1985 exemption) if the property had not been Lou's principal residence before the transfer.

The Act is a two-sided coin. Profits from the sale of a principal residence are not subject to capital gains tax. For that reason, any loss incurred on selling a principal residence is not deductible from other income. You can't have it both ways!

## Divided Use Deduction

Some houses are used for more than one purpose at the same time. Very often, home owners like Annie use the main and second floors as a principal residence while renting out the basement, an income-producing use. All rent received must be included in Annie's income, while expenses incurred *specifically* in earning that rental income are deductible from her income. These expenses include bookkeeping costs and the cost of newspaper ads. In addition, that portion of the expenses incurred for the building *as a whole*, such as realty taxes, insurance, mortgage interest, heating and utilities, which can reasonably be attributed to the rental use of the property, also can be deducted from Annie's income. Deciding how much of the property is used for rental purposes (and therefore the proportion of the building expenses that are deductible from other income) commonly is based on either the number of total rooms rented, or the percentage of the total square footage that is rented.

Irv rented two rooms in his eight-room house for a monthly charge of $150 each. During the year, he spent $80 in advertising to rent the space. His gross income will be $150 monthly for each room, $300 per month, or $3,600 for the year. His net income will be $3,600 less the $80 in expenses, less a further one-quarter of the overall expenses for the house.

When part of a home is rented out, the principal residence exemption for the whole house can be maintained, if and only if no capital cost allowance (depreciation) is claimed on the rented portion of the house. Revenue Canada Taxation permits this arrangement, even though part of the property is being used for a non-principal residence purpose — to produce rental income. If depreciation is claimed on the rental portion of the property, capital gains tax may be payable on the portion of the house rented out, when it is sold.

## Change of Use Exemption

Property used as a prinicipal residence may, for any number of reasons, be converted entirely into income-producing property. When John was transferred to a new job out of town recently, he decided to rent his home rather than sell it. Similarly, Gary rented his old home (a principal residence) rather than sell it when he bought a new home, which he designated as his principal residence. Despite the anticipated capital gains consequences, the Act provides a limited exemption for changes of use, when a former principal residence is converted into income-producing property.

On his tax return for the year the change of use occurred, 1986, Gary must file a special election which deems the change of use not to have occured. To do this, Gary must sign a letter that contains a description of the property, and state that he is making the change of use election. Then, Gary can designate his former home as his principal residence for 1986, and continue this designation for three more years after that, even though Gary does not live there any more. *Gary can do this, even though he will be designating his new home as his principal residence as well during those four years.* While this change of use election is in effect, Gary cannot claim capital cost allowance (depreciation) for the property against the rental income received. Still, taxpayers like Gary who rent out a former principal residence, can have two principal residences, in effect, for up to four years!

During that four-year period, Gary can sell his former principal residence, and the total capital gains will be exempt from tax. After the four-year exemption has lapsed, his former principal residence can only retain that designation if Gary actually uses it again as his principal residence. The four-year limitation period can be extended in very limited circumstances.

Of course, with the changes in the treatment of capital gains tax introduced in the 1985 budget, any capital gains otherwise subject to tax after the four-year period expires, still could be exempt from capital gains tax. Many new avenues for creative planning are now available, in the wake of the $500,000 lifetime capital gains exemption.

To be able to continue the principal residence designation this way despite a change of use, the taxpayer must continue to be a resident of Canada.

## Mortgage Interest Deductibility

Interest paid on a mortgage arranged to finance the purchase of a principal residence is not deductible from other income. Interest paid on a mortgage arranged to finance the purchase of rented property is a deductible expense. If part of a house is rented, the divided use situation, a proportionate share of the mortgage interest will be deductible from rental income.

Canadians in some situations can deduct the interest expense on their home mortgages. To do this, a mortgage must be arranged for an unequivocal and unambiguous business or investment purpose. Further information on making mortgage interest deductible in Canada appears in *Hidden Profits in Your Mortgage.*

## Moving Expense Deduction

Canadians who move to a new community may be able to deduct their moving expenses from income earned at the new loation. To do this

- your move must be employment related, to a new location in Canada, even if for the same employer. Examples are a company transfer, change of job, or moving your place of business;
- your new residence must be at least 40 kilometres (25 miles) closer than your old residence to the new place of business or employment;
- your employment or business at the old location ceases.

Ian was transferred by his employer from Montreal to Calgary. All reasonable amounts Ian paid in moving himself, his family and his household effects can be deducted from his income earned at the new location. These include travelling costs; meals and lodging on route; transportation and storage costs; up to fifteen days' temporary board and lodging near either residence; costs incurred in breaking an unexpired lease; costs incurred in selling a former home, including legal fees and disbursements, real estate commission and any prepayment penalty incurred; as well as legal fees and disbursements incurred on the purchase of the new home, provided the old property is sold. Receipts must be kept, in case an audit is conducted. Where an employer picks up the full cost of the move or reimburses the employee for the full cost, no amount is deductible. Any partial reimbursement must be applied to reduce the amount of the income-tax deduction. Marvin recently incurred $5,000 in expenses when moving from Vancouver to Toronto. As he received $3,500 from his employer, Marvin can deduct only $1,500 from the income earned at the new location.

Moves into and out of Canada do not qualify for the moving expense deduction.

## Buying From A Non-Resident Vendor

Anyone purchasing property must determine the residency status of the vendor for income-tax purposes, as non-resident vendors are taxed differently when selling property. When a resident Canadian sells property, usually this is satisfied by the delivery of an affidavit to that effect on closing.

When the vendor is a non-resident, purchasers have a legal obligation to protect the interests of Revenue Canada Taxation. For the transaction to proceed as scheduled, the non-resident vendor must deliver a prescribed certificate from Revenue Canada Taxation on closing. Otherwise, the purchaser is obligated by law to withhold 15 percent of the purchas price, and send it to Revenue Canada Taxation. There it will be applied towards any income-tax liability the non-resident vendor may have. The penalty imposed on buyers who do not comply with this requirement is harsh. Although the entire purchase price was already paid to the non-resident vendor, the purchaser will have to pay an additional 15 percent of the purchase price to the government, presumably from his or her own pocket! Ignorance is no defence. Buyers cannot afford to turn a blind eye to the issue of non-resident vendors, if only for the penalty involved.

Most standard form offers state the rights and obligations of both seller and buyer when a non-resident sells property.

Whenever you know or suspect that the seller is or will be a non-resident on closing, notify your lawyer immediately. Let him or her set the wheels in motion early, so the appropriate certificate, relieving the purchaser from liability, will be available for closing.

## Making Mortgage Payments To A Non-Resident Lender

Purchasers who buy from non-resident vendors also must be careful if the vendor takes back a mortgage on closing. The same is true where the mortgage lender is known to be a non-resident. A little red light should be lit in your head, warning of possible dangers.

By law, a Canadian who borrows money from a non-resident lender must withhold and remit to the federal government what is known as "Part XIII" tax. Failing to do so makes the borrower responsible for any shortfall in the amount of tax payable to Revenue Canada Taxation on those mortgage payments. If the full amount of the mortgage payment previously was forwarded to the non-resident lender, this means double jeopardy for the borrower. The obligation to pay the money to the government rests with the borrower, not the lender!

Where a tax agreement exists between Canada and the country where the non-resident lives, the withholding tax generally is 15 percent. Otherwise, the withholding tax is 25 percent. The withholding tax applies only to the *interest* portion of a mortgage payment; it does not apply to the principal portion of a blended mortgage payment. When the interest payable is $500, either $75 or $125 will be sent to the government, the remainder being forwarded to the non-resident lender.

Whenever payments are made to a non-resident lender, be extremely cautious. The first time you withhold money to pay this tax, send it to Revenue Canada Taxation with a covering letter, explaining that the payment represents 15 or 25 percent of the mortgage interest payable to the non-resident lender. Also request that a non-resident account be established. In time you will receive a **PD7A** Remittance form from the federal government, which should accompany any future payments of withholding tax that you make. Be sure you explain to the non-resident lender what you have done as well, why, and how the deduction was calculated.

Paying Revenue Canada Taxation its due is not the end of the story. As a Canadian borrowing from a non-resident lender, you must file a **NR 4** Supplementary form as well as a **NR 4** Summary form on or before March 31 each year, for the previous calendar year.

Do not take this obligation too lightly! Remember, the penalty for noncompliance will come out of your pocket, not the lender's.

While the information contained in this chapter reflects the present state of the law, how it is applied may vary, depending on your specific situation. Professional guidance from a chartered accountant or a tax lawyer always should be obtained when dealing with income tax matters.

# 35

# *Now That You Own Your Own Home*

Isn't it wonderful! The deal has closed and the home is yours. Perhaps you have already started to settle into the house. What a feeling!

Buyers who followed the HOBS approach will have gone from start to finish in their transaction with a minimum of surprises and disruptions. Although the transaction was complex and had its difficult moments, you knew exactly what to expect every step of the way. You knew what you were looking for, in terms of needs and wants, communities and neighborhoods. Your finances were in order before any commitments were made. You also knew precisely what you were committing to, before making that commitment. In short, by developing your own home-buying strategy and sticking to it, you have been able to find the right house at the right price, maintaining and perhaps even generating further enthusiasm for your new acquisition.

What you have bought is a structure — and an opportunity to have it reflect your unique lifestyle. Much remains to be done to modify the home to your individual taste. Some needs may be more pressing than others — painting and wallpapering the house, or possibly ordering drapes and window coverings. Minor or even major repairs and renovations may be necessary. Floors and carpeting may require replacing as well.

Now that you own the home, apply the same, winning approach you used in buying it to improving it over time.

Establish a strategy — a master plan — to repair and spruce up the house over a number of years as an expression of your taste. Decide what you want to do, and when you want to do it. Then you can plan and budget for that work over the course of the year. Knowing what will be done next spring or summer, and knowing that it can be afforded, will keep your level of excitement high. Confidently, you will be looking forward to those upcoming changes, because they have been so well planned. Convert that successful home-buying strategy to a home-owning strategy, and start implementing it immediately.

Remember that the interest paid on your mortgage is not deductible in Canada against other income for the most part. As part of your home ownership strategy, set aside money and take advantage of the prepayment privileges you have negotiated in your mortgage. Apply the POPS principle — Pay Off your Principal Sooner, described in *Hidden Profits In Your Mortgage* — to save thousands of dollars in interest costs. The money that is saved can be applied elsewhere as part of your home-owning strategy.

Now you own a place you can call your own. You have worked hard, in many ways, to get to this stage. Enjoy your new home in good health. Congratulations!

# *Appendix A*

Items of personal property that might be included in a resale offer. Remember to be specific.
— refrigerator
— stove
— washer
— dryer
— dishwasher
— storms and screens
— drapes and drapery tracks, blinds, window coverings and shutters
— air-conditioning (central or window units)
— light fixtures (those to be *removed* from the home are listed; otherwise all accompany the house)
— hot water heater — if owned or rental
— gas/electric/oil furnace and equipment
— broadloom where laid
— garage door opener
— fireplace accessories
— all other permanent fixtures on the premises belonging to the seller, to be in good working order on the date of closing, free of liens and encumbrances.